Praise for *Born A...*

"*Born Aware* provides validation that acute spi
people from all walks of life ... Diane's book
free."—Eva Herr, author of *CONSCIOUSN
Conventional Science and the New Science of Quantum Mechanics*

"This is an important book for navigating and making sense of this grand transition to the emerging new world and new human."—John L. Petersen, editor and publisher of *FUTUREdition* and founder and president of the Arlington Institute

"A pioneering work on the subject of coming into this life fully spiritually awakened ... Whether you were born aware and need an enlightening tune-up or someone who had a spiritual awakening or a person just starting out on a spiritual path, this book will inspire you to tune into your soul on the deepest of levels."—Bernie Ashman, author of *Sun Signs & Past Lives: Your Soul's Evolutionary Path*

"For those who wonder why they are here, learn from *Born Aware*, where you will find a wonderful description."—C. Norman Shealy, MD, PhD, founder and CEO of the International Institute of Holistic Medicine and editor of the *Journal of Comprehensive Integrative Medicine*

"A fascinating account of people who are 'born aware,' with full knowledge of their past lives and spiritual heritage."—Colleen Mauro, author of *Spiritual Telepathy: Ancient Techniques to Access the Wisdom of Your Soul*

"The case studies in this book demonstrate that human life histories are dramatically affected by spiritual realities. There is so much of importance that can be learned from studying cases of this type."—Jeffrey Mishlove, PhD, host and producer of the *New Thinking Allowed* video channel

"This book is a great practical handbook for those who want to develop access to the subtler levels of consciousness."—Paulo Vieira de Castro, MSc, author, literary critic, and organizational wellness director at the Institute of Applied Consciousness Technologies

"*Born Aware* is a rich and original contribution to consciousness science literature."—Nelson Abreu, BSEE, vice director of the International Academy of Consciousness

Other Books by Diane Brandon

Dream Interpretation for Beginners:
Understand the Wisdom of Your Sleeping Mind
(Llewellyn Publications, 2015)

Intuition for Beginners: Easy Ways
to Awaken Your Natural Abilities
(Llewellyn Publications, 2013)

Invisible Blueprints—
Intuitive Insights for Fulfillment in Life
(Insight Publishing Company, 2005)

Contributing Author to

Speaking Out
(Insight Publishing, 2005)

The Long Way Around: How 34
Women Found the Lives They Love
(Carolina Women's Press, 2000)

BORN AWARE

Photo by Keith Papke

About the Author

Diane Brandon has been working professionally with her intuition as an integrative intuitive counselor since 1992, and she has been teaching others how to access intuitive information on demand since 1996. She also teaches classes and seminars on dreams, personal empowerment, creativity, and listening skills, in addition to wellness classes, and offers corporate consulting.

She's the author of *Dream Interpretation for Beginners, Intuition for Beginners*, and *Invisible Blueprints*, and is a contributing author to *The Long Way Around* and *Speaking Out*. Her private work with clients focuses on facilitating personal development and life fulfillment, and she brings dream work, guided meditation, regression, natural process healing, and other modalities into her work. She has produced three meditation CDs and formerly hosted a radio show, "Naturally Vibrant Living." Born and raised in New Orleans, she has an AB from Duke University and did master's work at the University of North Carolina, in addition to French studies in Geneva, Switzerland. She's also a professional actor, singer, and voice-over artist.

BRN AWARE

Stories & Insights from
Those Spiritually Aware
Since Birth

DIANE BRANDON

Llewellyn Publications
Woodbury, Minnesota

FIRST EDITION
First Printing, 2017

Book design by Bob Gaul
Cover design by Ellen Lawson
Editing by Aaron Lawrence
Flower graphic by Llewellyn Art Department

Llewellyn Publications is a registered trademark of Llewellyn Worldwide Ltd.

Library of Congress Cataloging-in-Publication Data
Names: Brandon, Diane, author.
Title: Born aware: stories & insights from those spiritually aware since
   birth / Diane Brandon.
Description: First Edition. | Woodbury: Llewellyn Worldwide. Ltd, 2017. |
   Includes bibliographical references.
Identifiers: LCCN 2017018540 (print) | LCCN 2016059611 (ebook) | ISBN
   9780738752228 () | ISBN 9780738751764
Subjects: LCSH: Spiritual biography. | Spirituality—Miscellanea.
Classification: LCC BL72 (print) | LCC BL72 .B73 2017 (ebook) | DDC
   204/.2—dc23
LC record available at https://lccn.loc.gov/2017018540

Llewellyn Publications
A Division of Llewellyn Worldwide Ltd.
2143 Wooddale Drive
Woodbury, MN 55125-2989
www.llewellyn.com

Printed in the United States of America

Dedication

THIS BOOK IS DEDICATED TO all those who have been spiritually aware since birth—the born-awares, who may have kept their memories to themselves—as well as to all those who cherish the spiritual, are spiritually oriented, and who aspire to maximize their spirituality for their own growth and for the benefit of the world.

Acknowledgments

THIS BOOK HAS BEEN A true labor of love. Every time I interviewed one of the Born-awares in this book and later transcribed the interviews and shaped them into chapters, I found that I was enraptured and inspired. I shared with so many friends how wonderful this material was; by its very nature and content, this material is hugely uplifting and enthralling.

First and foremost, I must thank the Born-awares you'll meet in this book. They were so gracious and giving to allow me to interview them and ask them to share some very personal information, information that in many cases they had never shared with anyone else before. Each of you was so pleasant and generous and I so appreciate your time and willingness to speak with me, as well as who you are by your very natures. You're such gifts and have enriched my life with your presence!

I would especially like to thank Julie Scardiglia, who was the first born-aware to spontaneously share her pre-birth memories with me. Little did she know at the time—nor did I—that her sharing these memories would lead to this project. It was because of her spontaneous sharing, followed by that of another person, that I realized that I was being given the idea for this book and was being asked to write it. So, without you, Julie, this book would very likely not have happened. Thank you so much for your generosity!

I shared the idea of this book with a couple of friends after Julie and another person shared their memories with me, bouncing the idea of such a book off of them. They were very encouraging and I greatly appreciated having this supportive feedback. Thanks so much to Kathlyn Bushnell and to Theresa Waltermeyer. Your support early on was critical to my feeling that this was indeed a worthwhile project to embark upon. (You'll meet Theresa later on in the book, as she is a born-aware.)

Gratitude must be expressed to Dr. Brett Hightower, who strongly recommended that I coin a shorter phrase than "spiritually aware since birth," in order to refer in a more shorthand manner to this phenomenon. With his suggestion, I might never have thought of the phrase "born aware."

I am so very appreciative of those who took the time to read and review the manuscript, even though it was in need of more minor revisions, and so graciously wrote endorsements for this book: in alphabetical order, Nélson Abreu, BSEE, Bernie Ashman, Erlendur Haraldsson, PhD, Eva Herr, John G. Kruth, Colleen Mauro, Jeffrey Mishlove, PhD, Laurie Nadel, PhD, John L. Peterson, Gary E. Schwartz, PhD, C. Norman Shealy, MD, PhD, Paulo Vieira de Castro, MSc. Thank you all so much for your kindness and generosity!

I would also like to thank Angela Wix, acquisitions editor at Llewellyn Publications. I'm so glad you were open to taking that second look!

The production editor, Aaron Lawrence, spent a considerable amount of time putting my text into a formatted version for publication and making suggestions and asking for clarification in some places. His work was prodigious and I very much appreciate his efforts.

Special thanks to all those at Llewellyn who contributed to the effort of making this book a reality are also in order. Publishing a book requires the efforts of many different people in different departments, and I may not know all of you, but your efforts are greatly appreciated.

And to you, the reader, I would also like to extend my sincere gratitude. I so appreciate your taking the time to read this book and hope that you find it worthy of your time and attention. Together we can bring positive changes to this world.

Contents

Introduction   *1*

Part 1: The Born Aware Phenomenon

Chapter 1: What Is the "Born Aware" Phenomenon?   9

Chapter 2: How We Can Benefit   17

Part 2: Individual Accounts of Those Born Aware

Chapter 3: Rosalie's Story   27

"For the first couple months of my life, I was bouncing back and forth between Spirit and 3D life."

Chapter 4: Jimelle Suzanne's Story   47

"I was very aware of a horrible light, blinding, blinding lights, and choking. I couldn't stand it. I just felt like I weighed a thousand pounds and I was choking."

Chapter 5: Heather's Story   59

"I was working for the Creator and … I was making things … and they were quite beautiful."

Chapter 6: Theresa Waltermeyer's Story   69

"I remember picking my parents and picking my father. I just wanted to be his daughter."

Chapter 7: Jemila's Story   81

"Oh, my God, what have I done?"

Chapter 8: Cheryl Ludwig's Story   93

"What in the world are these people thinking to not cover my eyes from the sun?"

Chapter 9: Matthew Engel's Story   107

"Okay, so I've arrived. Here I am ... I was feeling a sense that there was a force and a team in the spirit realm that was all involved in getting me here."

Chapter 10: Terese Covey's Story   115

"I agreed with my dad that I would be okay."

Chapter 11: Cynthia Sue Larson's Story   121

"Whoops! Wrong planet!"

Chapter 12: Dr. Stanislav Gergre O'Jack's Story   133

"I was in a rolled-up position and housed in a warm environment surrounded by a seemingly orange-red color illumination. ... something like being in a sauna. I could feel the warmth, the sounds."

Chapter 13: Rozlyn Reynolds' Story   143

"Shortly after being born, I remember seeing all the bright lights, faces looking down at me with masks on."

Chapter 14: Carmel Bell's Story   155

"I remember being in the 'soup' before I was born.... I was ... given a choice as to 'what' I would be in terms of being seen as good, bad, or indifferent."

Chapter 15: My Story   163

*"When I was born I remember thinking that I didn't want to be here
again. I knew that when I wasn't here I was with the Divine and I
wanted to be back with God. I also knew that when I wasn't here,
and was on higher levels, I had absolute knowledge and I resented
not having absolute knowledge while here. However, I knew that I
had to be here because there was something I was supposed to do."*

Chapter 16: Those with Initial Memories
From Ten Months Old   181

"I was born with awareness and a sense of what I know."

Part 3: Lessons from the Born Aware Phenomenon and Accessing Our Awareness

Chapter 17: Initial Lessons—Attributes and
Differences of Those Born Aware   201

Chapter 18: Spiritual Lessons from the
Born Aware Phenomenon   239

Chapter 19: Grooming the Higher Soul
Awareness and Other Recommendations   259

Closing Thoughts   285

Appendix A: Questions That Were Posed to Interviewees   289

Appendix B: A Meditation for the Higher Soul Awareness   293

Appendix C: If You've Retained At-Birth Memories   299

Bibliography   307

Introduction

WE HUMANS PRIDE OURSELVES ON our minds and on being aware. Indeed, awareness is considered by many to be a critical trait and a hallmark of being human. So when is it that we become aware?

Researchers and psychologists assert by and large (despite a new field called birth psychology) that babies are born as blank slates with regard to consciousness and awareness—that they have no self-awareness, aside from bodily awareness, until sometime later as their brains and minds develop, and that there is an amnesia preventing babies from remembering anything prior to the age of two or three. Is this really true?

And what about spiritual awareness?

As we know, humans can be aware, as in having cognitive awareness and self-awareness, without also being spiritually aware. Spiritual awareness typically opens up a vast new vista in consciousness and takes our awareness away from the regular quotidian and mundane human focus into the spiritual realm. For those who are spiritually aware, when does this spiritual awareness set in?

In this book we'll be exploring both of these types of awareness, as spiritual awareness can overlap with and amplify self-awareness.

With regard to whether babies are born with any awareness or not, I know firsthand that all babies are not necessarily blank slates at birth and that one can indeed be aware at birth and have thoughts and perceptions and remember them. I was. I have always remembered what I thought when I was born. And, as you'll see, I'm not the only one.

What does it mean to be born aware? And how does that affect one's life and awareness throughout the years? What is that awareness, if it's not connected to the human psyche and personality? Could one be both aware at birth and spiritually aware? Conversely, could one be born aware but not spiritually aware?

If we have people among us on this planet who were born spiritually aware, what can we learn from this phenomenon? Can it benefit us in any way? If it's desirable or beneficial, is there any way to groom this awareness or other attributes?

These are some of the topics we'll explore in this book.

If you're spiritually oriented, interested in metaphysics, curious about "the other side" (or where souls are when they're not here in a body), wanting to grow more spiritually—or even interested in consciousness itself—then the information in this book should be of interest to you.

In part 1 you'll learn more about this phenomenon and what it means to be born aware, as well as some of its potential benefits, including the higher soul awareness.

In part 2 you'll encounter the personal accounts of people who have been spiritually aware since birth, or who have been aware shortly thereafter, as well as a variation on these, including my account, and the differences having been born aware has made in their lives. You'll get some glimpses into the other side (where we "reside" when we aren't here in a body) and what some souls do (just some of the possibilities) when not here.

Finally, in part 3, we'll look at some of the attributes that those born aware have in common, as well as some of the differences, the spiritual and practical implications and lessons of this phenomenon, and the types of awareness we could potentially have access to. In the last chapter, I'll share some ways to groom what I call the higher soul awareness and some other born-aware attributes.

You'll also find a meditation in appendix B to access the higher soul awareness.

As you read each person's story, allow yourself to see if there are any commonalities among them and what the implications may be, as well as what appears to be significant. Allow yourself to see if any of your own memories are triggered. If so, in appendix C you'll find a discussion of what you could do if you've also been spiritually aware since birth.

As you read this book, it's important to note two distinctions:

- The phenomenon you'll be reading about concerns people who have been spiritually aware since birth (or shortly thereafter) and *have always retained those memories* (regardless of psychic gifts or past-life recall). Their memories are spontaneous and did not have to be retrieved through any artificial or after-the-fact means, such as regression, rebirthing, meditation, dreamwork, etc.

- One can be naturally intuitive, remember past lives, or see those who are deceased without also being spiritually aware or innately spiritually aware. One does not need to be spiritually aware in order to be intuitive or psychic. In other words, one can be intuitive or psychic without also being spiritually aware.

The genesis for this book came about quite synchronistically, and I feel that the time is right for this information to be made more widely known.

In the fall of 2013, I received a message during meditation that I needed to start connecting with more like-minded spiritual people, including those unknown to me and living throughout the world. I've known many spiritual people for several years, but this message was telling me to widen my net, so to speak, and to connect energetically with more like-minded people, irrespective of where they were located geographically. That began to occur spontaneously in monthly meditations that I had already been participating in with two friends.

Then, beginning in the winter of 2014 and within the space of three months, two people spontaneously shared with me an early memory. I had learned over the years that my birth memory was somewhat unusual. Now two more people had added their early memories to mine. I knew that I was being given a message to do something with this information, and the idea for this book was born. After I started writing this book, I was surprised to learn that six people I had known for many years and who were friends of mine also had these memories. (I'm fortunate, as some of the Born Awares you'll meet in this book had never known anyone else with similar memories.)

I began to conduct interviews over the phone, recording each interview. One interview was conducted via e-mail, with the respondent e-mailing back answers to the questionnaire. I knew that I wanted more people to interview for this book, so I started asking friends and colleagues if they knew of anyone else who had been spiritually aware since birth. I also approached individuals through social media whom I felt might have been born aware, and I posted a question on my Facebook page about what people's earliest memories were. Most of the people who contacted me or were referred to me did not have spontaneous memories from birth and instead had early memories that had been artificially induced from having been regressed, or memories that stemmed back only to one or two years of age or older. Slowly, however, I found the people you'll meet in part 2.

As I conducted interviews, I asked each person to share his or her memories before I asked a series of questions. I already had a sense of how being spiritually aware since birth had likely informed a person's life, based upon my own experiences and insights, and formulated questions accordingly. (You'll find a list of these questions in appendix A.) Each time I interviewed a person, I was fascinated, if not spell-bound, by the information I was privy to, and I quickly bonded with each born-aware I hadn't known previously.

When I began interviewing, all I was focused on was gathering information. At that point, I thought that was the primary focus of this book. However, as time went by, I started seeing how each person interviewed had a piece of the overall puzzle (the larger spiritual picture) and how each experience correlated with the others. My mind kept lighting up with realizations and ahas. Spiritual realizations, concepts, implications, and lessons ensued, and I felt they had to be included in this book.

Thus, a large portion of this book is comprised of the stories of those who were born aware, followed by the spiritual implications that were implicit, as well as some recommendations for utilizing and benefiting from this material.

These born-aware accounts need to be told. There are indeed people who were born aware living among us and I know that there are a lot more of us out there. Even if most people have not had these experiences, we can certainly all benefit from what we can learn from them.

Author's Notes

- Please note that all of the accounts reported in this book represent *spontaneous recall*—not memories that were retrieved after the fact via means such as regression, rebirthing, near-death experiences, hypnotherapy, etc. The memories shared are those that these Born Awares have always had throughout their lives.

- Please note that material inside of brackets [*i.e.*] represents the thoughts of the author, as differentiated from parenthetical information.

- Some of the opinions expressed by individuals in this book are their own opinions. There is no express attempt via this book to criticize or denigrate any specific religion or faith, as we all have our own spiritual path and way to connect to higher spiritual levels. In addition, people interviewed may use varying terms for God, such as Spirit, Source, Creator, the Divine, the Universe, etc. These terms are used interchangeably.

- The recommendations in this book are to be used with common sense. The publisher and the author assume no liability for any injuries caused to the reader that may result from the reader's use of content contained in this publication. Common sense is required and recommended when contemplating the practices described in the work.

Part 1

The Born Aware Phenomenon

1

What Is the "Born Aware" Phenomenon?

FOR YEARS, I NEVER SHARED my at-birth thoughts with anyone else. I wasn't trying to hide my memories; instead, I simply didn't encounter people or situations in which this type of topic was discussed. It never even crossed my mind to share my memories; they were just part of who I am and my norm. It wasn't until I had met more people overtly into metaphysics and after I had started doing my intuitive counseling work that the possibility of sharing these memories occurred to me. Even then, though, it still took more years.

Being born aware is just not a topic of conversation in our culture. This could be because it's a fairly rare phenomenon and/or because there's widespread doubt that babies are aware or think. Indeed, the concept may seem to many people, if not most, to be quite bizarre or impossible. As a result, this phenomenon is neither widely known nor understood.

Exploring What
"Spiritually Aware Since Birth" Means

In order to explain what the born-aware phenomenon is, I'll need to share how it played into the search for a title for this book. Because this phenomenon is not well known, it made devising a title somewhat of a challenge.

Initially in contemplating this book (after I realized that I was being given a spiritual directive to write it), I used the phrase "spiritually aware since birth." This phrase, I felt, truly captured what this phenomenon was. There are those of us, albeit very much in the minority, who have literally been spiritually aware from the moment we were born. I have always remembered what I thought when I was born, and my thoughts were spiritual ones (about the Divine, where I had come from on the other side, and having to be here on Earth). (You'll read my account in chapter 15.)

So being "spiritually aware since birth" entails exactly and *literally* what that phrase implies—that some people at birth have thoughts, perceptions, and/or memories that are spiritual in nature (an awareness of spirit; that this three-dimensional reality is not the only reality; of memories of the other, non-corporeal side; of a plan for their physical lives here; that they're here on Earth temporarily before returning to higher spiritual levels; etc.).

This means that our consciousness and soul don't begin (or aren't "born") when we are physically born into this three-dimensional world as newborn babies. We *come from somewhere else.* Some people call it "the other side." Others may think of it as heaven and still others as the afterlife or spirit world. It's where our souls and consciousness are when we're not in a body here in this more concrete and denser three-dimensional reality. Those of us who have been spiritually aware since birth have an awareness of having come from this other spiritual, non-three-dimensional, non-corporeal realm.

This awareness is not induced or recaptured after the fact when we're older; it's there innately in us at birth. Of those spiritually aware since birth in this book, some of us have clear memories of the other side, while others have more of a vague sense of it, and still others just know that we don't come from here or originate here (this planet or any three-dimensional place).

The awareness that is the subject of this book is a wise, knowing, and spiritual awareness that comes from our soul awareness and is not a product of the newborn's mind (which would be expected to be more that of a blank slate). You'll find the specific examples of what this spiritual awareness at birth encompassed and what Born Awares thought, perceived, and remembered as you read each person's account in this book. We all had our own awareness and thoughts at birth. Our "minds" and awareness were far from being blank slates or those of an infant or an unformed mind.

This, then, is what the born aware phenomenon is: an innate and conscious spiritual awareness at birth that is quite mature and clear and not a product of the chronological age of the infant.

Born Aware vs. Spiritually Aware Since Birth

While I embrace the term "born aware," it may be a bit of a misnomer. I discovered in the planning and writing of this book that there are people who remember their thoughts and perceptions at birth but were not also spiritually aware when they were born. Thus, not all people who have memories from birth are *spiritually* aware at birth. In this sense, the term "born aware" is not specific enough, whereas the phrase "spiritually aware since birth" fully captures the phenomenon.

That said, for the purposes of this book, please take the phrase "born aware" as shorthand for the full meaning—spiritually aware since birth.

Compared to Innately Spiritually Oriented

Many, many people can remember always having been spiritually oriented in their lives. They remember always having had a sense of coming from somewhere else, although not necessarily knowing where that was, as well as feeling that being here on this planet feels strange to them. They frequently can remember always having felt different from other people or, in their own view, "weird." I have known hundreds of people who feel this way and have spoken to client after client over the years who can remember always having been spiritual.

Such people are innately spiritually oriented; however, they tend not to have been spiritually aware since birth, as their earliest memories typically stem back to only the age of two or three and, in some cases, to one. They also tend not to have memories of the other side, but they have a somewhat hazy feeling of otherness instead. They may long to be somewhere else which they may feel is their spiritual home, have an innate knowing that there is a spiritual and non-corporeal place from which they came (without having any clear memories of it), naturally gravitate toward spiritual topics, have a sense of a higher power, and have spiritual awareness to some degree—yet lack the more direct, engrained, experiential, and somewhat clear awareness and memories of the other side. It's as if any clear awareness and memory of the other side had been erased and they've been allowed to retain a hazy spiritual orientation and tantalizing longing to be where they can't clearly remember, but know is better and preferable to here. While they often have some of the attributes of those born aware (which we'll delve into in chapter 17), they usually don't have all of the attributes.

We're fortunate to have so many innately spiritually oriented people on this planet, as their spirituality has enriched culture, taught and healed many, and helped to move humanity forward. That said, those who have been literally spiritually aware since birth appear to differ in significant ways from those who are innately spiritually oriented by nature and who lack natal memories.

Compared to "Life Between Lives"

People from ancient times have wondered about other levels of existence and what happens to us after our physical death—the death of our bodies. The idea of an afterlife has captured and fascinated people while also seeming to be far away and mysterious. This is because people by and large have theorized and wondered about other spiritual levels from their human perspective and while being firmly anchored in—even trapped by—and oriented to their existence on Earth and what they know of "reality" from this limited perspective. Various religions have taught a range of visions and versions of an afterlife—from heaven to several other concepts going by diverse terms.

Near-death experiences, which have increased in frequency due to the rise in medical technology prolonging and saving lives beginning in the twentieth century, have allowed "experiencers" (or "NDErs") to gain glimpses into non-corporeal existence and what it feels like to be aware while not in a physical body. While near-death experiences may not always allow experiencers the full breadth of non-corporeal existence in the afterlife, they have allowed increasing numbers of people to taste part of it and gain some sensory experience of it. Many NDErs come back from their near-death experiences dramatically changed, especially in awareness, and often go through an extensive period of time afterward adapting and adjusting to their new awareness, often struggling to find a way to incorporate it into their lives.

A fairly recent entry into the discussion of the other side has been material written about the life between lives phenomenon. There are several books in print about life between lives, most notably those by Michael Newton, a pioneer in this field, among others. This phenomenon is about glimpses people have gained into the other side through hypnotherapy. While undergoing hypnotherapy, subjects are taken to the past before being born or taken to the future after death. In this way, people who generally had no previous experiential awareness of the other side have been able to see what is now referred to as life between lives.

The information on life between lives has been widely disseminated and represents a wonderful service in introducing people to non-corporeal existence. However, it is a vastly different phenomenon from the born aware phenomenon.

Aside from the obvious difference—that the Born Awares' memories are spontaneous and were never lost and thus didn't need to be retrieved via hypnotherapy or other modalities—there are additional differences as well.

The term "life between lives" itself exemplifies one major difference, as it refers to and is predicated upon life here on this planet in a physical body as being the main focal point, main orientation, and primary perspective. In other words, it's a glimpse of non-corporeal existence from the human perspective on earth, with glimpses into existence on the other side, as a result, representing a deviation from humans' norm and engrained perspective. Those who undergo hypnotherapy and are the subjects of life between lives work tend to live from the perspective of their human lives incarnated on this planet, with their glimpses into the other side representing a deviation from their typical human perspective, although some may be spiritually oriented. Being here is customarily their norm and their glimpses into non-corporeal existence usually seem quite different, if not somewhat foreign or exotic at times.

By contrast, the main focal point for those of us born aware is innately the other side. We have a lifelong and inherent perspective of and orientation to the other side. Higher spiritual levels—the realm of the soul—are our true home, where we know that we originated and where we are anchored, and life here on Earth as a human feels strange to us. This is clearly the *opposite of the life between lives phenomenon.* We were born knowing that our true home and orientation is to the other side and that we are "strangers in a strange land" during our lives and sojourn here. We might refer to human life here as a temporary sojourn or interruption between our true—and customary—existence in spirit form ("temporary embodiment interrupting true, original spirit existence," for example), and we typically long to be back in our true home.

For those who have been taken to the "life between lives" via hypnotherapy, being here is customarily the norm and their glimpses into noncorporeal existence usually seem quite different, if not somewhat foreign or exotic at times.

In this way, the born aware phenomenon and the life between lives phenomenon are quite different, yet mirror each other from rather opposing perspectives.

I must add that the born aware phenomenon is far from being new. I would expect that many people have been spiritually aware since birth over the ages, even if this phenomenon is not widely known.

Benefits from Learning
About the Born Aware Phenomenon

The born aware phenomenon may be interesting in and of itself, but there are benefits to be derived from becoming conversant with it. There are personal attributes and hallmarks that come with having been born spiritually aware, and these will be explored as well. The commonalities among those of us who were born aware are both striking and significant. (You'll read about them in part 3.)

One of the most significant attributes is the easy access to what I call the higher soul awareness. You'll learn more about it in the next chapter. I can't speak highly enough about this type of awareness and its benefits and am very grateful to have been born with it. Even if you weren't born aware, you can access your higher soul awareness and benefit from it.

As I mentioned, the born aware phenomenon also has strong spiritual implications. I'll touch upon them in the next chapter and then more fully delve into them in part 3.

We'll next explore the higher soul awareness and why it's so valuable.

2

How We Can Benefit

LEARNING ABOUT THE BORN AWARE phenomenon can benefit our lives in a variety of ways. There are many note-worthy spiritual implications of this phenomenon, which can give us more spiritual information and enlarge our spiritual understanding. These spiritual implications include information in the following areas:

- A clear and mature natal awareness

- What is possible

- Direct access spiritually

- Easing of fears and feeling protected

- Awareness that we're here to do or accomplish something

- The greater drama and what is allowed

- An embrace of being whole-brained

- Dealing with the human side and our personal stuff

- Cocreation and awareness of higher spiritual agency

- Spectrum of consciousness

- Divine spark evidenced by a love of animals and nature

- Implications for parents

We'll be fully exploring and discussing these various spiritual implications and lessons of the born aware phenomenon in part 3. Our lives can be enriched significantly by these implications.

The Higher Soul Awareness

Those of us who have been spiritually aware since birth have been hugely affected by having been born this way. One striking characteristic is something we came into the present lifetime with that stems from our spiritual being—it comes from our spiritual souls and our awareness on the other side. It's what I call the higher soul awareness. Those of us who were born spiritually aware were in this awareness when we were born, rather than in the awareness of a baby, and we frequently find ourselves in our higher soul awareness, which has not waned over time.

One of the strongest benefits we can derive from the born aware phenomenon is that of the higher soul awareness.

What is the higher soul awareness and how is it beneficial?

One way of looking at it would be to consider that it's our awareness when we're not here in the earthly experience or at the least a remnant of this awareness. It is the awareness we have on the soul level that is not a product of our human consciousness, nor of our human anatomy, nor of our human needs, nor of our human persona. It's neither a product of nor limited by our human psyche or experience—and it's not connected to our personality in the present lifetime or any of our previous or future personalities from other lifetimes. That said, our higher soul awareness may 'contain' those human personas, and when we're on the other side we can access any of those personalities at any time, not just through a memory of them, but also in communicating with those loved ones on earth who knew us through the human persona.

My sense is that our personality and persona change from one lifetime to another, just as our gender, race, nationality, religion, etc., will. After our physical body dies and we transition back to the "other side," at some point we drop the persona (the human persona) of that lifetime and get into our higher soul awareness. There are sometimes things souls need to experience before dropping the human persona on the other side, such as going through a healing process if the lifetime had been particularly hard or if the person had endured a difficult and lingering illness before transition, but at some point thereafter the human persona is dropped. That said, souls can still access the human persona of the last lifetime—or of any lifetime.

Thus the higher soul awareness is not the same as the human persona or personality. It is distinct from the human persona. Some people, in attempting to grasp what it is, may liken it to being in an alpha brain wave state (or daydreaming) or dissociation (a defense mechanism that is protective during abuse and allows one's mind to "escape"), or even, to use a slang phrase, zoning out. However, it is none of those."

Instead, the higher soul awareness is an awareness that's transcendent and pure. It's oriented quite naturally to the perspective of a higher spiritual level and is quite clear and objective. It's neither connected to nor colored by our human side or experiences. It's also firmly rooted in the present (or eternal) and lacks the mental chatter of the human consciousness. It's present, unaffected by background noise, and tends not to waver. It also is devoid of negative human emotions. It further transcends space and time and simply *is*. It is anchored in or oriented to, again, the present or now.

That said, however, it is still somewhat limited, as we don't have unlimited access to absolute knowledge with it while we're still here in a body (which, you'll learn, really irked me when I was born). (Theoretically, because information is energy, we should have access to all information and knowledge, but this rarely bears out during the human experience for more than one reason, even though we have absolute knowledge on the other side.)

Over the years, I observed myself feeling a certain way about something in the world on one level, and yet on another level I felt something different. It took me many years to determine that what I was experiencing was my spirit awareness: my awareness that was split between what my human side could see and feel and what my higher soul awareness observed and knew. Often these perceptions, stemming from two different sources, would differ from each other. I posed the question to most of the Born Awares I interviewed for this book to see if they had also experienced that phenomenon of feeling different things on different levels, and there was general assent.

I also asked some of the Born Awares in this book to describe what their higher soul awareness was like. You'll read their responses in the individual accounts in part 2.

You'll read in my account that I have a sense that we have a "spectrum of consciousness." Our higher soul awareness is at the upper end of that spectrum, our human awareness is in the middle, and our sub- and unconscious lie at the lower end. Interestingly, our unconscious has a greater connection to and can more freely access our higher soul awareness at times than our normal waking human awareness can (because our unconscious is more porous and lacks the filters and distorted perceptions of our waking consciousness).

Benefits of the Higher Soul Awareness

Our higher soul awareness allows us to see and perceive from a higher perspective. It is one aspect that we have retained from being on higher spiritual levels that has not been drastically changed by being here in body and having a human side. Because of our human personal psychological stuff—the wants, needs, fears, mindsets, beliefs, etc.—when we humans are in our typical human consciousness, we frequently don't perceive clearly and objectively, because our perceptions are filtered through the distorting lens of our personal stuff. Someone with beliefs or prejudices, for example, will see through the distortion of those beliefs or prejudices, just as our fears and wants will often color and affect our perceptions. Our typical human filters for perception are not operative, however, while we're in our higher soul awareness. In other words, we can see things objectively because our typical human psychological "stuff" that filters and distorts perception is turned off, bypassed, or transcended.

With our higher soul awareness, we tend to understand quite naturally the higher meaning and purpose of events in life, whether personal ones or public ones, rather than funneling those perceptions through our very limited human awareness with its blinders, fears, wants, mindsets, and beliefs—and its attendant misperceptions and misinterpretations. For example, when I read or hear about an event unfolding on the world stage, I typically have an initial emotional reaction. However, I then naturally and involuntarily find myself looking at what the purpose of the event is from a higher spiritual perspective and what positive lessons and shifts it may trigger for people or for the world stage. This is not to say that horrendous events don't trigger my compassion or revulsion, because in fact they do. It's just that I automatically and almost imperceptibly shift into my higher soul awareness to get a sense of what the higher purpose may be and what good may come out of painful events—and this happens quite automatically without my deciding or intending to shift into it. I may then alternate between feeling compassion, for example, and shifting into my higher soul awareness. For those of us spiritually aware since birth, our higher soul awareness is our natural home, focal point, and orientation. It's the natural "seat" of our consciousness.

Our higher soul awareness can also lead those of us who have been spiritually aware since birth to transcend our human side to the point where we can see and observe ourselves objectively as well, as if we were observing someone else. So not only can we go back and forth between our human side and its perceptions (although filtered through our personal stuff) and our higher soul awareness; we can also observe ourselves somewhat clinically or dispassionately and get a sense of what we need to work on in ourselves, fine-tune, and improve upon as humans. (For several years now, when I have taught intuitive skills to others, I have taken students through advanced exercises trying to groom this objectivity. In one such exercise, I lead students to go to a higher vantage point and observe themselves in a situation that has been problematic, in the hopes that they will be able to observe themselves clearly and objectively. My goal was to enable students to gain clarity and objectivity to be applied to their accessing intuitive information that was reliable and not filtered through their personal stuff. I later came to realize that I was actually trying to take students to their higher soul awareness.)

Even though the higher soul awareness stems from our soul and transcends our human persona and perspective, it still pales in comparison to Divine mind, which far transcends and goes beyond what we could imagine."

Having such a natural access to our higher soul awareness gives us many benefits. We tend to feel innately protected spiritually and have access to spiritual wisdom—and not through thinking or learning or deductive reasoning, but through a strong knowing deeply embedded within us instead. It can lead us to feel a stronger connection to Spirit or Creator (and guides, angels, and other spiritual beings). It can restore or strengthen our innocence and purity and lead us to trust that we will always be okay. We tend to be born knowing some spiritual truths and may then have access to more as we move through life. For those who are spiritually oriented or interested in spiritual matters, I cannot emphasize enough the importance of accessing your higher soul awareness.

Would you have to have been born aware in order to have access to your higher soul awareness?

We can't typically go back in time and redo our birth and awareness at that time. However, that may not necessarily mean that we can't find ways to groom our higher soul awareness.

I'm sure some deeply spiritually oriented people may naturally find themselves in their higher soul awareness at times, even if not born aware. Some people who have transformative near-death experiences come back deeply changed, and some of them have a greater access to their higher soul awareness. Dr. Kenneth Ring wrote about this phenomenon in his book *Heading Toward Omega*. Some people undergo a spontaneous shift in awareness or spiritual awakening that leads them to an altered consciousness and concomitant easier access to their higher soul awareness. There's a book on this topic that is considered to be a spiritual classic—*Cosmic Consciousness: A Study in the Evolution of the Human Mind* by Maurice Bucke, which was published in 1901.

Thus, one may be able to access the higher soul awareness after the fact, so to speak.

In part 3, we'll look at some ways to groom the higher soul awareness without having been born aware or needing to go through a near-death experience that triggers it.

Next we'll meet some Born Awares—those who have been spiritually aware since birth—and learn about their lives.

Part 2

Individual Accounts
of Those Born Aware

3

Rosalie's Story

*"For the first couple months of my life, I was bouncing
back and forth between Spirit and 3D life."*

ROSALIE HAS ALWAYS REMEMBERED WHERE she was before she was born,
when she was in spirit form on the other side. Her description of the place
of Spirit is a beautiful one:

> *A feeling of openness, a feeling of flight, a feeling of communion, a
> feeling of a lot of other energies around me, a feeling of benevolence,
> a feeling of being someplace incredibly vast that I was a part of and
> that felt like a part of me, but felt so much bigger than me, and felt
> accessible. And it was very comforting and very wide open. I just
> remember the feeling of exploring and just feeling that wherever I
> went in this place I was safe. I was supported—just the feeling of
> ultimate comfort.*

Her memory of the other side included an awareness that she had an identity. "I definitely had a sense of identity, and I had a sense of identity of me as the soul and the width of it."

Rosalie has always had a sense of Spirit (Source, the Divine) and of her present persona as Rosalie (in this lifetime) as being part of a "large pot" of Spirit. In other words, she has always recognized that her soul or spirit encompasses more identities—from other lifetimes—than just her present one of Rosalie. She can differentiate between her identity and personality in this lifetime and her larger soul identity, even though her present persona is also part of her soul.

> To me, it just has always felt like the entirety and the completeness of me—everything I've ever been and everything I am all at once: every lifetime, every being I've been, every facet of my being... This is where words are going to fail me... I've been aware of myself as energies that also have not incarnated, but that's part of my soul, and so that's all me and it's like me in my completeness... How I would describe it is as a knowing that simply hasn't incarnated.

Rosalie remembers being in her mother's womb as well, at which time she identified herself as Rosalie the soul and not her present-life human persona. She was there with Spirit for a few moments to witness and experience the first heartbeat of her future body (in the embryo). She "recognized the significance and the beauty of what was taking place" and felt easy and delighted with being with Spirit.

She remembers her first heartbeat when it then occurred:

> I remember the feel of Spirit, of whatever it was that first set the beingness of my cells in motion. And I remember the feeling of Spirit breathing this spark into the electrical system that was my newly-formed heart [in her embryo as Rosalie]. And I remember that first heartbeat... So, for me... my life as Rosalie, while a part

of my soul, is very precious to me because it was a cocreation with Spirit, and Spirit put that first heartbeat into my heart.

She felt delight at the potential and possibility of her impending incarnation as the human being Rosalie and welcomed coming into this life. She remembers Spirit's reverence for the gift of life that she was to become. She regarded the spark of her first heartbeat as a miracle.

She doesn't remember knowing what she was incarnating to do, but she knew that her essence was brightness and joy and that she "came to be light and … joy." This memory has inspired her and given her strength throughout her life, especially in moments when she has felt discouraged.

Rosalie feels that she didn't stay in her mother's womb throughout her pregnancy, but instead sometimes dipped in and out, staying for moments at a time. She remembers staying in her mother's womb a little longer when it was closer to the time when she was going to be born.

She was quite aware of the differences between the world of spirit and the three-dimensional one here on Earth, just as she was aware of her soul as Rosalie encompassing her human persona as Rosalie. As the larger soul, Rosalie said, "I just knew I was vast … I knew in my beingness prior to two months [old] that I was this big soul who'd had a lot of experiences and who knew a lot of things."

She described Spirit:

I did have a sense of Spirit as an entity, meaning something beside me, as it were. Yet Spirit was everywhere….I'm going to use a lot of words to describe this, because I can't pigeon-hole it too much. I kind of felt that Spirit was separate, but part of me, but there was an energy that was with me that was part of me but that was also distinct from me and certainly bigger than me. … and a feeling of—from my perspective now where safety has been an issue in my life—absolute safety, joy, beauty, magnanimous love.

At-Birth and Early Memories

Rosalie also remembers being born.

> *Part of it was ... spiritual awareness and part of it was physical ... I remember exiting my mother's womb ... When I had this memory of my birth, the physical ... I remember coming out of my mother's womb and I remember the bright light, which irritated the s—t out of me ... I remember being pissed off. I'm like, "What is that?" ... So that was number one, and the other was, "Oh, my God, I am ... freezing." So my first physical memory was of pain and discomfort because of the light and the cold. I hated it. I was not happy. I was like, "Oh, no, I don't like this place."*

The bright lights felt to her like interrogation lights. However, in spite of the physical discomfort she felt when she was born, she remembers the "delight" with which she was received, because the doctors and nurses were laughing in delight when she was delivered. She hated the bright lights and the cold, but liked the welcoming joy that greeted her.

For the first two months of her life, Rosalie felt that she was bouncing back and forth between Spirit and her new physical life, with glimpses of being held and waking up in her crib, while feeling cozy and warm. However, she felt that until she turned two months old, most of her awareness was still with Spirit and that she spent more time with Spirit on other levels than in this physical reality.

> *At two months, after having come in ... I consider it my 51 percent day. I know that for the first couple of months of my life I was bouncing back and forth between Spirit and 3D life. At two months, I crossed the line of being more here than there. That's why I call it my 51 percent day.*

Before that, she only had hazy memories of being here.

*Just sort of like glimpses of waking up from naps and seeing my
mother or seeing my environment or knowing where I was in 3D,
but just bouncing in and out of that and being more in the place of
Spirit . . . just being aware of the differences between the two worlds,
as it were.*

During her first two months of life on Earth, as she was bouncing
back and forth between here and there, she was gradually spending more
aware time here, until her 51 percent day. At that point, she had become
more aware of this Earth plane and was more here.

While she was still in Spirit before her 51 percent day, she was aware
that she had other lives:

*The soul Rosalie was this big pot into which were all of these experi-
ences, awarenesses, knowings, and I could pick from them. And at
that point I didn't have a clearly differentiated sense of "this belongs
to this time and that belongs to that time." I just know that I had a
huge pot of beingness from which to draw on.*

She clarified her awareness a little more, and added, "I wouldn't call
it memories; I'd just call it awarenesses." Rosalie didn't see any of this as
past-life *memories* because she didn't see them as past. Instead, they felt
more to her like "awarenesses." It was all part of "who I am" rather than
who she was or used to be. So there was an incorporation or amalgam of
all her personas and experiences and awarenesses from various lifetimes as
coexisting in the present tense. (It was later on, during her teens and early
twenties, that she started to have spontaneous recall of specific past lives
and could discern them as such.)

*I was certainly aware at two and three months of lying in my crib
and feeling myself as an entity, you know, Rosalie, but feeling the
larger soul of me and just taking in what was around me. I remember*

my mother coming in to wake me up or get me out of my crib. My mother used to say to me when I was little that I would wake up smiling, and I remember waking up smiling because I would wake up and see her above me and I adored my mother. I adored the feel of her spirit, and so of course I would wake up smiling because there was this beautiful, loving being right there reaching out for me.

Her mother often referred to Rosalie as her "little ray of sunshine." At two months old, Rosalie liked both her soul Rosalie and her 3D human persona.

I was aware of the soul Rosalie and I was aware of myself Rosalie and … I dug them both … I enjoyed and appreciated and I loved both aspects of me, both the larger soul and the specific entity Rosalie.

She knew that she had a joyful nature and that it was one of her gifts, as well as that she had magic in her. This is in stark contrast to the self-esteem issues that have dogged her in her life that spring from abuse. She knows who she is on the inside (joy, magical), but feels she has trouble seeing who she is in the world or as compared to others she sees in the world or how others perceive her or her energy.

Despite these pleasant memories, Rosalie did undergo some abuse, which she remembers starting when she was three months and three weeks old. She was aware of someone standing outside of her crib,

… watching me. She didn't do anything that first time, but just kind of studied me. And I remember being aware of her and I remember not liking the feel of her. Now there wasn't anything malevolent that was happening, but my gut was saying this was not a benign energy and I sort of perked up and paid attention … And then subsequently not long after that … experiencing her rattling hard the side rail on my crib or reaching in through the slats to slap

*me. And I remember the feel of that and the feeling of the injustice
of it, of "why is she doing this? I'm not doing anything," kind of
looking for a reason in my mind and not finding any.*

So Rosalie felt that she needed to pay attention and be alert. [Rosalie's awareness of the injustice of this abuse thus indicates that babies with that higher spiritual awareness have an innate sense of fairness and justice.]

Unfortunately the abuse continued for years and had such a negative effect on Rosalie that she has intermittently contemplated suicide. A saving grace for her was having always been spiritually aware and aware of herself simultaneously as both a human being and a larger soul.

Once this abuse started, Rosalie's view of the world changed.

*I do remember between the age of two months, when I was more
here than there, and three months and three weeks when the abuse
started. I remember feeling differently about the world than I did
once the abuse started. . . . I was aware when I came in at two
months that I was magical, and I felt sort of a brightness, a
lightness, and a sweetness to life.*

She shifted after the abuse to feeling anxiety. She would wake up in her crib, feeling anxious and worrying about whether the abuser would come in and hurt her. Rosalie feels that she developed hyperarousal as a result, which often is a hallmark and symptom of PTSD.

Another early memory Rosalie has dates back to somewhere between the ages of six and eight months old and before she could walk.

*I was too young to walk, so my mother was holding me, but I was
old enough to hold my head up, and I remember my mother holding me and we were walking into a church. I don't know what the
occasion was . . . it wasn't like Sunday service. It was at a time when
the church was empty, and my mother went there for some reason,*

*and she carried me in her arms. And I just remember feeling… (It's
like I remember the toast that I had for breakfast; it's such a clear
memory.) I just remember feeling, "Oh, Ma, really? This place? Really? Ugh! Oh, come on, can't you see?" I remember hating the feel
of the place. It felt small and limiting and mean and inauthentic,
and I didn't want to have anything to do with it, and I was really
disappointed in my mother. And I felt kind of like a sense of dread
that I was going to be dragged into it. And I remember feeling that
because I have to say that I've always, always, always been sensitive
to the energy of places.*

When she was ten months old, President Kennedy was shot and Rosalie remembers that day and the feel of it, although not necessarily who
was shot.

*I also remember when Kennedy was shot. And this is another story
that my family loves to discount 'cause I was ten months old at the
time… I was with my mother in the basement of our home in Chicago, and she was ironing—and it was just the two of us downstairs.
And we had a little black-and-white TV down there, and I was
sitting in a high chair. And more than like remembering the news
reports per se, if you think that I feel energy and I feel the people
around me and I feel the places that I'm in. What happened that
day that I think a lot of people—just sort of your normal, everyday,
3D people—don't understand is that there's energy to consciousness,
both individually and en masse. And so what I remember from that
day was a horrific rip, just a gash and a shredding in the consciousness of humankind in terms of the spirit of it. Something got very,
very broken—and I felt it… It was big and it permeated. It wasn't
just my mother or my family or a neighborhood. It was the country
and the world, and when something that big happens and it's got*

*that big an effect on the…psyche of humanity, I mean I felt it as a
child. So I knew when Kennedy was assassinated because it was a
rip like no other… It's kind of like a before and after in my life, like
before Kennedy was assassinated there was a certain feel to life, and
then after he was assassinated there was a different feel to life.*

Another memory comes from when she was ten months old and was
on the changing table with a straw hat on her head. She was happy and
relieved because she was out of reach of her abuser.

Rosalie's first vision occurred when she was eleven months old, in 1963.
It was Christmas and it was before she started walking. She feels that she
had probably scooted off by herself because she found herself alone in the
living room, and she remembers standing up for the first time. After pulling
herself up, she found herself loving the new vantage point she had. At that
point, she had her first vision, which was a clear knowing, that she came
here to tell stories. Interestingly, at the same time she jutted her backside
out and felt that she became aware of her body. She knew that this was
significant because two of the things she has loved the most in this lifetime
are writing and dancing. So it was during her vision at eleven months that
she realized what her purpose was in this lifetime and discovered her love
of dance.

Rosalie had a second vision at the age of six that involved her future
partner. She has never forgotten that vision and has known that she would
meet him. This vision reinforced for her that her knowing was valid, despite others doubting her inner knowing and pooh-poohing her. There had
always been a stark contrast between her own inner knowing and the messages she received from her upbringing and her family, as well as the Catholic Church, which were to not trust herself or her knowing. Rosalie knows
that her inner knowing gave her confidence and trust in herself, regardless of
whether there was any rational basis for it or external evidence, because she

knows that this inner knowing comes from Spirit and from something bigger than herself. As a result, her inner knowings have been a comfort for her.

Innate Spiritual Awareness

When she was twelve, Rosalie would climb very high up trees and talk to Spirit (whom she said "wasn't that cranky, constipated God" from church). She has always talked with Spirit and feels even closer when she's out in nature.

Rosalie has also had experiences with what we would call ETs (extraterrestrials), starting when she was seven or eight, but these didn't always feel to her like typical ET experiences as portrayed in popular culture.

> *When I was younger, I was visited by family in other galaxies, shall we say. Occasionally it freaked me out. Mostly it didn't though, because it was just kind of like, "Okay, this is just another part of who I am." Yeah, I've been visited by ETs or whatever, and I think that I've been taken a couple of times too, but the experiences that I had when I was taken, I was taken by people who loved me and who were connecting with me from other family, as it were.*

Rosalie was the only person in her family to be spiritually aware, despite her father being somewhat mystical, and she often felt frustrated as a result of her isolation. When she later shared some of her early memories with her family, they not only failed to believe her but also derided her, which frustrated her even more. She felt a lot of frustration at her siblings and was furious at them for mocking her, leading her to feel that people around her were "knuckleheads who didn't get a lot of stuff." This stark contrast between her inner knowing and spiritual awareness and the derisive reception she received from others around her served as an ongoing source of both irritation and pain.

Past-Life Memories

Rosalie had several undifferentiated past-life memories from early on, as mentioned above, and later in her teens or early twenties she began to have spontaneous recall of some specific past lives that she could discern as such. She first started to have these spontaneous memories while studying at a community college and taking a basic history course. The course professor was in the process of translating some 5,000-year-old cuneiform tablets for a museum. One day he brought one of the clay tablets to class to show to his students, and he also started teaching the class cuneiform. When he wrote a sentence in cuneiform on the blackboard for the first time, Rosalie immediately knew what it meant, even though the professor hadn't yet taught the class how to translate it. At the time, however, this experience freaked her out (probably, she feels, because she was still affected by her Catholic upbringing). "How do I know this? This makes no sense." At the same time, she was also delighted.

She's had numerous additional past-life recollections since then.

For example, there was one life where I nicknamed myself Zeus. I was a gay Greek man in the time before Christ. I was beautiful. I mean I was a god … but I was depressed so I laid down on a rock, and I committed suicide by simply not breathing [because of a romantic disappointment]. And what that experience taught me was I would have to deal with whatever it was anyway and come back and do that. So I might as well just get it over with. While I absolutely believe suicide is anyone's right, I don't believe in it for myself at all because it's just a delaying of the inevitable, and it's cowardice and the easy way out [laughs]. And it's only temporary anyway, like you can't not deal with what's there to be dealt with. If you don't do it now, it's going to come back in another time in another place.

Rosalie remembers another life in the early twentieth century in which she was an eleven-year-old Quaker girl in Pennsylvania who walked into a pond and drowned. She remembers another in the late nineteenth century in England as a young blond, curly-haired, blue-eyed boy. She has recognized people from some of these lives as people she knows in her present life.

In the life in England, she was abandoned by her rich mother who took him (Rosalie) to a seedier section of the town they lived in and left him in the streets because she loved her wealthy lifestyle and didn't want to be bothered by taking care of a child. Some people took pity on him and gave him bread and coins, but he died in the street at about five years old. She recognized her mother in that lifetime as her abuser in the present lifetime, which gave her insight into her tortured relationship with her and why her abuser has always treated her with strong contempt and scorn.

Rosalie also knows that she's had several lives as a Native American and has lived pleasant lives as well as difficult ones.

In addition to those past life recollections, she has also had what she refers to as a "portion of living" (or what I would term a "fragment of incarnation"). After visiting the newly-opened Holocaust Museum in Washington, DC, and also seeing the film *Schindler's List*, her memory of this experience was triggered. While sitting in Union Station afterward waiting for her train for her trip home, she had a flood of memories.

The past-life experience—or fragment of incarnation—took place during World War II during the Holocaust. There was a woman in a concentration camp (one of the prisoners), who was eighteen or nineteen years old and who just wanted out of that experience and her life because she was so drained by it. Rosalie took the woman's place in her body, and she took on this mission with a conscious purpose. (Rosalie does not use the typical word "walk-in" to describe the experience, as she considers that word to be rude, belittling, and dishonoring of the actual experience and to smack of possession.) She viewed this as a gift of compassion to the soul she replaced, a soul too weary to stay in the physical experience of the concentration camp. Rosalie knew that the woman's leaving was not an act of suicide, but more of completion, and that there was higher purpose in Rosalie taking her place.

On the spirit level, Rosalie was very aware that she was going into "extraordinarily difficult, horrific circumstances." She remembers coming into the woman's body and into the concentration camp and feeling everyone around her. There were many others there who were exhausted and Rosalie knew that her spirit was fresh in comparison.

For Rosalie, that sojourn represented a partial lifetime in which her soul was gathering experience. She lived a couple of years in that concentration camp and ended up dying there. She wasn't distressed by her passing, because she feels that she came into that experience "purposely" and "willingly." She was in her higher soul awareness while she was there and knows that she was able to give light and hope to others in the concentration camp. (Her coming in as a more fully formed adult being and not as an infant meant that she didn't have to go through difficult formative years that could have pulled her more into the human psyche and its pain.) She died just before the end of the war and before the other prisoners had been freed. Thus, her experience in that fragment of incarnation was threefold: a gift of compassion for the woman who just wanted out, for her soul as Rosalie to gather more human experience, and to give light and hope to the other prisoners in the concentration camp and make their experiences there a little less difficult.

Innate Intuitive Ability

Rosalie has always seemed to just know things without knowing how she knew them.

I've always known things that I had no particular business or way of knowing in this life in 3D based on my experience to that time.

She's always been good at reading other people, although her ability to see the difference between how some people present themselves (their external face to the world) and who they are on the inside—especially those who are somewhat negative on the inside—has bothered her.

Inauthenticity, to this day, is just the bane of my existence, because what happens is I get one message from their conscious outer self and then I get another message from the real them. And when they're at odds it's annoying to me. I'm constantly having to reconcile that and it's a lot of energy, and it doesn't work for me.

Rosalie resents having to use her energy to reconcile those two conflicting energetic messages she receives when people are inauthentic. In addition, she found it frustrating that the people around her while she was growing up, including her family, couldn't see others' inauthenticity and duplicity, which would lead to Rosalie feeling discounted by others whenever she shared her perceptions.

Observing vs. Engaging

Rosalie has often felt that she is observing people and situations around her, as opposed to being engaged in them. She feels that with her family, particularly her siblings, she couldn't engage, as she was "cut from such a different cloth" from them.

Rosalie hasn't felt as if she was just passing through here, her Earth existence, because she considers this existence to be as valid as every other lifetime she's had. It was a choice she made to be here, and her being here contributes to her soul, although she's also quite aware that this is not the entirety of herself and who she is. She wants to experience everything she possibly can while she's here. (She feels that many New Age people tend to discount their human selves and experiences and focus instead on their larger soul or on the other side.) She doesn't see her Rosalie persona as ancillary to her soul, but, instead, as part of her soul.

Feeling Different from Others

Rosalie feels that her experience of life is different from that of most other people, primarily because of her knowing and awareness. She frequently says, "I know what I know," even if she can't quantify it. For example, about fifteen years before the widespread scandal of Catholic priests molesting children became news, she already intuitively knew that priests were committing these acts and she had a jaundiced eye about the church. Before the news broke, whenever Rosalie shared with others her sense of what was going on, she was accused of being cynical and anti-religious. This has put her at odds with others at times, but she feels that it's *because* of her spiritual awareness that she's different. She knows that she can't always share those intuitive knowings with others, and this frustrates her..

Additional Gifts

Rosalie has been blessed with several gifts: a strong intellect, intuitive knowing, creativity (especially with dance and writing), and her connection with Spirit.

> *One of my strongest gifts and sort of a special gift is that I know what I know and I'm connected with Spirit, and I have a perspective and an understanding of life that is just so much deeper than 3D life alone, which cannot be encompassed by any religion.*

View of Organized Religions

Rosalie is not fond of organized religion. As mentioned earlier, she did not care for her Catholic upbringing, and she distinguishes between the God that was taught about in church and her memory of being with Spirit.

> *And then there was Spirit, who created all of us and who created Earth and plants and animals, and who loved us and who was a creative, loving life force.*

She does not care for the dogma of religions, which she feels can make people's minds and spirit smaller. She feels that it's important for people to find a way to connect with Spirit outside of dogma and outside of a church's locus of control. Her father was a believer in Catholicism, but he was more into the mystery of the Divine than the dogma and rules of the church. Rosalie regards religion as an unnecessary evil and a spiritual playpen. She further feels that her religious upbringing was soul damaging. Buddhism is the only faith that doesn't feel that way to her.

View of Animals and Nature

Rosalie loves animals and feels that they're closer to Spirit than humans are and exhibit an awareness that's much purer than we as humans do. Likewise, she also loves nature, which she feels "is life itself." She feels very connected to the Earth and to its rhythms. As a result, she minimizes her use of technology and uses it only to the extent that she has to. She loves spending time in nature and feels that she connects with Spirit there. Before she starts to dance or to write, she'll go outside and either sit on the porch or walk out in the yard under the stars, which she feels connects her to herself.

Additional Personal Attributes

Even though Rosalie finds herself to be very different from others and often feels frustrated by others, she's very compassionate and emotionally sensitive. She feels that her compassion for others has both allowed her and led her to be compassionate toward herself.

She knows that she came into this life innocent and pure and that that part of herself is still intact. At the same time, however, she feels that's she's not naïve and that a part of her being has been affected by all the "hard and ugly" things she's experienced in this lifetime. Despite her background of abuse and how it has affected her, she's never lost sight of her awareness of the interconnectedness of life and of people.

Rosalie doesn't have a lot of fears, but the abuse that started at such a young age for her did create some ongoing subconscious anxiety. This subconscious anxiety was her norm for years, and she didn't realize that it wasn't normal by others' standards. (Of course this is true for many people who underwent chronic abuse at a young age.) Even though she's suffered from abuse-driven anxiety, she's always trusted that things would be fine in her life. This indestructible trust likely stems from her innate spiritual awareness and her very young vision that showed her that she would be writing. She has an ultimate belief about herself that she would always land on her feet.

Personal Experience of Different Levels

Rosalie has also experienced feeling one thing emotionally or psychologically and another, different thing on another level. Rosalie attributes this to the difference between her history of trauma from the abuse and what she knows on a spiritual level (i.e., that everything is fine). She feels that she can have an emotional reaction initially in the moment at times based upon her personal history of abuse, but her spiritual orientation then sets in, her higher soul awareness. She describes her experience of being in her higher soul awareness as the following:

> There's such a lack of finiteness. The human experience is so finite, there are no boundaries in the sense that you could box up who I am. But yet there's a place where there's edges to me or borders so that I know it's me ... and yet it's as diffuse as a cloud, but there's definitely a presence to it where the molecules are Rosalie, the soul of Rosalie. Like if I were hanging out with you in that space, I could tell me from you, and yet we would overlap. Kind of like overlapping clouds ... where they kind of permeate each other ...

Synaesthesia and Unusual Senses

While Rosalie doesn't have any of the more commonly known forms of synaesthesia (a condition in which two senses are combined, so that some people with the condition will, for example, see sounds), she has always had a spiral sense of time instead of a linear one. As a result, she says that things that are past or future "are just parallel to me along different points of the spiral." She always innately sees the patterns in things, especially if there's symmetry, such as in numbers. Coupled with this, she has a photographic memory and is able to remember long strings of numbers, like phone numbers. She has to be careful about what she allows herself to see because she can't get things out of her mind later on, as they're imprinted in her memory.

On Feeling Protected and Guided

Rosalie has always felt protected in her life by spiritual beings. She had a bad car accident many years ago when she was in college. This was prior to laws requiring drivers to wear a seat belt. When she got into her car, something told her to put her seat belt on, which she did, even though she wasn't typically a seat-belt wearer. Whereas she tended to lock her car door, a voice told her, "You better just leave your driver's door unlocked in case you get into an accident." She thought it was odd and viewed it at the time as a random thought, but she heeded that voice nonetheless. On her return trip, she got slammed from the rear by another car. It was an accident that left her with some injuries that haven't completely healed, but it could have been much worse. She feels that she was protected in this situation by the voice that had spoken to her.

She has additionally been aware of her guides at times throughout her life and feels providence has been walking with her and protecting her.

She has known that she came here to Earth to do something and that because she hasn't done it yet she'll be fine. Throughout her career she has had to travel, and she's frequently seen other people in airports who were afraid of flying. Nonetheless, she remembers walking on to planes feeling that her fellow passengers didn't need to be fearful because Rosalie was on the flight, and she knew it wasn't her time to go yet because she hadn't fulfilled her life purpose.

She feels that she has traveled places in her sleep and has been with other people for the purpose of doing something to help someone or as part of a community. These have been actual experiences that she feels are soul missions rather than part of a dream. There are good feelings around these missions even if the logistics or the situations around them are challenging. In these experiences she feels a sense of cooperation and coming together, as well as love and doing something for a higher good. She's also had visions of her future while sleeping.

On Being Spiritually Aware Since Birth

Rosalie feels that being spiritually aware her whole life is both a blessing and a curse. She feels on the one hand that it's a huge blessing and that she couldn't begin to imagine how she would feel or how small her view of life would be had she not always had this awareness. On the other hand, she feels that it's created a lot of loneliness and isolation, because other people can't relate to her or her awareness. That said, she feels that ultimately it's more of a blessing because her spiritual awareness has been one of the things that have kept her from committing suicide out of despair over the abuse she suffered.

She feels that even when she's in some sort of pain in her life, her spiritual awareness is still there. It may temporarily be blocked by the human experience of pain and can be very difficult to deal with, but her spirit awareness never leaves her.

I feel that it's important to see human emotion as not only a valid experience, but a way of deepening your connection to and your experience of your spirit self.

Life Purpose

Rosalie's life purpose has been in her mind throughout her life, and she feels that her view of it has been expanded by her experiences in life. She also shared that her work with me in our private sessions has further expanded her view of it. (Rosalie is a client of mine and shared that her intuition led her to me.) While she has always known that she came here to tell stories, she has found that the difficult experiences she's had to heal from in her life, especially the abuse, have deepened her sense and understanding of being human, and these experiences have deepened her compassion for others and her understanding of why it's so important to be kind. She feels that her compassion for herself through her healing process has extended out to others and that she's gained an understanding of what it is to be spirit in human form. She now feels that she wouldn't trade any of her life's experiences, including the traumatic ones, as they've deepened her sense of purpose and have brought her to where she is now in life.

4

Jimelle Suzanne's Story

"I was very aware of a horrible light, blinding, blinding lights, and choking. I couldn't stand it. I just felt like I weighed a thousand pounds and I was choking."

THIS WAS JIMELLE SUZANNE'S FIRST memory from when she was born. The heaviness she felt—feeling like she weighed a thousand pounds—was representative of her awareness of having trouble acclimating to being in a physical body again on this dense three-dimensional level. Her mother later confirmed that Jimelle indeed had a lot of phlegm and had been choking when she was born.

Jimelle feels that she has a vague memory before her birth because she felt that she hadn't spent any time in her mother's womb before she was born, and that her soul came into her new human body at birth. However, her first clear memories were right after she was born.

47

Innate Spiritual Awareness

Jimelle was always spiritually aware, which for her was an awareness of "they." "They" were always around her, although she didn't call her sense of this spiritual presence God or angels or guides. It was just "they."

She has always sensed them and can't remember a time without them. She would sense them and think, "Oh, they're here," and she could hear them communicating with each other about her. She could hear them say things like, "She's walking pretty well," "Her lungs are doing pretty well now," "She's developing right," and "I think she's going to adjust okay."

She would get very indignant and think, "Of course I'm going to adjust." However, at the same time, she felt good about them being with her, and she knew that they weren't physical beings here on the Earth. Their presence made her feel good and protected and comfortable. She now feels that they are her spiritual advisors and guides, as well as some relatives who had passed on.

She was aware of them early on discussing her progress because there was some question as to whether she would adjust well to being in a body again and back on Earth, because her coming here was sort of a last-minute thing. They were always looking after her because there was a question as to whether she would be able to do whatever she needed to do while being here, and they were trying to make sure that she was able to do it (referring to her purpose for being back on Earth). This could have been because her mother was older (47) when she had Jimelle and there may have been concern about Jimelle's condition and health as a result.

Jimelle stated that her awareness and thoughts at birth were similar to her present adult ones.

My thoughts were exactly the same as at present—very articulate.

Author's note: this is common among everyone I've interviewed who's had that spiritual awareness at birth or shortly thereafter.

If anything she was frustrated because she was unable to make her mouth work so that she could express her thoughts. This frustration over the dichotomy between her clear awareness and her chronological age and resultant inability to express herself was evident in two additional memories that she shared.

Early Memories

Jimelle's next memory after birth was of when she was nine days old. (She later asked her mother about this memory, and her mother confirmed it.)

It was very hot, there was something white over the top of me, and, interestingly, my thoughts were exactly the same as they are now, very articulate, thinking, "Oh, my goodness, what is this over me and I just do not like this heat." Terrible! And I was just really irritated with the whole thing. And I thought, "I could not see anybody and I was in this—whatever this is." I could not tell what I was in. And all of a sudden someone pulled back this white thing, which I [later] learned from my mother was a diaper ... And we were stopped at the border between states ... And there was my father. I didn't think of him as my father. I just thought of him as such a handsome man. He had this black curly hair.

Right next to him another face appeared, who was an official with a mustache and who wore an official uniform. She later found out from her mother that they had been at an inspection station at the border between Arizona and California where cars were inspected to make sure that no agricultural produce was on board (due to concerns about crops being endangered by pests or disease).

I was trying to tell my dad not to put that white thing over me again. I didn't like it. And so they talked about how cute I was and all of that, and I thought, "This is weird." ... And then the darn thing went

*back over the top of me, and I thought, "Let me out of here. I don't
like this." And I started getting very upset and I started crying.*

Jimelle remembers several additional things before she turned a year
old. However, the next salient memory came when she was about ten
months old, when they were visiting her grandmother in Texas. She had a
stuffed dog, named Bow Wow, which she carried around with her everywhere. She remembers going out to a shed one day on her grandmother's
farm, carrying Bow Wow, and climbing onto a box to try to look inside—
and inadvertently dropping Bow Wow into the box. She went back into
the house to try to get her mother to tell her what she wanted. Her mother
couldn't understand her, which really frustrated her. She then thought,
Oh, what is wrong with these people? She was finally able to get her mother
to understand by dragging her and pointing.

As should be obvious, her awareness as an infant and toddler was
not that of a baby, and this contributed to her frustration over not being
able to communicate her concerns or get others to understand her. She
described her awareness:

*I was like I am now. I thought I was an adult. I was not a baby in
my mind.*

She was very frustrated and irritated over trying to get the adults
around her to understand. There were times when she would think *these
people are just not understanding me.*

The discrepancy between her awareness age and her chronological age
created additional problems for her. She felt older than everyone else and
hated to be bossed by others.

When Jimelle was five she got sick and was in bed with a very high
fever, feeling worse and worse. All of a sudden there was a bright light
overhead and the room started to get dark. She knew she was starting to
go out of her body and noticed that she felt relieved. Her mother was crying.

Then a doctor came into the room and Jimelle asked him to turn on the light. He did something that brought her back into her body. Whenever she has told others about that experience, she just naturally says that the bright light she saw was actually her soul leaving her body, although she's not sure about that.

Attitude About Being Here

Jimelle didn't want to be here (in this lifetime). She resented her body, finding it too heavy, and would think *oh, this stupid body*. She would go out of body at night, enjoying the feeling of escaping from her physical body. She later told her parents that she really enjoyed sticking her toe into the mattress all the way down to the springs, but they would just look at her. She also resented having to breathe because she felt she had to work at it. So she would just hold her breath at times to avoid working at breathing. Once she held her breath for too long and passed out.

From a very young age, Jimelle has felt as if she is just passing through Earth and is here temporarily. When she was six or seven, her father was telling her about heaven, and she told him:

You know, I don't know the need for all of this. Why can't we just go back to heaven and be done with it? It's ridiculous, all this stuff.

Her father was concerned, of course, that she didn't try to leave here by ending her life in some way.

Past-Life Recall

Jimelle has had a natural spontaneous recall of some of her other (past) lives, and the boundary between her present lifetime awareness and that of some other past-life personas was so thin that she thought she was still a man (from another lifetime). When she was four years old, she wanted a cowboy outfit. Her parents bought her one, but when she looked in the mirror, she saw a little girl with blond hair in a cowgirl outfit looking back at her.

I was so shocked. I just felt sick to my stomach. Here I was, this little white, curly-haired thing wearing a stupid skirt, and my gun didn't even work.

She knew that she was a gambler and a drunk and could play poker. She knew she had abandoned her family and that she rode horses out in the desert. In this lifetime, however, she can't grasp how to play cards (although, interestingly, she's quite adept at intuitively reading playing cards). At one birthday party when she was little, all the children were riding horses and she demonstrated that she knew how to mount the horse and knew automatically how to post, gallop, and canter. She also knew that she had lived as a geisha and tried to make her eyes more like that of a geisha, in addition to wanting to put geisha make-up on herself.

She also remembered going to visit her aunt or grandmother by the railroad tracks and riding a buckboard. She later realized that this memory had not been from her childhood in this lifetime, but from another one instead.

So her awareness represented an identification with different personas from various lifetimes, as if she were still living them. She didn't see them as separate from her present persona as Jimelle. (These are similar to some of Rosalie's undifferentiated past-life memories.)

As an adult, Jimelle went through a period of depression. At the suggestion of a friend, she went to see a psychic, who told her that she (Jimelle) felt that God had arbitrarily chosen her to suffer, but that there were reasons behind all of what she had experienced in other lifetimes. This triggered a powerful healing for her, because this was the only way to make sense of what she was experiencing—the confusing mad rush of information from other lifetimes. Jimelle had many instances throughout her life of spontaneous past-life recall, including past-life connections to people she met in this lifetime, but had not been able to make sense of it until the psychic shared that information with her.

Innate Intuitive Ability

Jimelle has had intuitive experiences since she was approximately three years old. For example, she would know before people would come to visit. There weren't any earth-shattering instances, but she would have an inner knowing about things.

Synaesthesia and Unusual Senses

She also has synaesthesia (a condition in which two senses are combined, so that one sees sounds, for example, as mentioned previously). For Jimelle, this has expressed itself in two ways: with calendars and with colors and numbers. After learning about calendars in school, she always saw them from a vantage point up in the sky and looking down. She saw them on a ball, which represented the Earth with squares on it, and these had the month and dates inside with random colors. She has always seen the numbers one through nine with a corresponding color. (For example, she always sees green with the number three.)

Innate Spiritual Awareness

Needless to say, Jimelle has not just been spiritually aware since birth, but also spiritually oriented. She's had access to spiritual wisdom since she was little, although she wishes she had access to more. When she was ten or eleven, she remembers going with her mother to see the movie *The Search for Bridey Murphy*, a well-known film about reincarnation. Jimelle told her mother afterward that she knew the movie was accurate, but her mother didn't want to hear anymore on the subject.

Jimelle sometimes receives spiritual insight from "they" and from a grouping of spiritual beings. For example, she received information in February 2012 about possible upcoming earth changes. Some of this material included the following:

Wherever inequities exist with regard to the balancing of the planet Earth and the rising consciousness of the people, somewhat extreme activities will be experienced. It is not the intention to destroy—but to awaken. There is a choice and a destiny encoded within each being to experience Earth events for the purpose of growth and teaching for the individual experience and for those who observe it.

In 2012, an angel appeared over her bed. One of her guides woke her up and there the angel was. It was the most magnificent sight she has ever seen; she found it breathtaking. The angel was dressed in a deep wine color and she feels that those angels deal with past lives. Jimelle believes that this has been a theme in her life this time around—coming to terms with or recognizing past lives. She says that is the only way her present life makes sense.

Feeling Different from Others

Jimelle feels that her experience of life is definitely different from that of most other people who haven't always been spiritually aware. She can see and observe things very clearly and in great detail. She likened it to having a "great big magnifying glass that you can see all the little details with."

This results in her being able to see more than other people can. She feels that when she's dealing with most other people she has to be shallow and superficial, which she finds annoying, and it's difficult for her to converse with most people in a lighter, less meaningful way.

Observing vs. Engaging

Jimelle feels that most of the time she is observing what is going on around her in an unengaged way—unless she's emotionally involved with something or going through something emotional. In the latter instances, she feels that she is then involved and engaged. She's also good at reading other people unless she's emotionally engaged with them, and she has recognized some people as people she's known from another lifetime. When this happens, she gets glimpses of the other lifetime—where that person was and when they were together.

Additional Gifts

Jimelle has taught dance for a number of years, after having danced herself for several years, and she's often spiritually inspired to create certain dances and to teach a certain way. Jimelle is also a writer, having written spiritual poetry and fiction, including a metaphysical novel, *Blue Vision,* which was published in 2013. She's also worked professionally with her intuition and has done readings for others.

Views of Animals and Nature

Jimelle loves animals and considers animals to be precious, beautiful, and innocent. She has pets and also keeps food bowls outside for animals. A neighbor's dog sometimes brings hungry animals to Jimelle to feed and take care of. She loves nature and has houseplants. She's extremely compassionate and sensitive and feels that there is a part of her that is very innocent and pure, although she does lose her temper at times (as we all do). She feels that her pure, innocent part has guided her in her life, but she has trouble understanding those who lack that compassion and innocence.

View of Organized Religions

Jimelle was brought up in a religious tradition (Methodist and then Christian Science), but is not a fan at present of religion. She feels compassion for people who belong to religious groups who might need the security and sense of companionship that they have with other people of similar belief systems. That said, she feels that religion has nothing to do with spirituality and is only man-made rules, control, and power. Plus, she feels that religion, due to religious dogma, has caused a lot of wars, bloodshed, grief, and torture, which she finds appalling.

Personal Experience of Different Levels

Jimelle frequently finds herself feeling one thing emotionally and something different on another level, because she feels that she gets triggered emotionally at times. When that happens, she usually tries to figure out what the lesson is for her from the situation. Gaining the distance and perspective might not work for her in the moment and often takes hindsight.

When asked to describe her level of awareness when it's clear, she described it as a higher level and where you know stuff, which is a place of knowing and wisdom.

Jimelle had a dream several years ago in which she visited etheric schools (which is recounted in my book, *Dream Interpretation for Beginners: Understand the Wisdom of Your Sleeping Mind*). In these etheric schools, she saw various souls dancing in perfect unison. That was as close to a sense of oneness as she has ever felt.

On Feeling Protected and Guided

From birth, Jimelle has felt protected and guided and has had experiences in which she feels a higher being interceded to help her. Once she was right on the verge of having an unavoidable car accident when someone literally grabbed the wheel of her car and turned it, sparing her the accident and impact.

Even though she feels that she is protected, she also acknowledges that she has some fears that are intense. For example, she has a fear of heights. While on a visit to see the Grand Canyon, Jimelle found herself quite afraid of the height there, to the extent that she just wanted to go back to the car and sit in it. She said that she was taken aback by this reaction because she hadn't expected to have such a strong fear while there. She suspects that this fear came from some past life. Even while she's feeling some of these fears, however, a different part of her knows that she will be fine and has no reason to fear. (Note: this is an example of the difference between what the higher soul awareness knows and the human persona feels.)

On Being Spiritually Aware Since Birth

She feels that being spiritually aware her whole life is both a blessing and a curse. She loves her spiritual awareness and perceptions. However, not having had many people in her life with whom she could share her awareness and experiences, especially when she was very young, has felt like a curse at times. As she has encountered more people who can understand her experiences, being born aware feels like more of a blessing to her.

Life Purpose

Even though she has taught and advised others for years, she's still trying to determine what her life purpose is. That said, she had a dream years ago in which someone handed her a beautifully printed certificate on which was written, "Master of Nursing." Synchronistically, three days later her father collapsed and she had to travel and take care of him. She feels that taking care of others has been a theme in her life, so she has been a healer to others. As a result, she feels that may be her purpose.

5

Heather's Story

"I was working for the Creator and … I was making
things … and they were quite beautiful."

HEATHER REMEMBERS WHERE SHE WAS and what she was doing before she
was born. She was an angel and was in a place with her angel friends that
is difficult for her to fully describe, except that everything there was light
and beauty.

*There was beauty everywhere, beauty, beauty, beauty, and nothing
but beauty—and light and beauty.*

She worked with other angels doing creative work.

*Basically we worked in groups of four, and we were all kindred, and
we would build planets. We would formulate all kinds of wonderful
life forms. It was taking the energy of the Creator and building from
it, and that was what we did.*

The groups of four were like a "consciousness group of four," and they were communal as opposed to being what we would call individuals.

My recollection of it is somewhat hazy, but... I did have a sense that we were directed and that we were communal, meaning that the directions came... translated into the consciousness rather spontaneously and in a way that wasn't like, "Here do this, do this, do this," in a linear fashion like we think of things. It was not linear at all. It was very much just flooded into your consciousness, and the knowing of this is what I must do.

Heather knows that she is an incarnated angel and has always had a pervading knowing, which was innate in her, that everything is made of energy and is light and energy. She didn't understand when people didn't grasp that. She defines an angel as "nothing more than a being of light that constantly serves Divine will and carries out the Divine plan."

Before she was born, she was happy to go wherever God sent her and do whatever she was told to do. Being born in this lifetime was an opportunity that she was looking forward to.

At the same time she feels that she was lucky because there was an option for her:

... if, when I went through the birth and I was a baby, and I decided this just wasn't for me, I had an option to go back to my true self and not be in this world.

Right before she was born, she met with her spirit guide, who told her, "I'm going to be with you your whole life, and I'm your ancestor." She later forgot that he was her ancestor, but then remembered it subsequently during her life here. He was with her at her birth into this lifetime and has been her primary spirit guide throughout her present life.

Before she was born, Heather had no sense of her mother's pregnancy while her physical body was being gestated. Her consciousness didn't come in until right before she was born.

I was there at the time of the birth... I wasn't there before. I was doing what I was doing elsewhere, and then I got called in because it was time.

At-Birth and Early Memories

She doesn't recall the birth itself but knows that it was off-putting. She feels that she may have repressed any memory of it because it was traumatic and abrupt and wasn't done in a way that was very loving.

While she was in the nursery in the hospital with all the other babies, she remembers a wonderful man who came there. As he was looking at her, her soul connected to his soul. She couldn't see him, but she could feel his energy. She knew that he was important to her and always would be. That man was her father and she felt a strong connection with him and feels that this was the reason she decided to stay, because she knew that he would be there for her.

Heather has several other memories from her infancy, not all of which were pleasant. She remembers one incident when she was just a few months old and lying in her baby bed. A woman who helped to take care of her, and whom she loved, came into her room and started screaming when she saw a tick crawling on Heather. The woman was afraid of spiders and, even though ticks are not spiders, the physical resemblance must have been enough to scare the woman. That incident imprinted upon Heather and she also developed a fear of spiders.

Additional memories stemming from her infancy were also unpleasant and, moreover, abusive. Heather had her head banged against the side of her baby bed and there was emotional abuse that continued over a period of time.

Heather also has some pleasant memories as a baby. She remembers being held lovingly, as well as good memories of her father and other people being kind to her.

Feeling Different from Others

Early on, even before the age of one, Heather realized that she was different from those around her.

It just seemed like I was living in two different worlds and that they lived in one world and I lived in the other one.

She felt that she still had an innocent and pure light, but others didn't seem to recognize it. She also noticed that others didn't want to commune with nature spirits in the way that she did. However, she did feel that she had known her family before, in spite of how different she felt from them (except for her father, to whom she felt quite connected).

Innate Spiritual Awareness

Heather's innate spiritual awareness has been with her from the time she was born. She has always remembered the light and the oneness from a time before she was born, while also coming to learn at a young age, probably within a few months, that this was not true of others and that this physical three-dimensional reality was quite a different reality from the one of light and oneness from which she had come. She was both sensitive to and aware of energy, including people's energies, and she interacted with energies of people, which was how she related to others. However, she could tell that this was not what others did. She feels that she was always in that oneness with God until she was trained otherwise.

She has also had spontaneous out-of-body experiences for most of her life, starting at a very young age. Throughout her childhood, her spirit guide would take her out of body and they would go have enjoyable excursions. They would often do it night after night and it was great fun. She felt that she was living a whole other life while her body was asleep.

She has always loved nature and communing with nature beings—fairies, devas, and elementals. She loved toddling around outside at a young age and singing songs—songs that she feels she was channeling from nature spirits. This started around the age of two.

When she was young she was focusing on absorbing this reality, so as to acclimate to it, but she still got to feel the oneness through her connection to her spirit guide and guardian angels, as well as the nature spirits that she felt so connected and close to.

Heather feels that when she was very, very young, she was her true self (her true soul being) before she was contaminated (i.e., affected by this physical reality and its conventions). From her birth until she was three or four years old, she feels that she was in her soul being (what she terms her "spirit light," and what I would term her higher soul awareness) 80–90 percent of the time. Unfortunately others had a hard time understanding her and some of the things she would say. Her family would often look askance at her and she would be told that she had a wild imagination. Heather gradually came to realize that this wasn't necessarily a compliment and that she was experiencing life quite differently from others. On the other hand, however, she sensed that her father understood her and saw and recognized her light. This gave her the sense that she always had someone in her corner.

View of Organized Religions

Heather has always been compassionate and sensitive and feels that it was her true nature to love everyone and everything. Her conservative religious background trained her out of that, however, and trained her to replace compassion with pity, for both self and others. After several years she was able to reclaim her original sense of compassion, which she feels is more helpful for others than pity. Likewise she feels that she was born free of fears, but that her religious upbringing was steeped in fear. A pattern of worry in her family inculcated fears into her and created conflict for her. As a result, she felt brainwashed into fear, even though her true self knew better. She was affected by the atmosphere of fear and had to work through that over the years in order to get back to her more natural self that trusts and knows that she's protected and isn't in the grip of fear and worry.

As a result of her conservative religious upbringing, which was so at odds with her innate knowing, she eventually left the church in her teens. She was down on religion, especially fundamentalist ones, for a while. Later on, while in college, she started exploring and studying other religious traditions and saw the commonality among religions. She feels that at the core of every religion is light, but that some, especially fundamentalist ones, focus on the darkness.

Past-Life Recall

Heather has had dreams of other lifetimes, one of which was when she was a man who was French. After she woke up from this dream, she knew French for just a few minutes. She didn't necessarily know when she was little that these were other lifetimes, but she felt very connected to the experiences. While she was dreaming, she felt very connected to the French man, and the dream experiences felt very real. She knew that the man had gotten killed in the French Revolution.

Innate Intuitive Ability

Heather is naturally intuitive, and one early manifestation of this was her ability to sense and feel the energy of other people. She could sense whether they felt good or not, although she learned that others were not as perceptive as she was in this regard. One example was when there was a new official in town who was charismatic, handsome, and dynamic and whom her family thought highly of and spoke glowingly about. Heather, however, felt that the man was devious and crooked. It was later discovered that he had been embezzling funds. Heather was not surprised, even though her family was shocked.

Her grandmother was strongly intuitive and Heather was told at times that she also had "the gift." However, she would then be admonished: "but we don't talk about that." This may have been because of the conservative religious atmosphere that Heather was brought up in.

In spite of her natural intuition, Heather started to shut down some of her abilities in her early teens, primarily because she wanted to fit in more with others; her intuitive gifts diminished as a result. Once she started to pay attention to them again, they reignited and grew. She came in with a strong intuition, which she has honed—along with creativity, an ability to channel, and a strong intellect—and developed, although she feels that her left and right brain often battle with each other.

Her sensitivity has been life-long, even when she tried to squelch it during her teen years. She is also sensitive to the energy of places and situations, especially if there has been trauma or difficulty in a place from the past.

Attitude About Being Here

In spite of the fact that Heather had felt that it was an honor to come to Earth and incarnate, and that being here was an assignment, over time she started to feel a resistance. This was because of the difficult things she experienced, including the religious dogma she was exposed to, which to her was dour and strict and focused on the negative instead of the positive. Between the ages of four and five, she started to doubt that coming here was an honor and wondered if this was, instead, some sort of punishment because being here didn't feel good. After watching a show about aliens, she started to dream that a spaceship landed and took her back home.

At the same time, however, while she slept Heather got to visit other places and times and feel more at home. Her spirit guide, who was a Cherokee ancestor, would take her through time to visit her Cherokee ancestor family, and she felt more at home there. She also felt more at home and connected whenever she spent time in nature and could feel and connect with the nature spirits.

Heather does feel that she has lived other lives as a human. However, she feels that she got to spend time in between those lives on the other side as an angel, as opposed to staying on a more human level.

Personal Experience of Different Levels

While she feels that her natural mode may be to observe things around her, Heather feels that she was sent here to experience life and what it is, as well as what it feels like to be human. As a result, she is often engaged with what is going on around her. She sometimes finds herself feeling one thing on a higher level and another different thing on the more human level— or the difference between "the wisdom of your soul and … that human aspect" (or what I term the human persona vs. the higher soul awareness).

View of Animals

Heather has always loved animals. She feels like a mother to all of them, believing they're like angels because of their innocence and desire to serve. She's experienced them as being wonderful teachers who've helped her to feel more like herself. Likewise, her love of nature has been healing for her and has provided spiritual sustenance for her.

On Being Spiritually Aware Since Birth

She knows that her experience of life appears to differ from that of most others, whom she has observed to be caught up in the more mundane aspects of the world. She's able to rise above concerns in a fairly short period of time, while others seem to stew about them.

When asked about whether she feels that being spiritually aware her whole life has been a blessing or a curse, she shared that when she was young there were times that it felt more like a curse because she used to feel out of place and different from others. She now feels that it's primarily a blessing.

Similar to others who were born aware, she feels that she used to feel more of a discrepancy between her human persona, especially when dealing with something emotional, and her true self higher soul awareness. As she has grown more over time and has aligned herself with her purpose in this lifetime, she feels that they are more synced up.

Life Purpose

Throughout most of her life, Heather longed to be back on the other side and not be here. However, when she started to live her soul purpose with her spiritual work, she no longer felt that and shifted to feeling more content being here.

I feel home goes with me.

6

Theresa Waltermeyer's Story

"I remember picking my parents and picking
my father. I just wanted to be his daughter."

THERESA WALTERMEYER'S MEMORIES STRETCH BACK to before she was born.

*I remember volunteering. I wanted to come back down to Earth…
I knew something was getting ready to happen, and it was a time
when there was a lot of spirits getting ready to come down, and I
wanted to be part of it… My understanding was that I was going
to play a part in bringing people together—like I was a link.*

Theresa knew that this journey was going to be a very important one.

*The reason why I was coming down… had to do with the Earth and
how the Earth was going to be affected… I did know that it was the
people who were going to [negatively] affect the Earth—and that
would be really whether the Earth survived or not.*

Theresa could tell that chemicals and industry would be harming the Earth and its climate and that people needed to be educated about these things. She knew she was coming in because she had a role to play in improving this impending problem.

She could tell that a lot of other souls were incarnating then for this same reason. She knew that the Earth would still be here but could be severely damaged. At the same time, she knew that she was going to be very successful in the role she was going to play and in linking with other people who were here to help and that the Earth would be preserved.

Theresa remembers looking onto the Earth and picking her parents. Somebody was showing her different couples who could potentially be her parents, and she remembers picking her father and really wanting to be his daughter. She also remembers picking her mother, but she wasn't as excited about her as she was about her father. She feels that this could be due to the strong past-life connection with her father and having been with him in various other lifetimes.

When she was first shown her father as a potential parent, it was automatic for her.

> I knew that's where I needed to be … My father was very laid-back, very kind, … He loved everybody. It was just very easy for him to relate to everybody, and that was one of the gifts that I was going to need … when I got to Earth … to be able to relate to everybody and anybody.

She could see that her mother was very disciplined and organized and that the two of them together were a good match for her. She was strongly connected with her father's energy and feels that she had a little crush on him before she was born.

She's not sure who was showing her the different couples or whether it was male, female, or whatever, but she could feel the energy, which was a very loving, kind energy, which she feels was a spiritual guide.

These memories that stem from the time she was born have always been with Theresa in this lifetime.

When she was very, very young, she talked about this all the time to her parents and grandparents, but they looked at her like she had two heads.

Theresa knows being here in this lifetime was for both the role she was going to play here and for her soul growth. She still remembers what it felt like on the other side. It had a "very light warm feeling," and she felt "very whole" there. In one sense she was happy to come and be on this mission, while in another sense she was very content and happy where she was (on the other side on higher levels).

She also had a sense of what her life would be like here before she came in. She knew that she was going to be presenting to people in different locations. She remembers being in her crib and feeling that she was practicing by addressing large groups of people in different parts of the world, jumping from country to country. As she did this, people in different parts of the world were speaking different languages, but she could understand them. Even though she knew before she came in that she would be doing this, it was very strong once she got here.

Theresa also has memories of being around other human beings who didn't look like us. They had a luminous appearance, but they looked human, although she questioned if that's the way they presented themselves so she could relate to them. They were much taller and looked somewhat translucent. She remembers one specific being with long blond hair, who was a male. She feels that this was on another planet and that she was there for the teachings and to gain knowledge and feels that she stayed there for a good while. This training was in preparation for this lifetime and she feels that she will be using that knowledge and training. She hasn't had to tap into it and use it yet, but feels that when the time is right she will. So this was not another lifetime on a different planet, as much as it was training for her here in this lifetime.

She also remembers traveling from planet to planet throughout the universe, being led by two spirits who were accompanying and guiding her. They were doing this to observe things while on other planets, and she feels that this occurred on the other side before she came here to Earth as preparation for what she was to do in this lifetime.

At-Birth and Early Memories

Theresa's first memory after incarnating was of being born and coming to consciousness and looking at the nurse. She instantly didn't like her, because the nurse wasn't kind. She also remembers a group of people standing around her in the hospital, with her grandmother being one of them, and that there were spirit-forms behind them, which she feels were her guides. Each spirit was assigned to a person with regard to how that person would interact with her, and she feels that they were her guides giving direction.

Her next memory is of being in her parents' bedroom in a crib when she was about seven or eight months old, where she was practicing speeches. Her mother would make fun of her and say, "Look at her. She's addressing an audience." This practicing was a reminder of where Theresa needed to go and what she was to do. She also remembers wondering why she was put with that family and in that environment, because they were lower in income. She finally got an answer to that question later in life—it was because she was supposed to make her own way in the world, and she had to understand how people lived and know people from all walks of life.

She remembers always having a "humongous" family, both here on Earth and on the other side. For example, she would always see spirits around her grandmothers. When her mother started to get sick, an invisible friend showed up and would be with her from time to time. At present and in retrospect, Theresa feels that her friend was probably an angel sent to comfort her. They didn't do a lot of talking and she feels it was more inner intuitive knowing and meaning that were communicated. Her friend would sit on the edge of the bed if Theresa was upset or if she could hear her mother being sick in the other room and her father trying to comfort her. At other times, the angel would lay on the pillow next to Theresa, just to let her know that she wasn't alone.

Innate Intuitive Ability

Theresa was always intuitive and had a sense of knowing. When she knew that something was going to happen, she would tell her family in advance. A lot of people in her family thought she was different. However, her grandmothers were very intuitive themselves and understood her and didn't regard her as different. It was the family members who weren't intuitive and didn't understand who regarded her as different. A lot of the other children Theresa knew also thought she was different.

Similar to others with these early spiritual memories, Theresa has always felt that she was observing what was going on around her, as opposed to being engaged in things.

Innate Spiritual Awareness

Theresa has always been spiritual. She knows that the message she'll convey in addressing groups of people has to do with reestablishing the connection between everyone and everything, and the connection that needs to be made will be made through the energy of love.

It's when we strip away all the defenses we put up to guard ourselves and just truly open our hearts that we can connect to that pure state of love.

She would like to think that that will happen in her lifetime, but feels that there's a lot of work that needs to be done.

Theresa knows that her consciousness while still in spirit form was different from her consciousness as a person here on Earth.

I remember feeling very connected to every living thing on Earth. I remember being connected to human beings, animals, plants, rocks, like I was all a part of them.

This is a different feeling or view from her human consciousness, in which there's what Theresa calls "a little bit of separation."

Theresa still remembers being with God, yet finds it hard to describe the Divine.

It was just a wonderful, strong, loving [energy]... It's so hard to describe because the feelings are indescribable, but it was just... pure love where you were secure. I don't know if there are any words to describe it... Perfect—like you were in a state of perfection.

She remembers God not being in a form and yet having volition and directing things.

This awareness and memory have always been part of her, even after she took on human form. She has been able to tell when the Divine is directing her and showing her things because it becomes highlighted for her, literally. For example, if she's considering doing something, she sees the situation illuminated by light. She never lost her connection to the Divine. It was always consciously part of her—at least until the age of ten, when her mother died. At that point, she just shut down for a while.

When her mother died, Theresa felt betrayed. So for about ten years she discarded her active awareness of God, the universe, etc. What helped to rewaken her spiritual awareness was a psychic reading she had at the age of eighteen. During the reading, messages came through that rang true to Theresa, and this experience got her curious and questioning. She started to inquire about connections to the other side. Then, when she had her two children, becoming a mother opened her up as well. She didn't raise them in a religious manner—she feels that they came in aware as well.

Awareness of Purpose

Theresa was always inner-guided from the very beginning. She always felt different from others and still does. She's always had a memory of not being here in human form, and she knows that Earth is her temporary home while she's here on assignment. She's always felt that she was just passing through here, though she's known she has a purpose to accomplish before she can be on her way.

She feels that one of her purposes in this lifetime is to help people connect. She remembers being shown an area where there were all different kinds of people, and she knew she needed to be able to connect with all of them, from the guru down to the street person. She was supposed to learn from all of them because each person was going to have a lesson for her. She was to learn how to connect with all of them—including animals—in almost a telepathic way, via a glance at the eye where she could feel an energy going back and forth.

Past-Life Recall

Theresa has a recollection of some past lives in which she was addressing large groups of people. She knows that she had a past life in Africa and that she was black in two or three lifetimes. She also knows that she had a past life in Italy, probably in the Tuscany area, and loved living there. This helped pave the way for her to choose to be born in this lifetime to people of Italian descent. She's still very drawn to Tuscany even though she hasn't been there in this lifetime. She also remembers living in England in a past life where she came from a wealthy family attached to the throne, even though they weren't royalty themselves. These past-life recollections came to her in spontaneous déjà vu flashes and instant memories.

Theresa's past-life memories started coming to her in her twenties after she had her two children and started to open back up to her innate spirituality.

Feeling Different from Others

She's always been good at reading other people and feels that her experience of life is very different from that of other people. She feels that her perspective of life is different from that of other people because she doesn't get into the mundane and everyday. She knows that we all have to focus on survival necessities while being here, but feels that when she's truly here, she's still somewhere else, meaning that her body is here, but her consciousness is oriented elsewhere.

She also feels that her spiritual awareness has made her different from other people, in that she's more open, more loving, more guided, and more accepting. She has more empathy and more foresight on what may be coming in the future. She can also access more universal information, whereas most people who aren't spiritually aware usually can't, and she has more healing abilities. She's able to help people help themselves or heal themselves.

Synaesthesia and Unusual Senses

Music has always been one of Theresa's strongest gifts, and she feels that she can hear sounds that others can't hear.

> *I hear music in my ears that you can't hear on Earth or by instruments, more of a celestial music. That I don't know can be replicated. I can even hear music ... like if it's raining, I can hear a song in the rain, like from the tapping of the rain. I can sit outside and hear a song go through my head just by the wind, the trees, the leaves.*

She feels that she's hearing nature's song as opposed to music that the sounds of nature might evoke for her. In other words, it's not her response to nature and she isn't making these songs up. When she experiences this, it pulls her into nature and she feels that she could be a tree, the leaves, a stone, blades of grass, etc. The music pulls her in and absorbs her.

Theresa is very observant and can see things that other people can't or might tend to overlook. She's walked outside after it's rained when there were raindrops and she could see the way they edged all the plants and outlined everything. Far from ignoring it and walking on, she couldn't take her eyes off of the effect because she found it so beautiful.

View of Animals and Nature

She loves animals and feels strongly connected to them. She likes what they stand for and feels that different animals give you a different feeling, a different sense of energy, and that they reflect back to you what your energy is. She also feels that they're "part of a universal message" because they reflect back to us where we are in our lives in our growth process and what we're attracted to. She feels that they're very nurturing, very loving, and very unconditional, which is important to her because it makes her feel stable and balanced and loved, and she feels that their awareness reminds us of higher levels.

Theresa loves nature because it makes her feel alive and grounded. She loves the colors and the smells of nature, as well as observing animals in nature, such as deer and squirrels.

Additional Personal Attributes

She's compassionate and sensitive and feels that sometimes she may be too much so. She's aware of a part of herself that's innocent and pure, but at times it can be a bit of a double-edged sword. There are times when she's too aware—and yet the innocent and pure part of her feels that it's untouched and can connect with everything. This is the spirit part of herself that's still connected to higher levels and that keeps her connected, even though she feels tainted at times (by things here on Earth).

On Feeling Protected and Guided

Theresa always feels protected, but at the same time she does have some fears that are more instantaneous ones, although she always moves quickly through them. For example, if all the lights go off she'll feel fearful, but then will instantly remind herself that she's okay. Once she tells herself that she's okay, she knows that she is. She always feels protected no matter what situation she finds herself in, even if she feels uncomfortable. In those cases, she always knows that she'll come out okay. Her sense of being protected derives from feeling protected by the Divine, and the feeling of being protected and guided has always been with her.

View of Organized Religions

Theresa was brought up Catholic in an Italian family. However, she now has little to do with religion because she needs to connect directly with God and Spirit and she doesn't need to follow others' beliefs. She does feel that whatever brings someone to the Divine is right for that person. It just doesn't work for her. She's had to have and maintain her own direct connection to the Divine.

Personal Experience of Different Levels

She's frequently found herself feeling one thing emotionally, which she refers to as her "human experience," and another thing on a different level. For example, if some negative event is happening globally, she may find herself emotionally disgusted by it, but if she taps into another level she can gain the understanding of why it's taking place—the higher purpose of it. She may disagree with the difficulty of the event emotionally, but she understands that energetically it has to happen for people to grow and learn. She experiences this with personal situations as well and is sometimes unhappy that she has to take the high road all the time. She chafes under having to give in all the time in problematic situations with others when she doesn't want to give in; however, she also knows that she has to because she has a better understanding of what she needs to accomplish to take things to a better level. At the same time, it can aggravate her because the human part of her wants to tell someone else off.

Near-Death Experiences

Theresa has had two near-death experiences as an adult. The first happened after she had had her two children and was having some dental work done. She was given a strong medication for pain that took her very deep. She met her mother on the other side. She was told that she had a choice either to stay on the other side or to come back to her life on Earth. She chose to come back because her children were very young and needed her.

She subsequently had another near-death experience as a result of reacting to a medication. In this near-death experience, however, she was not given a choice and was instead told that she had to come back to her life on Earth because it wasn't her time and there was too much that she needed to do.

Theresa feels that being spiritually aware her whole life is definitely a blessing, although she feels that it has been uncomfortable at times.

Life Purpose

She still feels that her purpose in this lifetime has to do with bringing large groups of people together and helping to raise awareness, and she is working toward fulfilling that with her organization, World to Come.

7

Jemila's Story

"Oh my God, what have I done?"

JEMILA REMEMBERS WHEN SHE WAS born.

I remember the delivery room when I was being born, and I just remember that first moment of the crashingly bright lights and incredible sound and how overwhelming it was. And I just shut down because it was like major over-stimulation... That first moment was like, "Oh my God, what have I done?"

Jemila also remembers feeling a sense of compassion for the people in the delivery room because they were all agitated and her mother was really upset. She found herself thinking, "Oh, I'm sorry that everyone's struggling so much." It all felt like it was more than she could handle.

Jemila had a brother named John who was four years older than she was. Through a meditation when she was older, she remembered being in the womb with him and that they were going to come in as twins. They weren't very far along in the pregnancy when Jemila realized that she didn't feel ready to come back in. She told her brother this and that she would catch up with him later, and then she withdrew from the womb.

Attitude About Being Here

Jemila has struggled with an ongoing nostalgia for the other side and has thus wanted to "go back home." She hasn't wanted to be here and feels that being embodied is just too difficult. She doesn't have many clear memories of what it was like on the other side and feels that she was protected from having such memories because she has become so nostalgic even without them. She shared that if she were to have clearer memories of what it's like to be without the human limitations, she would have jumped out of here a long time ago. Her brother died young, at the age of forty-two, and Jemila had to fight the urge to go because she wanted to join him.

Early Memories

She remembers having some out-of-body experiences (OBEs) at night when she was two or three. She was looking at herself from the outside and from up in the air. She had a lot of stuffed animals, and every night before she went to sleep she had to arrange them very carefully in a circle all around her for them to protect her. She remembers seeing herself in the circle of stuffed animals.

When she was two years old, Jemila had a very bad case of measles, with seizures and fever convulsions, and she almost died. Her father was trying to keep her from swallowing her tongue, and she was outside of her body watching—and she remembers that she wanted to leave. In a way she was glad that she was sick enough so that she could abandon her body and go home, because it was so hard to be here and she felt that she had done enough. However, she realized that if she did it would completely devastate her father, and she knew she needed to get back in her body. So she did.

Innate Spiritual Awareness

Jemila has always known that this was not the only reality, although she just didn't have the vocabulary to express what she knew. When she was around five, she was taken to church and felt really ecstatic because she was able to put names and terms on what she had always known. After that, she remembers lying in bed at night and singing a church song and seeing "all these beings hovering over the bed." She felt very happy to have the connection with these hovering friends.

When she was nine or ten, she remembers occasionally being afraid at night and asking for help.

> *These really tall, brilliantly white beyond white shining beings would stand around my bed and just be there for me ... I couldn't describe them because they were so bright that it was really hard to look at them, but they were really benevolent, compassionate, beautiful presences. And I thought of them as angels.*

When she was really small, she remembers asking where her real family was. She was looking for darker-skinned people from India and felt that she didn't belong to her family in this lifetime.

Jemila has always been inner-guided and has always known that there is more than she can see and that there are deeper things going on that she might not understand, but she knows they have meaning. She knows she has some special role—some special assignment—to accomplish here.

She has always felt that this was not her true home and felt more angelic than human. She wanted to experience being human before coming in but was seriously questioning that decision after being here because her human experience was so challenging to go through.

A Need to Help Others

Jemila has always been spiritually aware and feels that this has been a dominant theme in her life. She knows that she came here to be of service. She frequently finds that she's able to give feedback or counsel to others from a higher spiritual perspective.

In elementary school, her best friend and she agreed to meet at night after they'd gone to sleep, and they would fly around their town and look in on things that were happening. Jemila remembers being at rooftop level and tuning in to what was going on inside the houses. If there was any strife or unhappiness inside the houses, Jemila would send a blessing or positive energy "to help smooth things out for the people." Since then, she's had friends who were going through difficult things at night, either physically or emotionally, tell her that they could see or sense her in their rooms. She's known throughout her life that she often goes out of body at night and will come to with a thump in her bed and have a lingering memory of being somewhere or even of lying down somewhere and spooning with someone and comforting them, even people she doesn't know. She knows that she has gone to those who might have needed to be held, and she can remember having done that.

Jemila's natural inclination has been to help others—a carryover from the angelic realms. When she saw the film *Wings of Desire*, a film about an angel who had come to Earth, she wept because she felt so strongly that that was what had happened to her.

> *… agreeing to come in and then crashing and then being here and being so confused by everything, being so over-stimulating—and yet still wanting to experience that.*

There were parts in the film in which there were angels walking around or sitting down next to people in everyday places, and she has felt that she does that all the time, whether awake or asleep, because she senses needs around her and tries to provide comfort to others.

Innate Intuitive Ability

Jemila had intuitive and psychic experiences from the time she was young that came in the form of visual images and a kinaesthetic sense. She would see colors around things and would just know things about people that she had no way of knowing. Particularly strong for her has been psychometry. When she holds an object, information just floods in.

She's also a natural medium and has had passed-on spirits spontaneously appear to her and convey messages to their loved ones. She had a dramatic experience with this when she was young. She was very close to her paternal grandmother, who came to visit about once a year and with whom she felt very much in tune. Her grandmother died one afternoon when she was about nine, and Jemila's mother told her what death meant, that she wouldn't see her grandmother again. Jemila was devastated. That evening when Jemila went to bed, she cried, thinking she wouldn't see her grandmother again—and then suddenly her grandmother appeared in the doorway of her bedroom. She only saw her from the waist up and she was hazy, but Jemila definitely recognized her. Her grandmother was beaming, even though she had been very depressed and unhappy in life, and she told Jemila, "Oh, don't cry for me. I'm so happy." Unfortunately, Jemila knew that she couldn't share that experience with anybody.

Jemila's father was devastated by his mother's death, and Jemila remembers that she made a point of sitting next to him at her funeral and holding his hand and pouring reassurance into him.

While she was growing up, she felt that she didn't belong to her family, who didn't understand her seeing colors around things or hearing voices or having "imaginary" friends only she could see, but she knew they were real. Her family would tell her that she was making up stories or embroidering. By the time she was in 5th or 6th grade, she had been branded as a liar and told that she lied all the time. This was painful for her. She knew that what she saw was real, but now she began to doubt it. She now knows that her family had their own fears and preconceptions and that she was bumping up against them, and doubting her was the only way her family knew how to handle it.

Jemila's maternal grandmother lived with them because Jemila's mother didn't want to have another child and had had a nervous breakdown when she was carrying Jemila. She sat in a rocker and wouldn't talk to anyone for months at a time. So Jemila's maternal grandmother came to live with them to help out and take care of Jemila after she was born. When Jemila was ten or eleven, she was talking about some of the things she had intuitively seen and felt. When her grandmother heard her, she said, "You have to stop talking about this." Jemila's grandmother had been strongly psychic herself, but it had been largely beaten out of her in Sweden before she came to the United States. Her grandmother told her, "You know they'll put you away. They'll tell you you're crazy. You'll get into all kinds of trouble. You have to try to stop seeing and feeling these things." As a result, Jemila did a pretty good shutdown for a long time.

When Jemila was fifteen, she took yoga classes, which she loved. Her yoga teacher was wonderful and had studied in India and was instrumental in Jemila starting to open back up again. She invited Jemila and her brother to go with her to Milwaukee to attend a meeting of the Theosophical Society. Jemila had never heard of the Theosophical Society, but went to the meeting. During the meeting, there was some discussion of auras, and Jemila had an aha moment, realizing that that was what she had been seeing around people. She was happy to have a label for what she had experienced and was thrilled that people were discussing it with interest and respect and as if it were real.

When she was thirty-eight, her older brother John died. The next morning after she had made plane reservations, she sat down and meditated, asking her brother to communicate with her and let her know how he was doing. Suddenly a burst of light appeared in front of her in the fuzzy oval shape of an aura around a body, and the aura was "full of rainbow shards of light, just flashing." She then heard his voice, as clear as a bell, telling her, "You gotta check this *out*! This is so cool!"

She feels that he then did something astonishing for her. She knew that her parents were really afraid that he might have died alone, needing help, and he told her, "Tell Mom and Dad that I was okay and that I had help." He then showed her what had happened, as if he had popped a DVD in the player and showed her the whole scene so that she was able to experience it from his point of view.

He had had a heart attack and then fell on an icy street corner, and she could see that the heart attack was so huge that his spirit left his body before his face hit the pavement. Aside from the initial shock of the pain, there was no other prolonged pain or suffering. He was out of his body looking down and was agitated, thinking that he needed to do something to get back in his body, when a being appeared on his right side. The being told him that his heart had been struggling for a while and that it was badly damaged. Jemila saw her brother dialoguing with this being, with John asking if he shouldn't do something to get back in his body. The being told him that it was past the point where being in his body would be helpful. John then asked if he should ride along in the ambulance, and the being told him that the best thing to do would be to just let it go—and then added, "I came for you. Would you like to come with me?"

Then John said, "Oh, okay," and left with the being. This reenactment that her brother communicated to her was later validated when she learned that his face had indeed been scraped up from falling face first onto the pavement.

Jemila found this experience very reassuring and beautiful, although she couldn't share it with her father. She was able to tell her mother that she had seen John and that he was fine, and she knows that this helped her mother somewhat.

Additional Personal Attributes

Jemila often finds herself observing things and events around her as opposed to being engaged with them, and she has always felt as if she was just passing through here. In fact, she jokes that she would just like to pass through here a little faster.

She's usually good at reading other people, although like most of us she's feels that she's not when someone triggers strong emotions, especially when it comes to romantic relationships.

Past-Life Recall

Jemila has had some spontaneous recall of past lives. For example, once when she was receiving Reiki healing, she had a powerful memory of being a monk and being on the top of the Potala Palace in Tibet and consciously withdrawing from her body. As the monk, she was drifting upward into the sky and looking down on her (his) body that was now lifeless. At that point, the memory stopped for her.

Additional Gifts

Jemila has always had natural healing and intuitive gifts. She has done some energy healing work in which she was guided (as opposed to having learned a specific energy work technique), and she has sensed many other beings in the room guiding her healing work. She has also received medical information about animals. She's always been very creative as well, painting incessantly when she was little and later doing extensive acting as an adult, in addition to singing and writing and hosting a long-running radio show.

View of Animals and Nature

She loves animals and feels very in tune with them, and she has worked with them in various ways. She's had wild birds sit in her hand and has helped pets transition, supporting and easing them in their passage to death. She's also communicated with animals and done healing work on them. She knows animals have a huge capacity to love and connect and function on an intuitive level all the time.

Jemila also loves nature and wishes she had more time to sit by a brook and listen to the sound of the water rushing over the stones and be around really old trees. She loves to be in the mountains, especially the old mountains, because they feel like home to her. She feels that being in nature gets her in the flow of the present moment, allowing her to breathe in the energy of the planet and tune in to life.

On Feeling Protected and Guided

Jemila has always been sensitive and compassionate, wanting to ease the pain and suffering of others and comfort them, and a part of her has always been innocent and pure. She has definitely felt spiritually protected in her life and "lovingly supervised" by spiritual beings, who have encouraged her and reassured her that everything will be okay.

Jemila sometimes hears a guiding voice that tells her what to do. The only exceptions to this have been when she's been mired with human drama and emotions.

She once had a significant experience while walking back to her car at night in the deserted parking lot of a theater. She encountered a young man who had previously been following her around that evening in the theater. He started to walk toward her, and she decided to look for the good in him, instead of being fearful. He accosted her and said to her, "It's not safe for you to be walking alone in the dark out here."

She thanked him and added, "But I'm always so protected." He asked her where she lived and she gave him a vague answer instead.

His energy then shifted completely, and he told her, "You will be of tremendous service to people in the performing arts. I bless you and I thank you, and yes, you are protected." He then walked away. Jemila then realized that there had been an angelic presence in a form that had appeared mildly threatening, or at least confusing, until she greeted him peacefully. Ironically—or synchronistically—this incident took place right after she had read a book about Peace Pilgrim.

View of Organized Religions

Jemila was not brought up from a young age in a religious tradition, although her parents had been raised in a temperance tradition because alcoholism had affected ancestral family members. Her parents did take her to visit various Protestant churches for her to experience, and Jemila loved this.

After her family moved to California, there were many different people of all different types of faiths within a couple of blocks of her house, so Jemila was exposed to a variety of faiths. Her mother emphasized that there were many different spiritual paths and that all of them were good. Both of her parents expressed tolerance and appreciation for different faiths, as well as races, and her mother was quite spiritual, although not religious.

At present, Jemila doesn't actively participate in organized religion, but she's fine with it. Occasionally she'll attend a mass with a friend or attend a Unitarian service. She has sung, chanted, and danced with Sufi groups, but she doesn't have a current Sufi group to participate in. When she recently went to a dance conference of Sufis, she felt that she no longer belonged and that it wasn't her present path, so she feels in flux with that for the time being. If she needed to use a label at present, it would be Buddhist; however, she feels that her present path is pretty much unlabeled.

Personal Experience of Different Levels

Interestingly, Jemila has said the same thing that I have over the years: "on one level I feel this and on another level I feel that." (I'll be discussing this further in chapter 15, when I share my story.) This schism may be attributed to the difference between what the higher soul awareness knows and what the human psyche on the human level knows and feels.

Feeling Different from Others

She feels that her experience of life has tended to be different from that of just about everyone she meets, although she's met some kindred spirits along the way. It's been rare for her to know people with whom she could share her spiritual interests and experiences. One major way in which she has been different from others because of her spiritual awareness has been in the way she loves. She loves in a "really big way" that is "almost impersonal." It's personalized, but is also paradoxically impersonal. She loves to hug others. When she hugs someone and feels a chakra-to-chakra connection, she feels that she goes to a really high place with a powerful transmission of energy that feels to her like a cosmic transmission.

On Being Spiritually Aware Since Birth

Jemila feels that being spiritually aware her whole life has been a blessing. However, at the same time, it's felt like a curse when she's not been believed or affirmed in her spiritual awareness and experiences. The experience of being spiritually aware in and of itself has been a blessing. She just wishes that she had had a spiritual teacher or guru when she was young to teach her how to deal with what she felt and knew.

Life Purpose

She has tried for years to determine what her life purpose is, but she's realized that "so much of every day we spend with other people" is part of that, because there's always someone who needs to be listened to or comforted. Throughout her life she has gone out of her way to comfort others, and in her radio show she put a positive vibration out there for over twenty years, to which people strongly responded in a welcoming and appreciative way. She feels that her listeners felt "loved and comforted and cared about from a person they've never even met." She thoroughly enjoyed this positive exchange of energy.

8

Cheryl Ludwig's Story

"What in the world are these people thinking
to not cover my eyes from the sun?"

CHERYL'S FIRST MEMORY COMES RIGHT after she was born and being driven home from the hospital on a bright, sunny day.

> I have a very vivid earliest memory... but on the day I was brought home from the hospital, the sun was shining in my eyes and I remember thinking so vividly, "What in the world are these people thinking to not cover my eyes from the sun?" It irritated the—I was just like, "Are they stupid?"... I was just so upset. I didn't cry about it, but I was mad and I couldn't get the words out.

She even saw her face "squinched up" from the sun. She then thought, "What in the heck was I thinking?"—meaning coming back here to Earth. She knew that she was supposed to come here, although she didn't know or remember all of the reasons. She knows that it had to have been her decision to come here since she didn't think, "What in the heck were *they* thinking." She has intermittently questioned being here, and this has been a bit of a repeated leitmotif for her in her life.

She knows that she was really mad about her eyes not having been covered and doesn't know if any damage resulted, but to this day she's light-sensitive. She has seen several photos taken of herself when she was little and she's squinting in every one of them.

Early Memories

Cheryl has been an empath from her infancy and always knew when people were hurting inside. Even as a baby she would gravitate toward the person who was hurting the most in the room. She could sense that there was a glow inside of them that was a "soft, soft amberish and goldish glow with white sparklies through it." She could connect with the inside of them, in the heart. She would crawl over to the person in order to soothe them. (Those close to her even noticed this.) After she would crawl over to someone, she would then pull up to them, stand there, and wait for them to pick her up—and then she would silently tell the "sparkly ball" that she loved them and that they would be okay, and she would hug them until they could feel better. She couldn't do it in big groups of people, who might find it distracting, but she did this with smaller ones.

She also remembers feeling that she knew she could fly, and thus climbed out onto the roof at eighteen months old. Fortunately someone saw her and a neighbor got up on the roof and retrieved her. She remembers being upset that she wasn't going to be allowed to fly.

When Cheryl was three and visiting relatives, she was taken to a viewing of a family friend in a funeral home. She asked what was going on and why this friend was in a box. Because she was too little to see into the casket, her grandfather then lifted her up to see his deceased friend. When she looked into the casket, she could see the man turn his head toward her and wink with his left eye and then turn his head back again. She can still see it clearly in her mind. She said to her grandfather, "He is not dead. Didn't you see him just wink at me?" Her grandfather assured her that his friend had indeed passed away. Cheryl was quite upset that they put him in the ground and were burying him alive and he wouldn't have any air to breathe—and then he would really die. This was a memorable encounter (someone passed over communicating with her) and is still vivid in her mind. When she was a little older, she realized that she had been seeing his spirit.

Feeling Different from Others

Cheryl has always felt different from others, especially when others didn't understand the things she could. She even asked if she had been adopted, because she felt so different from her family. She was just told that she had a wild imagination.

Innate Spiritual Awareness

Cheryl has always been spiritual for as far back as she can remember, and she has always known that there was something more than this physical reality. She's felt connected to the Divine and guides and angels. She's often wondered why she came here, as opposed to a "star nursery." In fact, her awareness was not attuned to this Earthly world, but rather to other levels. She describes her orientation as other-worldly. Author's note: This is not the same as daydreaming, but more of a conscious attunement to the nonphysical and the "other side."

A Need to Help Others

In kindergarten, she gravitated toward the other kids who seemed shy or who were hurting or being bullied. Even though she herself was shy, she felt that she needed to help those who were hurting. She could relate to them and get on their level so that they would feel comfortable in coming out of their shells. To this day she finds herself wondering why people think the way they do.

Innate Intuitive Ability

Cheryl has come to know herself as an empath who can feel others' feelings. Feeling others' pain has been difficult for her, especially when she can't do anything to mitigate or assuage it. She's always been compassionate and sensitive to the point where it's felt that it's too much.

She has been naturally intuitive from a very young age. In addition to being an empath, she's had precognitive dreams, including one of her grandfather's passing in which he told her that he would be leaving her and hugged her. She would also have spontaneous precognitive knowings about things, like specific people calling her.

She has been inner-guided from the time she was little and always noted her dreams. She also had positive relationships with fairies from the time when she was old enough to walk. When she was somewhere between eighteen months and two years old, her grandparents planted a small maple tree in their backyard that was about her height. They would put Brach's candies in the crooks of the tree and told her that the fairies had put them there. However, she actually saw the fairies, which she describes as about an inch to an inch and half tall with wings similar to those of dragonflies. They were graceful and seemed fragile. There were both males and females who were quite young, and their clothes were "sparkly" and they glowed with iridescence and pastel rainbow colors, but no dark colors. The boys were wearing shirts and short pants that were above the knee. She also saw a different type of fairy that glowed, but without discernible clothes.

After a while she stopped seeing the fairies until she had an accident in her thirties and has started sensing them around her again as an adult. She recently saw a film about the Cottingley Fairies (the fairies two girls purported to have seen and photographed in Great Britain, although they later recanted and claimed just one of the photographs was real), and she recognized a similarity to the ones she had seen. She has recently been trying to reestablish contact with fairies and has felt a measure of success with a planting of zinnias. The particular type she planted typically grows to only one to two feet tall and hers are over five feet in height.

Past-Life Recall

Over the years, Cheryl has sensed some of her past lives. For example, she feels that she lived as a Native American, and in this lifetime she has innately had tracking skills while out in the woods. She's also always been drawn to the Central and South American, Egyptian, and Asian cultures, where she feels she's had other lives as well.

She's also had some spontaneous past-life memories. For example, in one she's inside a cave with other people on a cliff in a rain forest. The cliff is a darker rock and it's raining. When the water runs down the rock, it's darkening it. She has a spear in her right hand, not because she's hunting, but simply from a habit of readiness. She's in a relaxed frame of mind, as opposed to always being on guard, and is simply watching the rain falling and feeling at peace. The cave itself is up high with little access to it, but getting up to it is nothing to her and the other people in the cave because they're all very nimble. They're careful, but agile, in their ascent. She usually only has this memory when she goes into the woods, which makes her want to recreate it. She knows that her eyes had an angle to them and knows that this life took place in a rain forest in Central or South America.

She also remembers a house that she feels is probably in the United Kingdom. It's on an inlet of the ocean where there are big rocks with moss on them. The house was low and made of stone with white mortar and with a slate roof with smoke coming out of an opening. It was very cold there and everyone wore wool, but there was a beautiful countryside.

Innate Concern About the Environment

When she was five, she started drawing cities that were on fire and told her family, "I've got to stop the pollution." She also told them that when she grew up she would grow her own food and live in a cabin and that "if we don't do something, it's going to be awful." She could see the future effects of environmental degradation, although it wasn't very pronounced at that point.

Feeling Different from Others

Cheryl has always been good at reading other people and feels that her experience of life is different from most people. She not only naturally picks up on others' emotions and pain, but she has also been able to sense negative energy or intent. She's always felt different from others, primarily because of her spiritual orientation. She has felt that she can't share her perceptions and thoughts with others unless they weren't superficial. However, she's found that more people appear to be opening up spiritually, which she's observed as a trend in the world, and now she can relate to them more. She feels that some people may not be on the spiritual level that she is, but their spirituality has led them to be open and somewhat receptive.

Retention of Innocence and Purity

She has been able to retain her childlike nature and is in touch with the part of herself that is innocent and pure and appreciates wonder and beauty. She feels hurt when she sees innocence and purity betrayed, whether of animals, nature, or people. As a result, she's more comfortable being around young people and the elderly, as well as those who are spiritual.

Additional Gifts

Cheryl is also an artist who sculpts, paints, and makes pottery. Her artwork contains teaching messages and spiritual images. She loves to create and is naturally whole-brained as well, being equally artistic and organized. She's also a creative thinker who thinks of things to invent.

View of Animals and Nature

She loves animals and feels that she understands them and they understand her. They've always communicated with her, and she's done some animal communication work. She recently bought a betta fish she felt was calling out to her to be taken home, and within a month the fish was kissing the side of the tank when she stood near it communicating with him. She's felt that when she touches an animal and looks into his or her eyes, there's a bond between them. When she looks into an animal's eyes, she feels that she's connecting with their spirit, soul, and heart and can sometimes access a memory from another life with them. She can also see the timeless and present awareness in an animal's eyes. It would be very difficult for her not to be able to be around animals.

As mentioned earlier, she's always loved nature and is quite attuned to it, to the extent that she has felt that when she's outside she can see nature breathing. In fact, she feels that nature is her haven. She can see God in nature as well as the "absolute perfection" in nature.

Synaesthesia and Unusual Senses

Cheryl experiences a certain phenomenon when she's outside and looks at anything in nature, such as a grouping of trees or bushes. Her eyes will fix into somewhat of a stare, and almost instantaneously she's in a zone and can see an intricate series of concentric circles made out of a glistening spider-web type material. They range from the tiniest web up to the outline of the biggest tree, and they are all joined together and pulsating and breathing. If she blinks, the image will stop, but she's able to go right back into the stare and see the same thing again anywhere she looks. She likens it to the concentric growth rings seen in a cross-section of a tree, but transparent and massive. The traditional image of a radio tower emitting radio waves is similar to what she sees. She can also reach out and pluck one of the circles and then hear music. She's seen these concentric circles outside for a long time and doesn't understand why other people aren't seeing them. She feels that she's seeing the interconnectedness of everything and the continuum and the living, breathing spirit of nature.

To Cheryl, nature is everything. It has a soothing energy, and she has to have her regular time in it. She feels that in order for her to exist on this Earth, she needs to have it. She feels that she's a part of it and it's a part of her. If she doesn't get outside for a period of time, she feels out of sorts and discombobulated, like she herself is a plant that can't be boxed in.

Cheryl experiences the universe as very musical, whether she's outside at night looking up into the sky or when she's "out floating around in the universe." Because of this, she acquired a keyboard and has tried to recreate the sounds she's heard, which are very soothing sounds. She hears sounds when she's out in space and touches things. When she saw the film *Contact*, she cried during the part when there was music while they were out in space because she felt that someone else knew about what she had been experiencing. She also sees colors at random times, for example when driving.

Additional Personal Attributes

She's always tended to observe people and things around her, as opposed to being engaged with them, and has tended to hold back around most people, especially those with whom she doesn't resonate.

View of Organized Religions

Cheryl was brought up Presbyterian and attended services while growing up, but only for the major holidays like Christmas and Easter. When she visited her grandparents, who lived in a small town in the mountains of Virginia, they would all attend a Lutheran church, which Cheryl loved. As an adult, she's now intrigued by religion and has studied the major religions of the world, looking for what the commonality is among them.

That said, she sees a lot of hypocrisy in organized religion and feels that she's much more spiritual.

Near-Death Experience(s)

Cheryl had a near-death experience during surgery after she broke her neck in an accident.

All of a sudden during surgery I shot up like a rocket in the universe… way up into the galaxies, and it is just so beautiful, all the stars and the planets—and I hear… I hear music out there. It's a musical universe, for lack of a better word; like if you touch something it's musical.

All of a sudden she found herself sitting in a massive hand. She couldn't see it, but she felt it and knew that she was a teeny thing in this massive hand. She walked over to the edge and saw the Earth way, way down below and it was "the diameter of a pencil eraser." Then she looked up and all the knowledge in the world was there all around her, "but not in bookcases." She knew she could look up and know anything she wanted to know by just thinking of what she wanted to know. She then heard an androgynous voice ask her, "What do you think?"

Cheryl replied, "Earth is so much smaller and just really doesn't mean a lot, does it?" There was no answer, but she felt a huge unconditional love—"the most love in the world ever."

All of a sudden she was out of the hand and suspended in space. A woman was standing in front of her wearing a purple glowing long-sleeved dress that was illuminated and had a rounded collar around her neck. (As an artist, Cheryl has since tried to replicate the dress, but hasn't been able to.) She had a very pristine, China-doll face with very perfect features and hair that was "wavy golden, illuminated down to the bottom of her gown." They spoke to each other, but not with their mouths or lips;

instead, they communicated "heart to heart" (or telepathically), and she heard it inside of herself. Cheryl asked, "What is your name?"

The woman replied, "You can call me Ruth." Cheryl sensed that the woman didn't really have a name.

She looked behind the woman and started to see a whitish-golden glow from something like a hallway, and there were shadows that were silhouettes of people. She tried to peer around the woman to try to see who the people were. The woman then held a pointed finger up to Cheryl and said, "It is your choice, but you have a purpose."

Cheryl then looked down at the teeny Earth below and said, "Why in the world would I want to go back to that teeny-tiny little place that is full of hurt, anger, greed, jealousy?" And Cheryl named every negative thing that wasn't love that was in stark contrast to the total love she felt in this place. "Why? Why would I go back there?"

The woman replied, "I said it is your choice, but you do have a purpose."

Cheryl then asked, "What is my purpose?"

The woman said, "*That* is part of your journey." Cheryl said that that was no direction at all. The woman then informed her, "Your grandmother will miss you terribly." The next thing Cheryl knew she was flying back down to the operating room and saw that one doctor was going out to tell her family that Cheryl had passed away, but a nurse ran after him telling him to wait because Cheryl had been resuscitated. She saw them run back into the OR and perform blood oxygen tests to make sure she wasn't brain-damaged because she had been dead for twenty minutes. She felt that coming back into her body felt like putting on several hundred pounds.

Another significant thing Cheryl learned from her near-death experience dealt with the interconnectedness of everything and everyone.

When I died there was this massive, massive, bigger than ever entity... I have also seen where we are all sparks of this light out

there, with this fine weave of connectedness… We are all absolutely
connected. So then I also think of this collective consciousness.

Personal Experience of Different Levels

Cheryl is aware that her higher soul awareness sometimes conflicts with
what she feels on the human level of the psyche.

That's what makes it hard to be here, because you have that side of
yourself that's still very, very intact—the spiritual pure self. And then
you get bombarded with this human stuff and it's like oil and water
that's not mixing right. The oil is the stuff that's heavy.

She feels that no matter "how difficult it may be to be living in the two
worlds, it's much better than living in only the one" (the one here on earth
lacking spiritual awareness and restricted solely to the limited human consciousness and persona).

On Feeling Protected and Guided

Cheryl has felt protected and guided throughout her life from the time
she was little and was able to see spirits and fairies. She's felt the absence
of them if they're not around her and has tended to feel alone and unprotected in those times. Even though she feels protected, at the same time
she acknowledges that she does have some fears. When she feels embroiled
in human concerns, she loses her center and has to regain it. Sometimes
her fears will be triggered, but she ultimately knows that she's protected.

On Being Spiritually Aware Since Birth

She's glad that she's always been spiritually aware because it's made her life
easier in some ways, although it's led to her feeling isolated at times. The
experience of being in a body has also been difficult for her, aside from

feeling so much heavier, because she misses being able to think *it* and be *it* and do *it*, as well as blink and time travel really quickly.

Life Purpose

Cheryl has wanted to know what her life purpose was for a long time. In fact, she was disappointed when she was told during her near-death experience that part of her journey in this lifetime is to discover her purpose. She knows that it has to do with her sensitivity and with being able to hone in and know when to help, as well as continuing to be an artist. She would love to see each person in the world change something in themselves from the negative to the positive and plug into love.

She had a vision some years back when her awareness jetted outside of the Earth. She looked at the Earth, which was about the size of a softball and really beautiful.

> *And I was just hanging out in space looking at it and kind of looking around it. Well, all of a sudden these pinpoints of light that I talk about, which is the human beings at core—that spark within each of us—started connecting. Everyone started seeing the light.*

As each person saw the light, he or she would reach out and hold hands with another person who was seeing the light. Cheryl was "whirling around the Earth" and saw every nationality in their national garb starting to hold hands as they were seeing the light. This continued until it got to the last person, who was a construction worker wearing a white t-shirt, a yellow hard hat, blue jeans, and work boots. When he, as the last person to do so, saw the light and connected to another person and held hands, all of a sudden the Earth went into an exquisite glow that was a beautiful iridescent, golden glow that had a lot of "sparklies" in it. Suddenly every person on the Earth was enveloped in this light glow, and the light shot straight up into space and then fell back down onto the ground. She didn't get to see what happened after this, but she still gets chills when she recalls the beautiful glow resulting from everyone on Earth seeing the light and connecting to each other. This is a beautiful vision—and Cheryl knows it will happen.

9

Matthew Engel's Story

"Okay, so I've arrived. Here I am...I was feeling a
sense that there was a force and a team in the spirit
realm that was all involved in getting me here."

MATTHEW ENGEL'S FIRST MEMORY STEMS back to right after he was born.
He remembers lying in an incubator in a hospital room on the day he was
born and looking at the room with yellow walls and thinking, "Okay, so
I've arrived. Here I am." This memory has always been with him.

He also remembers feeling that "there was a force and a team in the
spirit realm that was all involved in getting me here."

Matthew has a sense of coming here and incarnating on purpose and
knowing that he would be taking on "certain challenges." He knew that
there was "Divine arrangement" with the circumstances, arrangements,
and details for this lifetime. He knew that he was coming into this lifetime
both for a specific task he was to carry out and for soul growth. He also
remembers a little bit of anxiety on his part just prior to entry. He likened

this to a kid getting ready to go down a tall slide and feeling flutters of anxiety, although being ready to do it, and pulling back a little, but then having someone push you down. He remembers feeling this way just prior to being born.

His next memory is from the day that he was brought home from the hospital. He remembers seeing his mother getting into the car for the ride home. The car was pulled up to the curb. He could see all of this as if he was hovering over the scene, observing it. He's always had this memory as well.

His later preverbal memories were more those of flashes. For example, he can remember sitting in his high chair in the kitchen and what the kitchen floor and the dishwasher handle looked like.

Innate Spiritual Awareness

Matthew always had a sense of a higher power that was there for him and around him, although he wasn't aware of a reference to God until he was three—which came from family—and the higher power he sensed was more like a team of spirit guides or a council. He also had an awareness of the spirits here on Earth, composed of family and teachers who would be here to receive him "on the other end." If he's experienced anxiety at times, he's had a sense of being reminded via a message, "Don't worry. You're going to connect with this one or that one."

He was always spiritually aware and had that consistent sense of a higher power, as well as a greater purpose—along with the knowing that there were things he was here to do, learn, and work out. His mother was studying metaphysical information and it was often dinner-table discussion, which provided a less hostile environment for his spiritual orientation. He feels that he chose his mother for that reason because she would be providing him with a spiritual template in this lifetime, which could be a good foundation for him, even though it was up to him to work with the information and develop it himself.

Feeling Different from Others

Matthew has always felt different from others. He vividly remembers being in preschool where there was a round cement track with kids' toys (such as tricycles and big wheels) and standing off to the side watching the other kids go wild, playing and "letting it all out," while he felt like an old man who was in the body of a young child (which he felt from as early as three or four years old). He watched the other kids play while he observed, and he wasn't drawn to participating. He felt very "floaty," and the other kids' wild energy felt very foreign to him. This was not an atypical feeling for him, and he frequently found himself feeling this way, as if his center was more sedate and serene than the other childrens'. Anything that was wild and loud felt foreign to him. He identified with his parents on some level when he was little, but not with other children his age.

Matthew felt this way throughout his childhood and adolescence and into his twenties. He felt disconnected from his peers in the sense that he felt older. As a child, he got along best with kids who were older, and as an adult in his twenties he had a lot of friends who were ten to fifteen years older than he was.

In addition, he found himself wondering when he was young, "What if my mother isn't really my mother? What if my father isn't really my father?"

He also felt disconnected from his body and feels that he was never very athletic, although he enjoyed eating and swimming and being in the water. Because of his buoyancy in water, he felt like he was less connected to his body.

Innate Intuitive Ability

Matthew has always been inner-guided, and his first intuitive experience happened when he was in the fifth grade, which was a precognitive, clairvoyant one. He also knew around that time that his father, who had divorced from his mother when he was around three, was having marital problems in his second marriage and that the marriage wouldn't last. And it didn't.

From a young age, he was also aware of people's intentions, motives, and emotions, as well as their energy. He could sense whether he could trust them or not. He was also very perceptive and clairsentient from the age of about five. Around the age of sixteen, he started to consciously connect with Spirit and receive information.

Past-Life Recall

Matthew has had spontaneous recall of some of his past lives. For example, he vividly remembers World War II in Europe and feels somewhat obsessed with viewing images and news clippings of Europe between the 1920s and 1940s, including the style of clothing, furniture, or textiles. He started channeling at the age of eighteen and received information on that lifetime. He was a female double agent spy, who was very charming, articulate, and shrewd, and he lured in some of the SS officers and took photos of them and passed on information about them. He (she) was also astrologically savvy in that lifetime. He's had images of slipping notes into clothing. He remembers books on spirituality and astrology being burned and remembers writing down snippets of information and references from some books, such as dates and planetary transits, and keeping the pieces of paper. He knows that he died just before the end of the war in 1944 in a bombing, and he was in his early forties.

He also feels a strong connection with England throughout the Middle Ages up until the Victorian Era. He loves Victorian houses and finds them to be quite comfortable.

Additional Gifts

He has always been good at reading other people, being able to sense where they are coming from. At the same time, he's felt that his experience of life has been different from other people who are not spiritually aware.

He's creative and was involved in theater, has a good intellect, and is very attuned to color and color's vibrations. He's always been an out-of-the-box thinker with an independent mind; he has asked "why" from the time he was little—resisting convention—which got him into trouble because he didn't buy into groupthink. In his early teens he got into some trouble because he would call adults on their stuff because he could just see through their inconsistences.

He's worked as a mental health counselor, although even before this he's had a knack for understanding people from a psychological standpoint. He feels that he was sort of an armchair therapist at ten years old.

I think that my real gift lies in integrating the psyche with the spirit—taking psychology and the ego and putting that in context of the soul's evolution and the consciousness of the spirit and the karmic and the spiritual soul evolutionary journey.

In his work, he feels that he's able to "really dive in with people and grasp their story both psychologically and spiritually."

Observing vs. Engaging

Throughout his life, Matthew has felt somewhat disengaged, as if he was observing people and things around him rather than engaging with them. He always felt as if he were just passing through here (this life on Earth). Everything feels very temporary to him.

View of Animals and Nature

He's always loved animals and describes himself as a lifelong animal person. He's consistently bonded deeply with his animals, which he describes as a merging sort of energy connection. He's found animals to be a great source of comfort and companionship, and he feels that the animal souls he has drawn throughout his life have always been very humanlike. He feels that he's had soul contracts to be with certain animal souls and there's a deep intuitive bond where they feel each other. When he looks into an animal's eyes, he feels love, sensitivity, and compassion, along with a sense of merging and "boundarylessness."

Matthew also loves nature, and since he was young he remembers loving the fall leaves and their colors, as well as things blooming in May. He felt that the seasons somehow "brought a spiritual connection to the Earth." He feels, though, that it wasn't until he visited California prior to moving there (he grew up in the Northeast) that he really began to connect with the Earth. On that visit, he felt a strong connection to the land, including the ocean and trees. He feels a Divine connection to trees and can feel their spirit energy.

On Feeling Protected and Guided

Matthew has always been compassionate and sensitive, except, of course, when he's personally triggered by something. He says it is like having his human side and his shadow. The human side has also brought some fears, but in the larger picture he's always known that everything would be fine and that he'll be protected and he trusts in this. He's always felt guided and protected.

View of Organized Religions

He comes from a Jewish tradition, and although his family was not practicing the faith, and he didn't receive religious training, he was exposed to it through his family. As a result, he feels that he didn't have the typical religious indoctrination and thus resisted the efforts of one grandparent to do that. Because of his innate spiritual awareness, he simply felt no need for a religious organization to tell him the difference between right or wrong.

I have always felt that truth, higher truth, right, wrong—whether it's in the darkness or light or whether it's just making the right decision or making the wrong decision—all of that has to come through our own heart, through our own soul, through our own wisdom, through our own compassion.

Matthew understands from a spiritual, sociological, and psychological perspective why some people may need religion to tell them what is right and what is wrong, and he attributes this to the age of the soul.

I do understand kind of a younger soul or baby soul type of an energy that just doesn't know what to do. So they need someone to tell them what's right from wrong.

He views this as a soul age type of difference, where younger souls may put the hierarchy of a church or synagogue or deity in a "very parentified role" due to a lack of awareness within. However, he's never felt that he needed that because he could make his own decisions from a place of integrity, while acknowledging that his human side could lead to self-interest at times.

Personal Experience of Different Levels

Matthew has consciously experienced the difference between what his human psyche may feel and what his higher soul awareness knows throughout his life. He feels compassion when he sees someone in pain from some hurtful and unjust situations, while his higher soul awareness can also perceive what the lesson may be in those situations and why they're taking place—in other words, "it is as it's meant to be."

Matthew described his higher soul awareness as:

... something that's peaceful, as something that's centered, as something that's wise, as something that's accepting, as something that's in a place of Divine acceptance, surrender, peace, love, and just knowing that it's all okay and that everything we experience is just

temporary. And it's happening all according to plan and that we
each sign on for it very, very consciously.

Access to Spiritual Wisdom

Matthew's spiritual orientation has included his awareness of some spiritual truths. For example, he knows that we're all here for a purpose and that there are no victims (because we've chosen our paths). He knows that,

> *... there is a level of depth, there is a level of understanding, there is a level of compassion, there is a level of healing, there is a level of rebirth, there is a level of illumination that can happen through every experience of darkness.*

He also knows that "the soul very consciously agrees to incarnate with whatever set of circumstances it experiences in the physical earth world."

On Being Spiritually Aware Since Birth

He feels that being spiritually aware his whole life is a blessing. There are times when he wishes he could do things on a more mundane level because some things might be easier, such as finding a partner or working in a career that wasn't built around helping people and that paid really well. At the same time, however, he knows that he wouldn't be happy going into a state of unconsciousness or unawareness.

Life Purpose

He has chewed on what his life purpose is for years and feels that it is to be a teacher, healer, guide, channel, facilitator, messenger, therapist, and sage. And these are exactly the things that he has been doing in his work here.

10

Terese Covey's Story

"I agreed with my dad that I would be okay."

TERESE REMEMBERS A CONVERSATION HER parents had when she was an infant. Her father put her on her stomach in the crib and her mother voiced concern that Terese might not be able to breathe in that position. Her father told her mother, "She's fine. Don't worry. She'll be fine like that." Terese remembers agreeing with her father and knew that she would be okay and would be able to breathe.

Terese always had the knowing that she was here for some important reason. Around the age of two, she was consciously aware of feeling that there was guidance and protection for her and that there was somebody there. Even before that, she had a sense of these things, although her specific memory of feeling didn't come until she was two.

Early Memories

When she was about three, Terese had a very vivid dream about UFOs. In her dream, she was outside in the front yard at home making an angel in the dirt with her arms and legs. (Grass had not yet been planted there.) All of a sudden, a UFO landed. She was abducted, along with some others close to her, and she still remembers fine details of the spaceship. Terese is still not sure where this dream came from or what had triggered it, but the dream has stayed with her and she has never forgotten it.

When she was seven or eight, she was attending a Bible study class at her church, but some of what was being said didn't feel right to her. All of a sudden, she saw a glowing figure and sensed it was Jesus. She sensed that He appeared to her to let her know that what she was sensing—that some of the information wasn't correct—was indeed accurate. This was one of the few times that she has actually seen a presence, as opposed to sensing one.

Terese has sensed that she lived on another planet or in another galaxy, but she doesn't have any specific memories of it. She's always felt that she didn't belong here on Earth and that this was not her true home and that she didn't belong to her family. Instead she's known that she's just passing through here.

Innate Intuitive Ability

She has always been inner-guided and intuitive, as well as innately spiritual. She has felt energies around her from the time she was born, especially the energies of other people. She could always sense what others were feeling and found that confusing as a child because how she sensed someone was feeling would sometimes conflict with how the person would say that they were feeling. She's always been good at reading other people.

From about the age of four, she started to feel very different from others. She also developed a fear of dark energies, which came about due to energies she sensed in her mother's house. (Her parents divorced when she was five, and Terese then lived with her mother for two years before her father gained custody of her, along with her brother, when she was seven.) Her mother had some mental illness issues and dabbled in the occult. Terese feels that her mother didn't know how to protect herself and may have invited in some negative energies. Terese could sense negative energies in the house and there were some psychokinetic events—drawers opening and closing, the faucet turning on and off, a rocking chair starting to rock, etc.—and all of this scared her.

As a result of the poltergeist and other fearful experiences, Terese shut off her own intuitive abilities when she was eleven. However, in her twenties she attended massage school and her interest and intuitive abilities opened back up again. In her work as a massage therapist, she often intuitively picks up on information about clients, including some negative information that she doesn't want to pick up on at times. (She once intuitively picked up that a client was a child molester.) She's a natural medium and sometimes has crossed-over spirits who are connected to her clients visit while she's working on them.

Observing vs. Engaging

Terese knows that we're here on Earth in order to experience, remember, and raise the vibration. She frequently finds herself observing people and things around her, as opposed to being engaged with them, and has been this way from a young age. She actually prefers to observe instead of getting pulled into other people's drama. She gets pulled in on occasion, but she knows that her experience of life is different from other people who haven't always been spiritually aware. Throughout her life she's been called different, eclectic, or weird. That used to hurt her feelings, but it doesn't bother her anymore. Indeed, she now takes comments like these as compliments.

Innate Spiritual Awareness

Her innate spiritual awareness leads her to avoid getting caught up in drama. If she goes through something difficult, she'll later question what the purpose of the experience is for her and what she's supposed to learn from it. If the situation concerns someone else, she'll ask how the other person is a mirror to her.

She's been blessed with healing ability and uses that in her work, and as an empath she is able to read other people. She feels that she has the ability to create whatever she wants by working with her higher soul awareness.

View of Animals and Nature

Terese has always had a deep love for animals and has been able to connect with them. Pets that aren't usually friendly to strangers will come up to her. She feels that animals can usually understand things that people don't, that they are more open and loving and nonjudgmental.

She also loves nature and feels more connected to Source when she's out in nature. She feels that it renews and balances her, and she will feel unbalanced if she goes for too long without being in it. She also feels a communication in nature that she doesn't completely understand at present. She's teared up at times when looking at various beautiful places in nature. She also loves trees and bonds with them.

On Feeling Protected and Guided

Terese has always been compassionate and sensitive, but feels that she's working on being more compassionate, especially in cases in which people are harming animals or children. (She was molested more than once as a child and knows the harm that can cause.) In spite of what she experienced, she feels that a part of herself is still innocent and pure. She's always felt protected—that everything would be okay.

View of Organized Religions

She started attending a small, nondenominational church with her family when she was about one. As a teenager, she started to become disenchanted with it because she started seeing more judgmental attitudes and controlling actions. When she was eighteen, she decided that church wasn't for her.

At present, Terese feels that religion is too rigid and that it "doesn't help people dance to their highest level." She feels that many religions teach people to rely on the teachings and that members can't speak to God directly. She still finds too much judgment and control in most religions. However, if she had to belong to a religion, it would be Buddhism. She is not in favor of religions telling people, "This is the way to do it," because she feels there can usually be more than one way.

Personal Experience of Different Levels

Terese has found herself at times feeling one thing emotionally or psycho-logically and another thing from a higher perspective, which she found confusing. Once she started delving into spirituality and metaphysics more, she understood where this was coming from. She's very grateful now for discernment and being shown the way. She's leery of people and groups that present themselves as spiritual and yet steer people in what she feels is "the wrong direction."

On Being Spiritually Aware Since Birth

She feels that being spiritually aware her whole life is definitely a blessing. She may not have had the guidance she's had in her life or been able to know things intuitively and spiritually had she not always been spiritually aware. She sympathathizes with people who don't have that innate spiritual aware-ness, and she feels that her life would have been miserable without it.

Life Purpose

She knows that her life purpose is to be a healer and a teacher. Throughout her life, she has helped people and guided them, and she continues to do the work she feels she came here to do.

11

Cynthia Sue Larson's Story

"Whoops! Wrong planet!"

CYNTHIA WAS BORN REMEMBERING WHO she was on the other side before she was incarnated into this lifetime. She had a sense at birth of feeling, "Whoops! Wrong planet!" She remembers where she was before she was born in this lifetime:

> *… being in a state of pure beingness, pure spiritual essence, where all is understood telepathically.*

She really missed the sense of community on the other side where there was no need for spoken language.

> *I have such a huge community there … a friendly, strong community of individuals who I love and who love me, who are always there for me, who I can be with instantly.*

Early Memories

Cynthia's first more specific memory is from when she was an infant, probably less than three months old. She was lying on her back looking around and seeing soft, harmonious, somewhat blurred pastel colors all around her. The colors would move if someone entered the room, and she could hear murmurs of voices. She could also feel the energy of people before they entered the room.

Cynthia found using language here on Earth to be difficult because no language was needed where she was before she incarnated. When she learned to speak, it would take her a while to answer questions. On the higher levels, there was no need to ask questions and be answered by someone, because if someone wanted to know something the answer would just be there with a lot of love and support. "We're heart to heart, we're spirit to spirit—we're just together."

If she thought of someone, that person would instantly be there with her. She remembered that as the way it really is in our true spiritual reality on the other side—her norm, whereas being here, which is not our true spiritual home, felt foreign.

When she was old enough to sit up, she would close her eyes and just rock. She was later told that there had been concern that she might be autistic because she had seemed to be in her own world. While she was doing that, in her mind she was back on that higher level in pure being-ness, the real reality:

> *. . . where things are the way they really are . . . It was so smooth and beautiful. It didn't have the harshness and the jangliness.*

She could see, sense, and feel energies from the time she was little and they felt "jangling," which was shocking to her. There could be loud noises and people could be in bad moods, which were upsetting to her. It was quite disharmonious, which was in stark contrast to where she had come from.

Cynthia has always missed that place like crazy, and she misses the feeling of knowingness. To her, the best thing one can be is dead again.

At the same time, she's always felt that she is on a mission here, and she's felt a strong sense of purposeness to it.

Future Life Memory

Cynthia has also had a memory of a future life in a "dystopian future" about five hundred years from now. This memory came to her as a "leak-through" (what I tend to call a bleed-through), with the information being gradually revealed to her. As a spirit, she had gone there to visit to check it out because it had been very popular and she had questions about it. Her innocent question led her to an insight.

> … it feels to me that something could go wrong with that kind of a future, where people don't have to worry, they don't need to make decisions, everything's decided for them, they're so taken care of. How could that have gone wrong?

The next thing she knew she found herself in that future life.

It wasn't the paradise that some might think it would be, although in some ways it was similar to the present time. Robots and artificial intelligence were commonplace, and most people enjoyed those benefits. There was a central artificial intelligence that had components that were highly protected, and it would regulate people's thoughts. In some ways, it was like a science fiction nightmare.

This experience has informed Cynthia of her sense of being here in the present lifetime for a reason, that of raising consciousness on this planet. She feels that the thought of a future with robots and artificial intelligence might seem tempting and inviting. However, she experienced its downside and feels that she's here at the present time to help people "understand the value of consciousness—that our thoughts and feelings literally change the world." She saw this as a young child.

It's been very difficult for her to be here on this Earth, although having a fearlessness about death, coupled with her strong sense of purpose, has actually helped her to stay here.

Innate Spiritual Awareness

Cynthia has always been aware of loving and beautiful beings around her who would give her guidance. There was no sense of gender or age attached to these beings; she sensed their guiding her and they were loving and beautiful. In some ways, she felt like a robot with information fed to her.

As a young child, she had her own way of falling asleep, which she would do by tracing her thoughts backward. She later learned that this was not recommended by some spiritual teachers, unless one has mastered meditation, because it was thought to possibly lead to insanity.

Cynthia's spiritual awareness has always been a part of her, with no starting point of when she was either exposed to or started thinking about the universe. She's always known that this physical plane was not the only reality, and she has always been inner-guided. She's also always felt different from others. She had assumed that on some level people knew about what she knew and just weren't talking about it, yet came to learn that they truly didn't have her awareness, starting with members of her immediate family. Fortunately her grandmother was quite spiritual and did understand the things that Cynthia did, and she was close to her grandmother as a result. For example, her grandmother had experienced angels firsthand, as Cynthia had. Cynthia feels that having her grandmother, who understood some spiritual matters, gave her a huge boost and made being here a little easier.

Cynthia's spiritual awareness and orientation have always been huge for her. She's had access to spiritual truths and feels that they tend to be somewhat obvious and simple, rather than always being lofty truths.

While she always felt loving beings around her, she was also attuned to the Divine and to oneness.

Attitude About Being Here

Before she experienced her grandmother's spirituality, it was so difficult for Cynthia to be here on Earth that she felt that there had been a "terrible mix-up," resulting in her being on the wrong planet. Around the age of four, before she started school, she stopped feeling this quite as keenly.

Cynthia feels that her true home is on a small planet:

> ... very close to the heart of nothingness itself, [where] anything you say could become manifest, you could change the way you are, I guess you might call it "shape-shifting," ... anything you can describe you can be.

It's a very small civilization, a small place with,

> ... not too many people, right next to the heart of nothingness itself ... It might be called "Manifestation Masters" but with such wisdom, such love ... There is no injurious thought ever.

There are many reasons why Earth feels wrong to her. Where she came from, there was no disharmony like here.

> ... people were in alignment. What they think is what they say is what they do.

There's a lot of compassion there and "everyone is treated as a part of you, with such grace." And it's a real place, although it's like a secret place that's "next to the great creative powers." If you know it exists "and you are able to be there, then you can be there."

Cynthia continued to feel dismayed about being here, and when she was about four or five years old she strongly felt that she needed to do a reset. She felt that death would be the way to get back to where she wanted to be. She noticed that there were fast-moving cars frequently going down the street she lived on, and she had heard people talking about this as an issue of safety. She began to think that she could position herself just right when a fast car was coming so that she would be hit and could go back to where she came from. She then had an angelic intervention.

Time slowed down and she saw bright beings of light who were actually there. She had always known they were there and had sensed them, but she hadn't actually seen them. They surrounded her and told her that she had a big choice to make and that she could choose fast or she could choose slow. She was given picture images like she used to have before she incarnated here; they were like thought bubbles with all the knowledge in them. She would feel good that she was going to be given information and all of a sudden she would be in the bubble and know it all.

They showed her different realities. One was of what she was planning to do, and they told her that it was her choice and showed her what it would look like if she did that, including the devastation to her family. It would create sadness and a dark space in their lives that wouldn't go away, with ongoing depression for some. They also let her know that she could choose to start over that way, but she would have to come back and do those first four or five years all over again. That didn't look good to her.

Then they showed her the slow path that included a long life and meeting like-minded spiritual people, including those who were born aware and those who really do understand that the spiritual truth is real; they showed her that she was here for a reason, that she chose her family, and that there was no mistake.

She was surprised and incredulous, but knew they were telling the truth. She found it confusing, yet also clarifying. She was able to ask all her questions, but then as she came out of it she felt that she was waking up from a dream that you don't fully quite remember. Yet she felt happy that she had chosen the slow path. She did make demands though. She had said to them, "You've got to promise me that there will be people like me that I will know."

They replied, "Yes, of course." She feels like it took a long time before she met people like that, but it did happen—and it made a huge difference for her, knowing that she wasn't alone.

Innate Intuitive Ability

Cynthia has been intuitive from a young age, and her angelic guides would tell her that everyone knew what she was thinking. She felt that this had to be true because she knew what other people were thinking. Even her family, who weren't intuitive, could pick up on what others were thinking. She felt that she could especially read what one person, who she felt was a stronger sender, was thinking and feeling and where his feelings would go next. If he was in a bad mood, she could pick up on it and she knew she had to tidy up and pick up all her toys from the front yard, the living room, and the hallway, so that there wouldn't be disharmony and so that she wouldn't get into trouble. She would put her toys into her room and shut the door, and then read a book or do something else.

She's always felt that she was observing people and things around her, as opposed to being engaged with them, and this has been natural for her. She feels that she was frequently "blissed out" as a child because her nervous system "was so engaged at such a heightened state of vibration." She found answering questions posed to her to be difficult because she was more naturally attuned to things and tended to flow with things, feeling the answer with others. This was another reason why she found human ways here on Earth to be strange.

She has certainly always known that she's just passing through here and is here temporarily. She's also always been good at reading other people and feels that she intuitively knows people's hearts, regardless of what their faces may show. She can read right through what may be shown on the surface to see what's inside, and this is true for her not just with people, but also with animals.

Feeling Different from Others

Cynthia feels that her experience of life has been quite different from that of people who haven't always been spiritually aware. She feels that understanding a shared process, as opposed to an ego-based one, is one difference. This is in addition to being inner-guided, being able to raise one's consciousness effortlessly, and being able to relax and find things coming together effortlessly. She feels that most people who aren't spiritually aware are very much out of harmony and that their heads and logic can lead them, instead of their hearts. They fall into the trap of feeling like they're all that matters, being in a "gimme, gimme, gimme" mode and are thus not being real, as opposed to being able to feel a part of what's around them.

Additional Gifts

She's been blessed with strong intellect and creativity, in addition to her spiritual awareness.

View of Animals and Nature

She feels that animals are very wise and have the same levels of depth that people do. She's very selective when choosing a pet, "the way you would be about any spirit coming into your family." Cynthia knows that an animal can be a part of her family by a mutual process of co-selecting. She knows that they can be so much more than just a dog or a cat, and she needs a pet that's a being of the highest level in her family.

She communicates telepathically with animals (pets, wild ones, and those she's never met), and she knows that when she has a higher level being as a pet, the level of telepathic communication is crystal clear and there's great co-operation. (She's written about this topic in books.) She feels that animals are ensouled, having individual souls instead of a group one. She also feels that we can live lives both as animals and as humans.

When she looks into an animal's eyes, she feels that it's very close to that wonderful paradise she knew before she incarnated here; they can serve to remind us of who we really are. She further feels that this is the way animals prefer to communicate. This is why wild animals trust her and animals she's never met before will follow her commands. She can feel them sensing, "there's a being here who's real." She's observed that a lot of animals are not so positively impressed by humans.

Cynthia likewise loves nature and feels that she can go to the highest levels when in nature, where she can feel the vibration of harmony and unity that feels very healing to her. She loves the aspect of nature that is untouched by man and without manmade intrusions of disruptions. This feels very peaceful to her.

On Feeling Protected and Guided

Her natural state is to be compassionate and sensitive, although she feels that she has toughened up in order to be on this planet. She has adjusted socially and can speak her mind. She knows that a part of her is really innocent and pure. She's always felt protected and guided and knows that things will be okay in her life, and though the acculturation on this planet is to buy into fear and there are times when she can get pulled into the confusion, she remembers that the fear doesn't feel right and isn't real. As a result, she has a lot of empathy for how people get confused here and don't understand that the ultimate reality is one of love. She works in several ways to help others and knows that she also helps others in her sleep.

View of Organized Religions

She was not brought up in a religious tradition because her family tended to be agnostic or atheist. So she wasn't exposed to organized religion through her family. However, she went on many family trips to places in the world that were sacred sites with high energy. The locations were those where few Westerners had been to, but Cynthia could feel the high energy and spiritual quality. She was able to visit Pacific Islanders and Africans who lived in remote areas. So unbeknownst to her family, they ended up giving her some wonderful spiritual experiences on these travels. (The purpose was to see how others really lived.) When they visited places in Africa, for example, where there were no roads or electricity and the people didn't speak English, Cynthia was thrilled because she could feel the resonance again with others, and she could communicate without speaking the same language; there was a universal feeling of love. She felt that the people living in those remote areas could really read her heart. She could also see that the sacred feelings they had for their sacred places were of a very high vibration. She could feel, see, and sense those energies and the experience was bliss. As a result, her family gave her one of the greatest gifts she could have received.

At present, Cynthia views religion as "handrails and a guidance system for people who need comfort and inspiration." She feels that many people don't have the knowingness that she has so they need a set of rules to keep them on track, like "training wheels to take you to a certain level, but you wouldn't win the Tour de France with it."

Personal Experience of Different Levels

Cynthia frequently finds herself feeling one thing on her human psyche level and a different thing on her higher soul level awareness. She feels, however, that this whole planet is that way. She's aware of her higher soul awareness and feels that it's quite angelic and *one with all*, but she feels that words are inadequate to fully describe it.

In her present spiritual practice, Cynthia makes a connection to "that beautiful oneness, Divine source, Spirit consciousness" and invites it to lead her in her life. She basically welcomes it to run her life. She feels that it's always her choice and she just needs to remember to make it. In her work, she helps others feel that oneness, and she has produced a healing meditation to help others feel it.

On Being Spiritually Aware Since Birth

She feels that being spiritually aware her whole life has primarily been a blessing overall, although it has also been challenging at times, especially when she was very young. Coming into this life remembering how good it was on higher levels makes it more difficult to be here. She feels it keeps those of us born aware on our paths because we usually know why we came here, but the fact that most people are unaware on a higher level makes it difficult. That said, Cynthia feels that this is a time of great awakening and that more people are remembering their spiritual selves.

It has been difficult for her because she hasn't been able to share what she knows because it's been somewhat of a forbidden topic for so many people. She has continued to do her work, however. She works with deva spirits (nature spirits) around the planet and communicates with them She feels that we can communicate with dolphins and spirits that may be driving natural disasters, such as wildfires, for example, in order to get various groups of aware beings (devas, dolphins, etc.) to help with those natural disasters via their consciousness. In other words, she can communicate with spirits who can be facilitators in healing various situations, including natural disasters, through their consciousness. She feels that there is a quantum nature (a discontinuous one) to all of reality and that we can work with it, meaning that quantum physics (which includes jumps in reality) can be used to create jumps of healing. Cynthia has studied physics and feels that there can be "a discontinuous jump for all of reality," including with healing and this can be applied to healing the damage done to the environment. Aligning 12.5 percent of a collective consciousness with a vision or intention of healing—for example, choosing clean air or restored wildlife—can trigger a discontinuous jump of healing.

She feels that we're getting closer to this quantum threshold among the population in the United States, with 8 percent of the population nationally currently meditating, while 10 percent on the West Coast is. Undoing the damage done to wildlife and the environment via quantum means would obviously be a better means of cleansing than natural disasters.

Cynthia feels that this has implications, as well, for releasing fears because healing can occur instantaneously. She endeavors to discuss the quantum paradigm and what consciousness is all about with scientists, including theoretical physicists who study the multiverse, to further our awareness and bring higher consciousness into the mainstream. This work is in alignment with what she knows her purpose to be.

Life Purpose

Cynthia has been keenly aware of the subject of her life purpose since she was little. She's known that she's here to help raise the level of consciousness in order to avert the negative reality she saw five hundred years in the future. She's seen the consciousness here on Earth as a web of consciousness, "like a beautiful net full of shining jewels at all the cross-points, and with just thought alone it starts raising up and lifting."

She works with each individual soul she can touch and reminds them of higher levels and vibrations, that they can feel them, including the joy, love, connectedness, and belonging, and that we can attain them.

12

Dr. Stanislav
Gergre O'Jack's Story

"I was in a rolled-up position and housed in a warm
environment surrounded by a seemingly orange-red-color
illumination … something like being in a sauna.
I could feel the warmth, the sounds."

STANISLAV REMEMBERS BEING IN HIS mother's womb. He felt that he had
lived in a cave and came to realize that this came from his memory of
being in his mother's womb when she was pregnant with him. He's always
loved to go spelunking and his experience in the womb must have created that pastime. But he didn't get to go spelunking and experience caves
firsthand until he was in his fifties. It felt so comfortable to him that he
felt like he was home.

He could remember thinking while he was in the womb, and he re-membered being "in a rolled-up position and housed in a warm environ-ment." He could even remember an orange-red color and could feel the warmth and the sounds. This was his earliest memory.

Early Memories

When he was about six months old, his mother was hospitalized with tuberculosis, at which time his father abandoned the family. He heard his father tell his grandfather, "You made me get married. You raise the kids." His father's leaving them saddened him.

He remembers being taken to visit his mother on "drive-by visits," since they couldn't be physically close to her, and feels that he was less than one year old because he was always being carried. He could understand everything that was being said. He remembers coming back from one of these visits and being cold. He sat in front of the heat register once back home with his legs pulled up to his chest, trying to get warm, and heard his step-grandmother say, "Look at the little one. He's reminiscing. He's missing his mother."

He remembers thinking, *I don't miss my mother. I'm cold. I just want to get warm.* He knows he was less than two because his mother died before he turned two.

He also remembers being bathed by his step-grandmother in a large pot on a gas stove, with his grandfather holding him up under his armpits. This was before he started to walk.

He remembers his grandmother being somewhat large-breasted, and when he was between the age of six months and one year she would put his hands there if he was cold. He remembers being cradled as she would do this.

Stanislav grew up in what he terms a ghetto in Detroit, with financial restriction and exposure to abuse. His grandfather and step-grandmother were verbally abusive with each other, and she tried to poison his grandfather once, as well as Stanislav a couple of times when he was fourteen and fifteen.

While he was growing up, he always found himself wondering why the people around him were so stupid. He saw people drawing conclusions in matters about which they had no information. He started to question why he thought the way he did and, after a family member began calling him stupid regularly, he began to feel that he was. His thoughts and life experiences differed from those of the norm. He now feels that the way most people think may be typical, but not normal, as that to him means "healthy and stable and believing in a 'God force.'"

Innate Spiritual Awareness

He had many spiritual experiences as a child and couldn't always distinguish between what was real (or stemming from this three-dimensional reality) and other, more spiritual ones. He could see people, for example, that other people weren't seeing. He was told that he had a tremendous imagination and wondered at times if he was making things up. Sometimes he wondered if there was something wrong with his eyes because he had no one who could explain these phenomena to him.

When he was between the ages of seven and eight, he finally began to share some of his experiences with his gypsy grandmother, and she explained some of this to him from her perspective. When he was eight, his grandfather told him that he needed to be baptized and start going to church. Stanislav refused to do that, however, because they lived in a racially and culturally diverse neighborhood, and he didn't believe in any one religion. He knew that there was a God and told his grandfather that, to which his grandfather replied, "Fine, you already believe in God. You don't have to go to church." He always had a belief in a creative force because even as a child he would question where he had come from.

He's been inner-guided from a young age and was always spiritual and nonviolent. (His grandfather distilled liquor when Stanislav was little to make extra money, and Stanislav didn't care for the behavior of people when they were drinking.) He also felt that this wasn't his true home. He didn't know, however, if he was the only one who felt this or whether others did as well. The negative aspects on this planet—e.g., the unkindness, the profanity, the thievery, and constant fighting, etc.—felt foreign to him. He also constantly felt that he didn't belong to his family. He didn't look like his father or other male family members and wondered if they had gotten him from some other family.

Innate Intuitive Ability

He was intuitively gifted from a young age, being able to see spirits and people who were passed on, to sense energy, and to experience precognition. This confused him, especially his precognitive ability, until he met Theosophists and learned from them.

When he was twelve, his father showed up a second time. (He had last seen him at age eight.) His father wanted to take him to a meeting and it turned out to be a metaphysical one. His father, who had given up gambling, smoking, and drinking, took him to a Theosophical Society meeting. Through this group Stanislav was able to meet Krishnamurti (a well-known spiritual teacher and author) and also studied major religions of the world. He could see major disparities between the beliefs of religions and the behavior of people who believed in those religions.

He felt different from others in some respects when he was little, but when he was twelve he started to feel different in a more comprehensive way. He also started having out-of-body experiences then. He wanted to escape the pain of negativity from a family member and the difficult living circumstances, so he learned to meditate from the Theosophists. He discovered that if he meditated in a really focused way, he was no longer in his body. He could explore and go down the street, go up in space, or go to other planets. He also started to write in a way that made him question where the information had come from—and he later came to realize that he was doing automatic writing, which is a form of what is now called channeling. His automatic writing started when he was twelve and has continued to increase over the years.

He has always observed people and things around him, as opposed to being engaged with them, and this is constant for him. He feels that he frequently needs to move around in order to see if he's still alive. He was stunned when someone got mad at him for assuming he had been reading her diary, because he was answering questions she hadn't asked yet. It turned out that he was just naturally and unconsciously reading her thoughts. He realized that he needed to see if her lips were moving before responding. This also happened in his work as a therapist, when he talked about things that his clients were thinking but not outwardly verbalizing.

He's always felt that being here on Earth was like a "strange beginning," as though he wasn't human. Instead, he feels like he was a drop of energy with a beginning but no end. He thinks of planet Earth as his second womb (after his mother's womb) and as part of an ongoing existence. When he was seven or eight, he heard the word "infinity" and asked others to explain it. He's still striving to understand it but feels that life must be like a Mobius band, with no beginning and no end—that his body had a beginning, but not his awareness or soul. He feels that he's part of an indescribable energy, and sometimes he feels like he's a "molecule of a whole species and that there is no such thing as separation." He feels that we use our sensory system to try to describe our relationship physically to another person, but at the same time we're connected, rather than separate.

From a young age, he could distinguish between his body and his soul and at five started to view his body as a garment for his soul. This is another reason why he enjoyed going out of his body and exploring, because he wasn't hampered by his body. When he was exploring other places while he was out of body, he would tell himself to draw where he'd been and what he had seen when he woke up. When he would be traveling to a different country as an adult, he would sometimes recognize places he'd been to while out of body.

Feeling Different from Others

He's good at reading other people and feels that that's why he became a therapist. At the same time, he feels that his experience of life is vastly different from that of people who haven't always been spiritually aware. He feels that about 98 percent of people are very narrow in their views, or "fundamentalist," as he terms them. He learned in school that the typical cone of vision for humans was fifteen degrees, and he resolved to broaden his range of vision, including physically, intellectually, and spiritually. He also feels different because he consciously strives to help everyone he meets to look at him as a member of their family—that there's a oneness to our species. His ability to access information is another way in which he feels different from most people.

Additional Gifts

Stanislav has been blessed with a strong intellect, spiritual awareness, and creativity. He doesn't always feel comfortable with claiming his intellect, however, because he has seen the arrogance of others who felt that they were smart, and he prefers humility. He's strongly creative when working with his hands, and he has won awards for industrial design.

View of Animals and Nature

He views animals as his obligation. He feels it's important to take care of them, be kind to them, and protect them, and he feels that they have an unbelievable communication. He was walking his dog once and became angry, and his dog yelped, having picked up on Stanislav's thoughts and emotions. Another time a strange dog he had seen only once before led him to his own lost dog after Stanislav had telepathically asked the dog to help him. He's also been able to receive messages telepathically from animals.

He feels that nature is "an entity in itself, a form of life." If it has a soul, he feels that it differs from ours because when he eats plants he doesn't have a sense that he's hurting them. He's familiar with the work of Cleve Backster, whom he's met, and feels that plants have some kind of energy, which may not be the same as a soul, but may be soul-like. He also feels that Earth is a living entity.

On Feeling Protected and Guided

From day one Stanislav has always felt protected and guided, and he relies on his visions in his dreams to guide him as well. He feels that if he's focused on God, nothing will bother or harm him. He's had a lifelong faith in God and has felt that if you commit yourself to good things, there's always a pleasant answer to everything. As a result, he's always felt protected and tends not to have a lot of fears. He's stood up to protect others, putting himself at risk, and feels that if a crime is being committed, he has the power of God with him, which protects him.

He's both compassionate and sensitive and feels that a part of him is still innocent and pure. He's been married three times and his wives have told him that he's sensitive. If he hears people use negative words, he actually feels it impact his chest.

View of Organized Religions

His family was Greek Orthodox and some of his male ancestors had been Greek Orthodox priests, but he was not compelled to go to church, as previously noted. So the household was Christian, but the emphasis was on God, rather than on religious figures who are intermediaries. He feels that God is the originating source, rather than "a copy or something dispensed through human beings." He looks at the true definition of religion, which is "to make one, to bind together." He feels that regardless of whatever religious label people may put on themselves, if they're not living the true meaning of it, they're not religious.

Near-Death Experiences

Stanislav has had more than one near-death experience. In one, after having eaten poisonous mushrooms, he went to another world where he spoke to several people, some of whom were already passed on and others who had recently arrived. He recognized one as an acquaintance and asked him where they were and what he was doing there, since he lived in New Zealand. He then saw a Duesenberg convertible and a tall, slim woman. He concluded that it was probably a dream and told himself to memorize all the details so that he could record them later. This experience lasted for three days. He saw that same tall, slim woman several times after his near-death experience and many years later met her in person—she's his present wife.

He's also had several experiences with UFOs, including one on the ground in Michigan, which was about a hundred feet away from him. He never panics or is fearful when he encounters one. Instead he feels awed and is very grateful for the experience.

Work with Anomalous Phenomena

Stanislav researches subtle energy and works with physicists on this subject. He's a conduit for anomalous subtle energy through the medium of photographs, which are termed spirit photographs and are taken unintentionally with the lens cap of the camera still on. This first happened quite spontaneously when he attended a concert by well-known musicians, who were friends of his, some years back. He had taken photos since he was a child and always carried a camera with him. He took several photographs while attending the concert, which he ended up developing. When he looked at them, the developed photos had several spots on them. His initial reaction was that the developer had ruined his film. However, after the photographs had been enlarged and studied, it turned out that there were some human-like forms on them.

Since then, he's continued to have photographs spontaneously taken on his camera—even though the camera was in his camera case and had the lens cap on. Since this first happened, he's taken over five thousand anomalous photographs, and his work has been featured in the books *Science and Human Transformation* by Dr. William Tiller, *The Orb Project* by Dr. Klaus Heinemann, and *Orbs: Their Mission & Messages of Hope,* which is also by Dr. Klaus Heinemann. His photographs have also been featured in the video "The Life After Death Project."

On Being Spiritually Aware Since Birth

He feels that being spiritually aware his whole life is definitely a blessing and feels that his life purpose is to help to bring about world peace. As an adult, he has had some health issues but has never been concerned because he still has work to do here on Earth and knows it's not his time yet.

13

Rozlyn Reynolds' Story

"Shortly after being born, I remember seeing all the bright
lights, faces looking down at me with masks on."

ROZLYN REYNOLDS' FIRST MEMORY COMES right after being born. She remembers all the bright lights in the delivery room and the faces with surgical masks on looking down at her. She also remembers recognizing her parents' voices right after birth, beginning with her father's voice, as her mother was sedated and not alert. It was after her mother woke up that Rozlyn first heard her mother's voice. She remembers being put in a bassinet and hearing her father's voice while she was in there. She was also aware of three angels with her, whom she always senses around her, as they have always been with her.

Pre-Birth Memories

Rozlyn has memories from before her birth in this lifetime.

I can remember very clearly being outside of this dimension, yet looking into it and seeing myself the same way, like remote viewing from a very distant dimensional field, and I can remember looking and seeing myself in other lives and doing other things. I can also remember very clearly before I was actually born—delivered into this life—of being with them [the angels] and just watching everything… everything going on in the world, not just with my family that I was born into… not even that, just things that were going on in the world—and not just in this world.

Rozlyn has clearly known from a very young age that this world was not the only reality.

Early Memories

Rozlyn remembers an earthquake hitting when she was just over a year old. (She lived with her family in San Diego in Southern California.) She was sitting in her high chair in the kitchen and her grandparents were visiting. She remembers the high chair moving back and forth and her mother jumping up and running over to grab the high chair in order to keep her from falling over. However, she was observing the scene from up in the air above it, with two of her angels with her, as opposed to being in her body observing it from that perspective. From that position up in the air she could see her physical presence below in the scene in her high chair, and she remembers watching her grandparents who were "freaking out," as she described it. They weren't from the West Coast and were terrified. She remembers being concerned for them, but one of her angels told her, "They'll be fine."

This was Rozlyn's first memory of being outside of her body. (She goes in and out of her body a lot.) It was also when she became more consciously aware of being protected and guided in her life here, although she's always had an innate sense of oneness. In fact, she doesn't always stay in this dimension of time and space.

When Rozlyn was three years old, her mother became very ill with hepatitis. Her father was not able to stop working, so he sat Rozlyn down and told her that he was making lunch for her ill mother and that she (Rozlyn) was to give her mother the meal at lunchtime. He told her to take care of her mother, who was aware but bedridden then, and to keep an eye on her throughout the day, but that she was allowed to go outside at 1:00. He took her outside and showed her how far she was allowed to go in the yard, which wasn't fenced in.

Rozlyn remembers sitting with her mother and talking to her angels and seeing God, and saying, "I need my mommy to get well." She felt light come in through the top of her head and go out through her right hand. She was holding her mother's hand and saying, "Let me help Mommy and let me take care of her." (Her mother had what was considered to be a serious case of hepatitis, and she made a somewhat remarkable recuperation within a couple of months, although her liver was permanently impaired.)

This was Rozlyn's first conscious memory of connecting to God in this lifetime, even though she had been aware of her three angels being with her since she was born and even beforehand. She sees Jesus as well, along with all other kinds of angelic presences.

Innate Spiritual Awareness

Rozlyn has always been innately spiritually aware. She knows firsthand that we can connect directly to God and that we don't need any intermediary to do this—nor any guru.

We are connected with our Creator and we source to Him for energy and strength, and we are being guided by our angels and guides— they are His emissaries.

She knows that we are a spirit having a physical experience and are just passing through here.

She has been inner-guided from birth and has felt different from others from very early on. She was high strung and high energy as a child, and she knew that her energy was different from that of other people.

She feels that Earth is not her true home because she would often leave her body and fly around. There is one place she always goes to.

> It's just a beautiful place … incredibly light-filled … It's full of white light, purple light, turquoise … I feel in that space like I am one with the space and with God … It's an incredibly powerful place of peace and healing. And it smells really good there [laughs]. I think of that place as heaven … There are some really interesting sort of white spinning columns, but they're not solid and they're like energy fields. And they're all a part of the energy and the love and the light of that place.

When she was ten years old, Rozlyn had a life-threatening bout of mononucleosis. She was quite ill and was bedridden for three months. During that time, she went in and out of her physical body. She remembers thinking that it was so much easier not to be stuck in her ill body, but she remembers hearing, "You're not done, so you have to stay here."

Past-Life Recall

She also remembers some of her past lives, and when she looks at them, as well as those of other people, she sees a "translucent string that runs between these lives," and they're in something like an energy bubble. At the same time, she sees her other lifetimes and personas as distinct, so she hasn't had an undifferentiated sense of memories bleeding into the present lifetime (such that they would feel more present than past).

She presently lives in the American Southwest, but she also went there as a kid. When she first got there, she remembers feeling that she loved the area and recalled living there before. She saw herself very clearly in a covered wagon coming across the United States at the age of sixteen. Her family and she came via a northern route through the Dakotas. She's never been there in this lifetime, but clearly remembers seeing the rolling land. She remembers:

> *... how desolate and we were coming across in this covered wagon, and I was married and very young and I was expecting my first child.*

She died in childbirth on the prairie in that lifetime.

When she was around ten or eleven, she realized that she had been hung as a witch in Massachusetts during the witchcraft trials. In this lifetime she can't stand for anything to be tight around her throat, and she would tell her mother from a very young age not to put anything around her neck.

She also knows that prior to that lifetime she lived hundreds of years ago on a beautiful island out in the ocean, which she feels was the Pacific Ocean. It was "an incredible energy field," and she could see herself moving her hand and creating colors and touching people and healing them. She feels that she was some sort of metaphysical doctor in that lifetime and in this lifetime she feels a strong affinity for the Pacific Ocean and feels at home and at peace whenever close to it.

Innate Awareness of Interconnection

Rozlyn feels very connected to her family and knows that they were together in her other lifetimes. She also knows that everyone and everything is connected.

> *I think of all of us as being interwoven fabric, and we're all connected. It's almost like a web. If one person moves in one section of it, we all feel it. And this is what people need to really get in the world, because we can't be killing and doing all of that stuff without*

doing those things to ourselves, because we are all inter-connected in this web. ... How I see this is like a huge, woven fabric, and when one person and one spirit, one mind-body-spirit is pulled out of that fabric, that hole is never really repaired.

She further likens that interwoven tapestry to an energy grid with everyone having an electrical and electromagnetic frequency.

Innate Intuitive Ability

Rozlyn has been strongly intuitive since birth. This often expressed itself as psychokinesis (mind over matter or moving objects with one's mind), and she would get into trouble as a result of things being broken. She would sometimes think, "I want this to happen," and it would indeed happen. She further had the ability to hear and see out of this dimension so she always talked out loud to other spirits and entities, other presences, and her angels, and she clearly remembers her mother telling her, "You can't do this in front of people because they'll lock you up." Her mother was fine with Rozlyn doing this with her, but not around other people. Rozlyn simply views this as being able to hear in different frequencies. She also has mediumistic abilities.

Rozlyn has also always been good at reading other people and intuitively knew things about others. When she was about six years old, her mother cautioned her that she couldn't just blurt out things that she intuitively knew about other people because it made them really nervous. Her mother wasn't upset about Rozlyn being intuitive; she just didn't want her to voice the things she was picking up on about others.

Feeling Different from Others

She is often observing people and things around her, as opposed to being engaged with them. Her experiences of life are different from other people's who haven't always been spiritually aware. She feels that people who don't share her innate spiritual awareness have no clue what goes on with her, and even people she's known and been close to for many years couldn't handle her spiritual orientation and knowledge and would find it unnerving and threatening, because they seem to want her to be who they always thought she was. At the same time, she still loves them for who they are. Having a different experience of life from most others feels like "an amazing disconnect" that you just can't explain.

Despite her innate spiritual awareness, her goal was to live a normal life, so for many years she tried to find a balance between her human side (with its logical mind and five senses) and her strongly spiritual one. Around the age of fifty, she decided to basically surrender and do what she felt God wanted her to do.

Additional Gifts

Rozlyn feels that there is a strong connection between musical talent, especially singing, and intuition. She's gifted musically and started singing professionally when she was ten years old. She continues to sing, although not professionally, whenever she needs release or comfort and finds it to be recentering and regrounding. She also loves to draw and paint and do crafts, although she's moved away from her artistic pursuits in recent years. In addition, she's an avid reader and researcher and focused on journalism in college. She has a strong interest in sociological and humanitarian issues. She doesn't focus rigidly on being either creative or logical and feels it's best to just flow in a way that works for you.

View of Animals and Nature

Rozlyn loves animals and is able to communicate with them, whether they're still here or crossed over. She feels that animals have tremendous emotions and a tremendous capacity to love in ways that humans don't utilize. She's seen that different species of animals do different things with regard to their energy fields and electromagnetic frequencies. She feels that an animal's world is very simple and noncomplex—just "love and be loved, exist, and live in your reality of what it takes to survive." They don't carry all the baggage that we humans do, and she finds that to be an amazing lesson that we can take from them.

When she looks into an animal's eyes, she feels connected to them, hears what they think, and feels what they feel, and she senses their prior experiences, including traumatic ones, which are stored in their hearts. She tries to help them release any painful ones in a healing fashion. She feels that animals have individual souls, rather than having simply a group soul. (Some people believe that animals don't have individual souls, but a group one for their entire species.)

Rozlyn feels that the Earth is a living entity and has a frequency that has a powerful component to heal—an amazing resource that we have but don't tap into or use. She feels that it's a perfect environment that provides everything—if it's not mismanaged.

On Feeling Protected and Guided

She's compassionate and sensitive and had to learn to erect boundaries so as not to be drained. She can place herself in a white light bubble of protection, love, and guidance and has used tough love when it was necessary to do so. At the same time, a part of her is still innocent and pure. She has not had many fears and instead has felt guided and protected by her angels and guides. She feels surrounded by the light of God's love, which protects her. If she ever feels negative energy, she asks her angels and guides for protection.

View of Organized Religions

She was brought up in a strict, fundamentalist Christian church with a lot of negative judgment and fire and brimstone. She continued attending the church until she was eighteen, but she had already started asking questions that may have been threatening or unacceptable to those in the church. She had also started being more open about what she could do with energy, which wasn't well received by those in the church. She had additionally started seeing more hypocrisy with people paying lip-service to the teachings, something she has since found with most religions.

She now feels that most religions have become like governments because they're manipulative and controlling—mind control and money control. She feels that religion is now about "nothing that anyone who believes in love" and is aware of that interwoven web connection of everyone (that needs to be honored) would do. She tries to be aware of how many people have been so mind-controlled by religion that they can't step out, while she also recognizes that there's a lot of social pressure from society, family, and friends for people to fit in and do the acceptable thing, which is to be part of religion and conform.

While she did have to reprogram some of the religious influence and doctrine inculcated in her, in a way she's thankful for her religious upbringing.

I feel a very powerful connection to the power of Jesus and how He lived His life... And that steps away from the traditional Christian—because unfortunately, let's face it—most Christians don't live anything like Jesus talked about... People who live in love and who make every effort to be compassionate, to help their fellow man, to help the Earth, to help animals—that's what we're supposed to be doing here."

She looks to Jesus as how we are to live our lives while we're here, although she knows that others who walked the Earth also lived this way.

That's what we're here for—to connect and to be in that interwoven connection and to love and to have compassion.

Personal Experience of Different Levels

Rozlyn frequently finds herself feeling one thing emotionally (on her human level) and a different thing on another level (that of her higher soul awareness). She can perceive the difference between these levels and reminds herself that as a human, while here, she's not perfect. She works on finding a balance between those two sides of her, even though she knows that being human (being here in a body) is pretty limiting. She also acknowledges that, while the higher spiritual levels are preferable, she still has to take good care of her body.

She described her higher soul awareness as:

That is when I am completely in connection with God and I feel the oneness—and I feel the oneness not just with myself and God, but with everyone else too. And that's very, very powerful. It encompasses everything—mind, body, spirit, emotions. It's the replenishment of energies and your soul being cleared by that connection and reestablishing your priorities.

Synaesthesia and Unusual Senses

Rozlyn has also always been aware that time doesn't exist in a linear fashion—but in a spiral, cyclical fashion instead.

Awareness of Being Here on Assignment

She knows that we're all here on an assignment to do a job. She distinguishes between a job she does to bring in income and her "job from God," which involves helping others.

On Being Spiritually Aware Since Birth

She has wondered off and on throughout her life whether being spiritually aware her whole life is a blessing or a curse, but she feels that it depends on how you perceive it and how willing you are to surrender to your calling.

When she has been willing to let go in her life and surrender to her inner guidance—what she is guided to do—it's a blessing. When she fights what she's being guided to do because the human part of her wants to do something else, it's a curse. When she can see things coming that may be troubling, she can send energy to it and light to it, but there can be a sadness. She knows that there are times when you have to surrender to acceptance and that it's not always easy.

She knows that her human side can be remarkably self-centered, and the realization that we're not really in control doesn't feel good.

You can vision, you can create the energy to manifest and bring them—you can do all of those things, but ultimately you are here on assignment.

Rozlyn feels that throughout her life she has sought to find a balance between what she's here to do (her assignment and purpose) and what she wants to do (stemming from her human persona). It's not that she doesn't want to fulfill what she came here to do, but that there are other things that would have been fun that she hasn't been able to do.

Life Purpose

She knows that her life purpose (and assignment) has to do with helping others and shepherding them in finding balance in their own situations. She had people, including adults, seeking her counsel and asking for advice from the time she was eleven or twelve years old. This has a ripple effect, Rozlyn feels, because if the people she helps then help others, then greater numbers of people are involved in the welfare of others and positive change is brought about. She has worked professionally with her intuition for many years, teaches intuitive skills to others, and does healing work. Her spiritual work with others is a large part of what she came here to do.

14

Carmel Bell's Story

"I remember being in the 'soup' before I was born…
I was … given a choice as to 'what' I would be in
terms of being seen as good, bad, or indifferent."

CARMEL BELL HAS ALWAYS HAD memories that extend back to before she
was born. In that non-corporeal place—a "soup"—she remembers a variety of aspects of what it was like and what she was doing there, including
"observing aspects of the Universe," having freedom of movement and
being able to go wherever she wanted to, being with other souls and walking and talking with them, "waiting for other souls to arrive," etc. There
was a "day-to-day learning" there and she would agree to work with other
souls for various reasons.

She remembers that there was preparation on the other side for her
coming into this incarnation, which unfolded for her in the following way:

I remember being in the "soup" before I was born. I remember following a vine that had flowers like lanterns on it and these lit up as

I walked. I was shown different branches and I knew I could choose to step on to a side path at any point. I was also given a choice as to "what" I would be in terms of being seen as good, bad, or indifferent. I was asked to be what is now known as a Medical Intuitive— not my chosen title but there you have it. One I was landed with.

There was a being with her guiding her in this process, who identified himself by saying, "I am your father, Jesus." She regarded him as both Jesus and Archangel Metatron.

Carmel embraced this incarnation.

I do remember a feeling of looking forward to this, but with a sense of this as a job that has to be done. I suppose a similar feeling to knowing you have to clean the bathroom kind of job. You like it when it's done and even when you are doing it, but it is a trial to start and even to keep going.

At the same time, she remembers having "a feeling of excitement over the adventures" she would have and the people she would meet.

Early Memories

Carmel's next memory after she was born was from when she was two months old. She remembers traveling with her family in the car and being in the back seat in a basket. Her caretaker, who was in the front, leaned back over her and Carmel thought that she was the most beautiful person. "She was like an Angel to me." Carmel remembers her smile and seeing the clouds in the sky, as well as feeling happy and safe in that moment.

She has many memories from her early years and feels that she has almost perfect recall, including being dropped on her head when she was six months old and the dress she was wearing that day. She remembers her caretaker crying a lot when she was a baby and that she spent more time with Carmel's older sister than with her.

At the age of eighteen months, she poisoned herself by mistaking a container of gasoline for lemonade, and she remembers the experience quite clearly. She also remembers being on fire at the age of four when there was a fire in the house (while she was recovering from a hernia operation at the time). She was badly burned all over her body. She had lasting effects from the fire and was told that she would never be able to have children, that her kidneys had also been destroyed. She has now healed from those effects. For many years—until she was twenty-one—she couldn't stand to be touched. Interestingly, her skin is now heat tolerant. For example, she can put her hands in boiling water to retrieve boiled eggs, and she can even touch fire. She can also sense fire and smoke, beating smoke alarms at detection.

Near-Death Experiences

The fire was her first near-death experience. During it, Jesus and Metatron told her her future husband's name, and she was also told that this life would be a difficult one for her. However, she was also told that she would have the resilience to meet every challenge, but that it would be much harder than she thought it would be. Her saving grace would be that her "soul mate, Bernie," would be with her and would help her. Interestingly, she has been married twice and both husbands are named Bernie. She was given a choice to back out of the deal and opt not to come back, but she decided to come back and live out her incarnated life here.

Though she was told before she was born that she would be a medical intuitive, she received more information about this during her near-death experience. She was told that she would be a doctor, but not a traditional doctor, and that she would see energy and understand it. She was then shown an image of a person and their auric field with all the grids and ebbs and flows. She gained a clearer understanding of life during her NDE, and it was difficult for her to come back.

This near-death experience changed her. In fact, her caretaker later told her that afterward she didn't recognize Carmel anymore and felt that she had given birth to one child and then had another, different one. Carmel feels that this caused a separation or rift between them, which has since improved.

Since my last NDE, a lot of this has been repaired, but it will never be the full and seemingly bonded relationship that other mothers and daughters seem to enjoy.

True to what she was told during her near-death experience at age four, Carmel's life has not been an easy one. She has had health crises several times and has also had two more near-death experiences. When she was seventeen, she had surgery and died under the anesthetic. Then, when she was forty-seven, she had a heart attack and was clinically dead for at least fifty-two minutes. She presently has a brain tumor, which a doctor says will be lethal, but she's working on healing it. She feels that she's been given the repeated health issues because she's supposed to heal herself, rather than giving away the power to another being. She's persistent and hasn't given up on healing herself.

Innate Spiritual Awareness

Carmel has always been spiritually aware and has always known that this three-dimensional Earth existence was not the only reality, that there is a creative force/being (that we term God). In fact, it used to distress her that everyone didn't innately know these things, since she has also always been inner-guided. She had many psychic experiences as a child and her life was lived intuitively. She has always known what was wrong with other people, physically and emotionally. She has always been able to see people both physically and energetically at the same time.

She knew that she ultimately didn't belong here and has searched for her home throughout her life, although she knows that it's not here on this planet. She's known that she's *on* this planet, but not *of* this planet. She remembers living on other planets and having other families there who were all a type of being or species different from the humans here. She remembers them clearly and still communicates with them.

Feeling Different from Others

In addition, she has always felt different from others, especially because of her knowings. For example, she never believed that skin color made a difference, and she knew that mankind had been to the moon and other planets, even before the landing on the moon in 1969. She has felt quite rejected by peers and family—she was even beaten up in school several times after speaking up about her beliefs.

Innate Intuitive Ability and Supranormal Gifts

She's experienced a variety of supranormal abilities and experiences that range from intuitive knowing to astral travelling to spoon bending and object flinging, levitation, though only a few inches off the ground, and hearing voices. (She finds it annoying that she was able to levitate only a few inches off the ground.) She's noticed that her abilities get stronger every year.

View of Organized Religions

Carmel was brought up as a Catholic and found that the religious beliefs of the church conflicted with her own knowings.

I had many arguments with our local parish priest because I refused to call God "Father" when I had a good father of my own. I could not believe that God would live in a cold building and be against people of different colors or beliefs.

The church taught precepts in terms of black and white—that intuitive abilities, as well as sex, were wrong—with which she disagreed. She wasn't shy about sharing her awareness and knowings, which put her at odds with her family. There was suspicion that there was a negative energy in their house and at one point the house was exorcised. The priest then turned his attention to Carmel.

Carmel is not in favor of organized religion and actually considers it to be "horrifying." She feels that most wars have been fought over religion or philosophy. That said, she does feel that Pope Francis offers a ray of light, since he is a departure from most popes, and is more aligned with authentic spirituality.

When she was fourteen, she was taken to a psych unit. A family member, whom Carmel feels is like her in some ways, had the process stopped. When she turned fifteen a few months later, she decided to leave home.

Additional Gifts

She has many gifts. In addition to her intuitive gifts, she also has a strong intellect and is very creative, having engaged in singing, dance, and crafts. She speaks several languages, has an almost photographic memory of everything she's read, and she speed reads, being able to read an 800-page book in a day. She also has some forms of synaesthesia. She sees the words people speak as colors and used to see objects and colors floating through the air in the dark.

View of Animals and Nature

She loves animals and feels that they deserve respect and compassion, as well as equal rights (which is how she treats her pets). She feels that animals can be as smart (and as dumb) as humans and that they feel emotions just as we humans do. When she looks into an animal's eyes, she can see the animal's soul and purpose, as well as any illnesses in the body. (Because she's a medical intuitive, this ability comes naturally.) She also loves nature, but feels that she doesn't understand it as well as she understands people and animals.

Retention of Innocence and Purity

Carmel is compassionate and sensitive and knows that a part of her is still very innocent. She's taken aback when she encounters people who look for ulterior motives in others. She knows that she says what she means and *vice versa*, but she finds others' motives hard to understand.

She has very few fears and sometimes feels protected. She always used to feel protected and guided, but that has waned for her in the past couple of years due to the brain tumor and resulting health challenges.

She has always tended to observe people and things around her, as opposed to being engaged with them. At the same time, she has always been good at reading people.

Feeling Different from Others

Carmel's experiences of life are very different from those of most other people, as are her philosophies. She feels that her innate spiritual awareness has made her different, as has the way that she challenges other people. She knows that she is responsible for every moment of her life—"every thought, every action. The only person who will punish me, per se, will be me."

On Being Spiritually Aware Since Birth

Carmel feels that being spiritually aware her whole life has been both a blessing and a curse, especially due to the negative reactions she's had from other people. She would not want her children to follow in her footsteps.

Life Purpose

She has always been in touch with her life purpose, which was reinforced during her near-death experience at the age of four, and because of this she works as a medical intuitive. When she's not doing her work as a medical intuitive, she finds herself feeling "lost, empty, and depressed." She also has a book out, *When All Else Fails*.

15

My Story

"When I was born I remember thinking that I didn't want to
be here again. I knew that when I wasn't here I was with the
Divine and I wanted to be back with God. I also knew that
when I wasn't here, and was on higher levels, I had absolute
knowledge and I resented not having absolute knowledge
while here. However, I knew that I had to be here
because there was something I was supposed to do."

I'VE ALWAYS REMEMBERED WHAT I thought when I was born. I never
thought that this was unusual, until perhaps the past ten years or so. I've
come to realize that it's quite unusual and that I'm extremely fortunate. It
has informed and shaped my life in many different ways.

When I was born, I remember thinking, "I don't want to be here
again." I knew that when I wasn't here (on Earth) and was, instead, on
the "other side" I was with God (the Divine, Spirit, etc.). And, quite simply, I preferred to be with God. I also knew that whenever I was here I

couldn't have access to absolute knowledge because that wasn't available to me here, and this also upset me.

Despite these strong feelings and my resistance, I knew that I had to be here because there was something I was supposed to do, which I thought at the time had to do with performing. So I pursued acting and singing for many decades.

My awareness at birth was not the awareness of a baby. It was quite mature and clear—what I term my higher soul awareness.

I had a memory of what it had been like to be with God and I longed to be back there, although my memory is not sharp or clear. I feel that I wasn't allowed to have a more extensive memory because it was already so hard for me to be here. What I could remember was being on a much higher level where there may not have been physical forms and where things are more abstract or composed of primarily perceptible energy. There was warmth and love and comfort and bliss, although these words can't begin to capture the positive feeling of it. It also felt that there were no boundaries and that everything was unified and merged without limits, although we had discrete souls and a point of view. There was pure aware-ness that didn't stem from a body or psyche. Being with the Divine felt like being protected—the ultimate in a positive experience—which was somewhat exhilarating. It was the epitome of being enriched and secure and accepted without conditions, and God was the ultimate awe-inspiring but not fear-inspiring power—and just the ultimate. I had access to every-thing there, including absolute knowledge.

When I read Dr. Eben Alexander's book *Proof of Heaven,* I was struck by his description of being with God because it came the closest to what I remember.

I don't have any specific memory from before I was born, except for being on the other side on higher levels with the Divine. I feel that I didn't spend much time, if at all, in my mother's womb until birth.

Innate Spiritual Awareness

My feeling of a connection to God has been with me throughout my life. It's the one overarching and supreme truth and knowing in my life that has never gone away. I've felt a lifelong yearning to merge back with God, one that is ever present with me, because the separation while being here feels so unpleasant and arid. I know that love and being deeply connected to others in a positive way is the closest we can come to being back with the Divine while we're here. I've been consciously aware that my search for absolute romantic love—a soul partner—has been triggered by my desire to have the next closest thing to being back with God and merging—again, while I'm here.

I've always had a strong spiritual awareness and orientation. I didn't have to learn how to be spiritual. It's always been innate in me.

I've always loved to sleep, because I feel that when I'm sleeping I'm not here. I may have been told before coming to Earth this time that I could always tap back into higher levels while I was sleeping. I'm not consciously aware of all the places I go to while I'm sleeping, but it's the closest I can come to being on the higher levels while I'm here—at least while I'm sleeping. Of course, I'm unable to bring back a conscious memory, but the unconscious visits recharge me. I feel that I'm worked on and soothed while sleeping, probably in the deeper levels of sleep. So sleep for me is a spiritual experience, and it refreshes and recharges me. Dreams have always fascinated me and dream interpretation is one of the areas that I specialize in with my intuitive and spiritual work with clients.

When I was little, my aversion to having to be here and my desire to be back on higher levels led me to frequently look up longingly at the sky at night and hope that a spaceship would come and take me back home.

On Feeling Protected and Guided

I've always felt protected and guided because of my direct connection with God. I've met many people and spoken to so many clients who aren't that fortunate. As a result, they appear to have fears and tend to feel vulnerable more easily than I have. (I would love to devise a way to help others feel that connection to the Divine so that they, too, could feel protected and guided from any fears or anxiety.)

I've never felt a need to know who my guides were because my connection has always been solidly with God, and that is my spiritual source and sustenance, as well as my source of guidance. Instead of specific, lifelong guides, I've felt that some may come in on an as-needed basis. If I had to name a lifelong guide, it would be God.

I don't tend to have many fears, except for an innate fear of drowning or suffocating, which I feel came from another lifetime in which I drowned.

Early Memories

My next memory came when I was sitting in my high chair in the kitchen. I remember watching a roach crawl across the floor. When I shared this memory as an adult, I was told I couldn't possibly remember it.

I remember feeling from early on that I wasn't really living my life, but was, instead, sitting in a room watching it being projected on a screen after having lived it (similar, perhaps, to a post-transition life review). I felt this way for the first few years of my life. This was apparently my way of pretending that I wasn't really here. I seemed to be passing through here as an observer, but not of or in this life (or three-dimensional reality).

I could have stayed in this other-world orientation and denial of this reality for a long time, which represented a source of comfort for me, but emotional pain served to pull me into my human emotions and into my human persona as Diane. I was bullied regularly for years, without respite, from the time I was very little. The pain pulled me into my human persona, and I found myself more "in" my life here on Earth as Diane.

The emotional pain from being relentlessly bullied and not having any recourse to anyone protecting me had lasting effects and conspired to make me quite insecure emotionally. I became a strong people pleaser, very concerned about how others were perceiving me, and it took me many years to heal this old wound to some extent (although never completely) and gain a measure of self-confidence.

Synaesthesia and Unusual Senses

I have a couple of more mundane forms of synaesthesia, a condition in which some senses are merged or connected. I've always associated personalities with some numbers, and I have tended to see calendars in rounded shapes with the months connected to each other in circles. I feel that synaesthesia may be a reminder of being on higher levels where any "senses"—after all, we're not in human bodies there—are merged, rather than separated. I also have somewhat of a photographic memory. I've always found it easy to remember phone numbers after having seen them. I have also had a photographic memory for text. When I was taking tests in school, I frequently had the experience of looking at the page in the textbook (in my mind) and reading off the answer.

Oriented Toward Meaning

Meaning has always been extremely important to me, and I've always looked for the meaning in occurrences—for example, the higher meaning or purpose of events. I have always had a need to understand things and have striven to do so. Things must also add up and make sense to me. I've never been content to look at things on the surface, or by surface appearances, which I find boring and trivial. One elementary school teacher wrote short predictions of what the students in our class would be when they grew up. For many, it was that "Johnny will be a fireman" or that

"Susie will be a nurse." For me, my teacher wrote, "One day Diane will solve the mystery of how the world began."

I was apparently quite different from others, even though I didn't always feel that I was. I was intermittently told by a family member that I had a vivid imagination and was called Sarah Bernhardt. My father had a huge amount of depth, and thus was my ally. He was a visionary with the IQ of a genius, and he was a staunchly independent thinker; I came to realize in my adult years that I likewise am a very independent thinker and can't succumb to or join in with groupthink.

Innate Intuitive Ability

While growing up, I was fascinated by "psychic phenomena" and sensed some sort of connection between spirituality and ESP. I never saw myself as intuitive, though, even though I had some spontaneous intuitive experiences when I was young. I knew at the exact moment that my dog died in junior high, for example, even though I wasn't in the room with her at the time.

I had another spontaneous intuitive experience in high school. While I was playing volleyball in my physical education class, my ring went flying off my hand. The entire class looked for it, holding hands and walking up and down the court—to no avail. The next morning on the way to school I had the sudden sense that I knew where it was. I parked my car in the back, went through the fence to the court, and walked right to it.

It wasn't until after I started working professionally with my intuition in 1992 that I came to realize that I'm highly intuitive. That awareness led me to realize in retrospect that I've always been inner-guided, something I apparently took for granted since it was my norm. I've always been an excellent read of other people and where they're coming from, in addition to being very sensitive to energy. In my work as an integrative intuitive counselor, the first thing I do in an initial session with a new client is to read his or her essence, which I partially feel. In my teens, I discovered that

I could sense if something was wrong with people, because I would get a feeling or sense of "broken energy" coming from them.

Thirst for Metaphysical Information

I had an insatiable thirst for information on metaphysics while growing up. In my early teens, I started chewing on the concept of "successive worlds." In college I discovered a book club (the Universe Book Club) which carried metaphysical books. This enabled me to start feeding my hunger for spiritual information. While an undergraduate, I found myself chewing on other dimensions and wrote a short paper on the topic. While growing up and even into my early adult years, I rarely came into contact with other people who shared those metaphysical interests. So, as a result, I rarely had people with whom to discuss these topics.

Additional Gifts

I was always sensitive and creative, in addition to being blessed with a strong, high intellect. I was placed in advanced classes in junior high and attended a public high school for the academically gifted. Music was always huge for me. When I listen to music, I'm not so much listening *to* it as in it—I'm *in* the music. I started taking private voice lessons around the age of thirteen and have sung for many, many years, in addition to both amateur and professional acting, voice-over work, and teaching both.

Additional Personal Attributes

I have a range of interests and have always loved to learn new things. I've been blessed to have never had any conflict between my logical left brain and my creative and spiritual right brain. If anything, I feel that people who focus on one and repress the other are limiting themselves.

I have never tended to identify with classifications or categories. I've always felt that I was a "child of the Universe," and I haven't felt strongly American or any connection to a particular faith, for example.

Observing vs. Engaging

I've always known that this three-dimensional reality is not the only one, and I've always been a strong observer of others and of what is going on around me. So the thread of not quite being here has continued to a degree throughout my life, creating a distinct dichotomy between my higher soul awareness (the part of me that is the observer and watcher and connected to higher spiritual levels) and the human part of me that has limited awareness and also carries emotional pain and insecurity.

View of Organized Religions

I was brought up Presbyterian (and was a youth group leader), but I've always felt that all religions are essentially talking about the same thing (about a Divine Creator and that this physical world is not the only reality), and I never saw any conflict between my spiritual awareness and knowing and the church I attended with my family.

I stopped attending church in my early twenties because I found myself very turned off by the hypocrisy I saw among many churchgoers, who appeared to attend church because it was the socially prescribed thing to do—espousing beliefs on a Sunday while living their lives far from those principles the rest of the week.

That said, religion has inspired many. Some of the most beautiful works of art, including painting, sculpture, architecture, and glorious music, have been created by and for those in religious institutions. Many of those following organized religions have what I would call a true faith, which is beautiful to witness. True faith, whether that in organized religion or not, is wonderful in its purity, and those with a true and honest faith often have warm, open, innocent hearts and a refreshing humility. The truly faithful can come from all walks of life and religions or beliefs.

As beautiful and refreshing as true faith is, and perhaps because I've always had a direct connection to the Divine, I feel that it's important for people to have and feel that direct connection, rather than going through the intermediary of a minister or priest or any other intermediary. Church dogma, to me, gets in the way of people connecting directly to the Divine, which leads to division and conflict among people from different religions and faiths. At the same time, however, I do acknowledge that it may be difficult for some people to establish that connection to what may feel abstract (a Divine being) and that they may need to go through an intermediary. The ideal, to me, however, is having that direct spiritual connection.

Past-Life Recall

When I was in college, I suddenly realized that I had lived before. On a date I saw the film *Romeo and Juliet,* directed by Zeffirelli. It was a visually beautiful film, and toward the latter part of the film, when Juliet discovers that Romeo is dead and decides to take her own life, she struggles with her death. As I was sitting watching this scene, very much caught up in the film's drama and her on-screen struggle, I suddenly found myself thinking, *You don't need to struggle. You just let go and you just leave without any pain. It's easy.* I caught myself up short and had an aha moment, realizing that I had to have died before to know this.

This to me was odd, because I had known from the time I was born that I didn't want to be here again. Obviously this implied that I had been here before in other lives. My conscious mind, however, was apparently influenced by the culture I grew up in and didn't connect with my deeper awareness, so I either didn't think about reincarnation or perhaps didn't know if I "believed" in it. This was a lesson for me about the difference between what our conscious mind thinks it knows—or believes, perhaps due to cultural or familial influences—and what our unconscious or higher soul awareness knows.

I have had a spontaneous sense of past lives throughout my life. I've always felt that I was a nun or monk in the Middle Ages and a chanteuse in Paris, probably in the life preceding this one. (When I started studying

French in junior high, it was like relearning a language I already knew. Even the idioms made sense to me.) I've also had at least two past-life dreams, one that took place in the Middle Ages and another in a temple in ancient times.

I've also had an undifferentiated past-life memory. I've always remembered going with my mother to visit a friend of hers. We would traverse cobblestone streets to a house that was close to the water, where we would visit a woman whose husband was a sea captain and who would serve us dinner on blue plates (Delft or Spode). I always assumed that this memory came from when I was young in this lifetime. When I was older, however, I asked about this memory, and I was looked at as if I had two heads. There was no such friend. I then realized that this memory had to be a past-life recall.

I couldn't differentiate these memories as being from another lifetime. They didn't feel like "past" lives to me, but rather like memories from my present life, not those from another persona or lifetime.

Once when I was regressed, I went to the lifetime when I was a chanteuse (Brigitte) in Paris. Through her eyes I looked at my present persona, Diane, which was an eye-opener, because as Brigitte I found Diane to be quite boring. Brigitte said, "Oh, she's so boring. She's too serious!" Seeing yourself through the eyes of a different past-life persona can be quite an experience.

Personal Experience of Different Levels

For decades I found myself saying to others, "On one level I feel this; on another level I feel that." This puzzled me, but after working with my intuition and refining my own understanding of the human mind and some spiritual concepts, I came to apprehend what it was stemming from—the conflict between what our human side feels and what our higher soul awareness knows and perceives. Our higher soul awareness is very clear and perceives much more objectively than our human self, without the human stuff that can cloud perception (those wants, fears, beliefs, mindsets, etc.). It can be somewhat of a pure "watcher" and "knower"—as if it were a detached pure awareness not stemming from a human psyche or body—and exists separately from and isn't influenced by the body or this temporal, three-dimensional reality. It's timeless and somewhat pure.

I never realized that it was unusual to be caught between awareness on the human level and another much clearer one on the higher soul awareness level. Yet I know that I've had a wonderful access to my higher soul awareness from the time I was born.

I've always been in awe of "the mind of God," which I feel surpasses what our puny human minds are capable of. It eclipses our human comprehension and is truly awe-inspiring. (From that perspective, I've always tended to smile when I've seen humans—whether in a religious tradition or not—stating what God is and what God does or believes or wants, as if we humans could dictate what God knows.) My experience is that God or Spirit is immense and huge, beyond our human ability to comprehend, but that as humans we want to define and categorize. How can one name and limit the limitless?

The higher soul awareness is hard to describe. It's not connected to my human personality, Diane. It transcends the human personality and awareness and is more of a pure awareness, like an "eye in the sky" that sees clearly and objectively. There is no human background mental chatter that intrudes upon it. At the same time it perceives on a higher spiritual level and is attuned to higher spiritual purpose. It's an awareness that all beings have access to, including (and especially) animals, and I connect with that in the eyes of animals (unless they're in pain or stressed).

Innate Awareness of Interconnection

I've always known that everything and everyone was connected. We may feel separation on this level. Many people get caught up in surface differences, such as gender, race, nationality, religion, etc. However, the feeling of separation is an illusion. We all come from the same place, despite any illusory differences on this three-dimensional level—not just other people, but animals and all of nature. On the higher levels, everything and everyone is connected with no boundaries or lines of demarcation, and Divine energy runs through everything and everyone.

We're all interwoven into a huge tapestry.

I always knew that everything was connected—people to each other, as well as to animals, plants, the planet, the solar system, the cosmos—that all, ultimately, was interconnected and part of the same whole, threads woven into the same tapestry, each color complementing and serving as a counterpart to each other. We are all individual notes sounding in harmony in the musical composition of the universe, the greater oeuvre of which we are not always aware.

Retention of Innocence and Purity

I've always been a people person and I've always been compassionate. I've always felt bad when other people were hurting and have always wanted to help alleviate their pain. I've always gravitated toward those who may be outcasts and who suffer as a result, wanting to help them feel better and feel better about themselves.

I tend to connect with people when meeting them and am drawn to know who someone is on the inside, as I'm not satisfied to know them just on the surface. My innate innocence led me to assume that all people were open, honest, and good people who also sincerely wanted to connect with others. I've had some hard lessons as a result, and I've had to learn discernment. Although I'm a people person, I'm a very independent thinker. I tend to be leery of groups, as I feel that they can become a hotbed for groupthink and group identity.

I have tended to be open and honest in my life. I was criticized as a child for being too open and for "telling my life story" to strangers upon meeting them. I was without guile and expected that everyone else was open and honest and could be trusted. I know that a part of me has always been innocent and pure, and I've always been connected to my higher soul awareness and my life on the other side. One reader, who was like a mentor to me, told me years ago that the deepest part of me was very pure and innocent like a baby's bottom. I am most comfortable with others who are also coming from a pure place, and I'm very uncomfortable with those who are not or who are into guile or deception or negativity.

View of Animals and Nature

I've always loved animals and nature. While growing up, I had stray dogs following me on several occasions. My third grade teacher let one lie on the floor behind my desk one day. I used to tell stories to our two dogs, and I had a pet frog very briefly. Connecting with animals feels like being back on the other side—like strong medicine for me.

I've been fortunate to have had some wonderful dogs, two of whom were advanced spiritually. I definitely feel that animals are ensouled and have individual souls.

I've tended quite naturally to look both people and animals in the eyes as a means of trying to connect with them as deeply as possible on inner levels. I feel that when I look into an animal's eyes, I connect with his or her awareness, which is a pure consciousness and a place and being without a form or classification. I connect with the pure essence and awareness. Animals are more naturally on this wavelength of pure consciousness and pure awareness than humans are.

To me, animals are pure and quite open and generally without guile. On a family trip to Disney World, two of us went to the aquarium, where we stopped to look at the manatees. I looked into the eyes of one and was struck by the depth I saw. My companion said, "They're lugubrious, aren't they?" And I replied, "No, they're ancient." The depth and awareness profoundly moved and affected me, and I've never forgotten the experience.

I know now that I was connecting to the higher soul awareness through that manatee's eyes. I've experienced this with many other animals, as this can be a gateway to the higher soul awareness and non-separation.

Animals are generally underrated. I feel that they are much more aware and intelligent than may be generally acknowledged (and research has been showing this with several species, as well as that some species have an innate sense of justice and self-awareness). Their awareness is to be respected.

I love to be in nature and feel its energy, and I love to garden (in addition to having many houseplants). For me, nature is respite, calm, peace, sustenance, purity, and companionship, as well as a gateway to the 'now' essence of higher levels.

Feeling Different from Others

I don't recall feeling "weird and different" until college and adult years. Being such a people person helped with this, especially throughout my young adult years. (I was quite sheltered while growing up and emerging into the real world was difficult for me.) Fortunately over the years I have found others who share some of my attributes and with whom I can resonate.

I tend to be an introvert, but I also love being around people I resonate with. I always need some alone time, which is when I fill up my inner reservoir and recharge.

Being a keen read of other people, I tend to immediately or fairly quickly sense where others may be coming from and if I can trust or not trust them, although I had to learn to pay attention to this. As a result of being somewhat empathic, I've had to learn how to erect boundaries with others at times, so as not to be drained.

I've always been uncomfortable around people who aren't genuine and who aren't coming from a pure place. I've even felt a fear around people who are powerful but lack compassion and a warm heart. People who are inauthentic, such as snobs or poseurs, are not those I am comfortable being around. Similarly, I am very uncomfortable with dishonesty and game-playing, as well as subterfuge, perhaps because knowing and learning the truth are so important to me, as well as my sensing that such people cannot be trusted. People who put themselves above others, including those with prejudices, or who are self-aggrandizing or lack ethics also make me very uncomfortable.

In contrast, when I encounter people with innate positive energy and warm hearts and who are coming from a pure place, I feel drawn to them and feel as if I can breathe more easily.

I started to feel different from others in grad school, as I understood better and claimed the artist in myself. It wasn't until my late thirties or early forties that I started to meet more people who had similar metaphysical interests. I was in a mastermind group for a couple of years with a spiritual teacher I greatly respected. I remember her telling me over and over again, "You're so clear." I didn't understand the significance of that at the time, although I now realize she was picking up on my being attuned to my higher soul awareness.

As I've delved more and more into my innate spirituality, especially since commencing my intuitive work, I've gradually felt more different from what we term the norm.

Experiential Spiritual Experiences

I tended in my younger years to seek spiritual *information* rather than *experiences*. I had a profound opening experience in grad school that involved hearing a voice in the middle of the night, an out-of-body experience, a subsequent dream with guides in it, and a memory of a prior dream that had presaged these experiences. It wasn't until I started working professionally with my intuition in 1992 that I had more hands-on spiritual experiences and found a context for that experience in grad school, which served to open me in some way to working professionally with my intuition. (I have not consciously had another out-of-body experience since then.)

After grad school, I found myself living in an older house that was haunted. I experienced various phenomena there, including sounds, objects being moved, and orbs.

Since that time, I have had many more experiential experiences with meditation, regression, journeying, etc.

Access to Spiritual Wisdom

My conscious awareness and knowledge about spiritual matters have certainly increased. I've come to know (again) that this is a very creative universe and there usually aren't hard and fast, simplistic rules about how the universe operates. I smile when I hear someone aver or opine about spiritual things always happening in a specific way because I can tell that they have no direct knowledge.

I've been privy to additional spiritual information through my work. For example, I've known that when we transition, or at some point after we transition, we drop the persona of the present lifetime and get into our higher soul awareness. In my intuitive sessions, when I'm asked to look at a client's loved one who had passed on, I always get the person in his or her higher soul awareness, rather than the persona. (It's puzzled me when I've seen mediums who usually tap into the persona of the deceased person, as opposed to the higher soul awareness.) At the same time, I know that all of our personas from different lifetimes and from higher level experiences still exist and that we always have access to them.

I know that we can bilocate quite easily on the other side, while also being able to project ourselves, whether our consciousness or the physical likeness of the body and the persona we had on Earth, to loved ones still here.

I've also known that not only are we all connected, but we live different lifetimes as many different things—both the good and the bad—in order to experience everything, the totality. This means that we are all equal souls and that sometimes we may be a teacher, guide, or higher being and at other times we might have a rather lowly existence, and we live as humans at times and animals at other times when we incarnate on the Earth. This is in addition to having lives in other parts of the universe (e.g., other planets and galaxies) in other forms. In this way, our souls can experience the fullness of a soul in all of its multiple expressions, both positive and negative, higher level and lower level. Because of this, the concept of karma that many people appear to adhere to—as payback for our transgressions from other lifetimes—has always felt foreign to me.

Again, I strongly feel that this is a creative universe. Our human minds may need the comfort of trying to come up with ironclad rules for how the universe operates. However, this to me is folly and illusion, because anything is possible.

Life Purpose

My spiritual awareness and orientation are ever-present in my life, for which I'm grateful. I'm still not sure what my specific assignment here is, but I know that I've been more synced up to my purpose ever since I began my intuitive counseling work.

I frequently find myself entangled in the human part of me, especially when a personal issue or want has been triggered. It's almost like having two different sides to oneself, although going between the two can be quite effortless or seamless at times.

On Being Spiritually Aware Since Birth

Those of us who have been spiritually aware since birth may not be the norm, but there have been wonderful rewards from being this way. The spiritual knowing is extremely important to me and the spiritual insights feed me. Even though at times it can feel like a curse, feeling like a stranger in a strange land, it's been more of a blessing for me, and I cherish my spiritual awareness.

I simply don't know any other way to be.

16

Those with Initial Memories From Ten Months Old

"I was born with awareness and a sense of what I know."

IN THIS CHAPTER, YOU'LL MEET three people whose first memories don't stem back to birth, but are still quite early, stemming from up to ten months old. Their accounts are both informative and instructive.

Diane Wulf's Story

Diane has always been aware, although she doesn't have many specific early memories. She has always distinguished between her "human self" and her "floating self."

Diane's memories tend to be based on texture or feeling. Her first specific memory was at the age of seven or eight months. She remembers sitting in a chair that was low to the ground and a sibling she didn't realize at the time was a sibling being on top of her and trying to hug her, while a bright light kept flashing. She wanted her sibling to get off of her. She remembers her feet being covered, which she didn't like because she liked being bare-foot. She also remembers that the chair itself had a funny feeling to it and that there were beads that you could spin with your fingers. (Years later she found this chair in her parents' basement. It was a bouncy chair with a canvas painted seat.)

Her next specific memory was around the age of ten months. She shared a room that had separate cribs with a sibling of hers. Diane remembers being able to stand at the time but not yet walk. She was uncomfortable, probably from a dirty diaper or diaper rash, and they were there for a long time unattended, with Diane wondering where her mother was. They were jumping up and down in their respective cribs, and their jumping made the cribs move. Diane remembers thinking that if she could get to the door by moving her crib, she could see her mother, and she succeeded in moving her crib closer to the door. She was too small to climb out and she remembers putting her hands in her diaper because her bottom felt uncomfortable and then wiping her hands on the wall. She was slapped for doing that. (A large part of her upbringing was physically and emotionally abusive.)

She also remembers being in a bathtub and not being able to climb out. She had to go to the bathroom and called for her mother, who didn't come. She then saw something floating in the water and she knew she was going to get punished for it. Her mother was angry and slapped her. After the bath, she remembers her mother pulling her hair and hurting her head as she was combing it. She was sitting on the couch afterward crying so hard that it rattled her chest and she had trouble catching her breath.

Feeling Different from Others

Diane always had a sense of right and wrong coupled with common sense. She would think, "There's so much emotion going around. Why, when this is so easily solved?" She always had the sense of not belonging to the family she was in and felt that she had to have been adopted because her mindset and thought processes were so completely different from those in her family. From a young age, she had the sense that where she was wasn't right.

She always felt a huge responsibility and called herself a "watcher," even though she didn't understand why. At the same time she always had a sense of direction, which she now knows was spirit direction.

Her family was very conservative and Catholic, which didn't resonate with her. She was uncomfortable with the box that her family put themselves in and thought, "How can you confine yourself to such a small way of thinking when there's so much more out there?"

She comes from a large family, and because she is so different from them, she was the only one singled out by her parents in an effort to repeatedly try to break her spirit. Her parents called her "corky," although she feels that they meant quirky. She could tell that there was something about her that made her parents uncomfortable, which led Diane to feel that she must have been adopted.

Innate Spiritual Awareness

She had an underlying awareness all along that God was Spirit, and she has always been spiritual. At a young age she felt that she had to dummy down in order to get along and function in society. So she squelched many of her insights and didn't share them with others while reminding herself that she needed to place a higher priority on getting along with others than being able to speak her truth.

At a young age, she felt that it was important for her to be around trees, which she loved and loved to climb. She felt that she needed to get up higher, as high as possible in a tree or on a roof and be able to fly up higher and watch the city from a higher and clearer perspective. She calls this her "floating self," and she knows that she was born with this awareness (the higher soul awareness). Because of the situation with her family, however, she couldn't always be in that awareness.

Diane has always been inner-guided. She knows that she is here on Earth perhaps because of the time period in the world. She knows that she needs to observe and that she will know when the time comes that she needs to step in and say what she needs to say or do what she needs to do and knows that she will be where she needs to be.

Her sense of purpose and being different were also food for thought for her. She felt that she had been placed in her family for some reason. Her parents died very young, and she found herself questioning what their role had been and whether it had been just to give birth to their children. They didn't really parent their children. She finds it odd that she could have the high intelligence and thinking ability that she has, given that her parents weren't very intelligent and weren't thinkers. So she has wondered why she was placed there because she just doesn't feel part of her family.

Additional Gifts

She is very intelligent and clear-sighted, with an apt, questioning, and independent mind, whereas she feels that her parents tended to conform. Her questioning and asking why ("What are you doing this for?") was not welcomed in her family.

Her awareness as a baby and small child was exactly the same as she has now as an adult. She didn't have to develop her clear and mature awareness; instead, she had it from her first memory, and she thinks of it as her sense of "what I know" and "this is my truth."

In addition to being gifted with a good mind, Diane has also always been creative. She's sensitive to energy and can sense things through the energy she picks up on.

Additional Personal Attributes

Truth has always been important to Diane. She frequently found herself thinking, "I don't know how I know, but I know this to be true." When she knows something to be true, she adamantly sticks to it, irrespective of what others may think and whether they like it. She has always had a way of being able to distinguish between truth, which she sees "in its true colors," and what she feels is fake or untrue, which she sees as blurry and with colors that are watered down.

It's rare for her to encounter other people who are similar to her, but when she does she can tell from connecting with that person through the eyes. She then gets this incredible sense of peace that can move her to tears. She can sense something like a glow over their heads and sense a tonality or clarity.

Diane went to Catholic schools, and she remembers being taught about the Garden of Eden in first grade and thinking, "This is not true. How can this be possible?" She felt that it was bigger than how it was told and that it was an unbelievably stupid story. She questioned herself because she was being taught this by authority figures, but kept returning to her sense of knowing about it. She knew that she had to keep her mouth shut because she knew she would be hit. *How can you limit yourself like this?* she found herself thinking.

She's compassionate to a fault and has learned that she has to dial it back, so that helping someone will not be at her own expense.

Diane is also emotionally sensitive. She frequently wears sunglasses and feels that it serves to be somewhat of a protective boundary for her. She knows that a part of her is really innocent and pure, at the same time that her awareness throughout her life has made her quite mature. That clear awareness, however, never prevented from her being whimsical and playful as a child.

Innate Intuitive Ability

Her sense of smell has always guided her because she can tell if a place feels like a good place or a bad one by how it smells. Likewise, her sense of smell will tell her whether a person is to be avoided or not. She has even gotten a headache if she's in the wrong place. For example, if she's been apartment hunting, she will know if a place doesn't smell right to her that it's the wrong place for her to live.

Diane is good at reading other people, but she hasn't met many people she can resonate with because most seem to be on a different path from the one she's on. She feels that most people have the potential to tap into greater things within themselves but don't because they are afraid and tend to wear the false layers created by the influence of their culture instead.

As a watcher, Diane has always been able to cut through and see what's really going on in a situation. She works as a law clerk though she has no legal training, and she knows aspects and details about law but has no idea where she learned them. The legal practice she works in does a lot of court-appointed attorney work and there has been pressure there for her to just be a soulless functionary, which she feels she can't be. She's been able to use her ability to read people and situations in her work to help others.

She can also tell when other people are aware and seem clear by looking at them, as well as sensing their spirit.

On Feeling Protected and Guided

Diane has always felt protected and guided from the time she was a baby, and she hasn't had many fears, although she doesn't always know who protects her. She thinks in terms of the Universe, which to her is all energy, rather than thinking of a supreme being that is a "lord." She feels that we're all part of the energy of the Universe and that everything always happens the way it's supposed to happen and is the way it is meant to be—and that even if we try to exert our will to make something happen, what will happen will be what is supposed to happen.

Observing vs. Engaging

She has always been an observer of people and things around her, feeling somewhat detached. She "watches things being played out" in front of her and knows that she's separate and untouchable. She often felt like Glinda, the Good Witch from *The Wizard of Oz* because she travels around in a bubble and will always be okay.

Despite the fact that Diane is a watcher and has always had her innate sense of knowing, she did go through a period of time, as so many others have, when she wanted to be able to fit in with others and be accepted. She had to work through that and realize that her separateness is fabulous and that she didn't want to be just a follower.

> *And I'm thinking, to these religious sorts, if you were created in God's image, as you say, then that means you carry God around with you. He has given you the responsibility of carrying Him around with you, so that is basically telling you, "Trust your instincts. Trust your spirit. Trust your own truth. God's not going to give you some big neon sign in the sky that's going to give you the answer."*

She knows that she has to trust her own instincts, her spirit, and her own truth. She feels that a lot of people are desperate for some sort of label that will explain what's going on and give them comfort and the answer.

View of Animals and Nature

Diane loves animals and feels that they're truth; they have something unconditional about them. They have no pretense about them and are clear and true, and she doesn't view them as a lesser form of being. She also loves nature and gardening, which she feels is our "touchstone to anything that has to do with the universe."

View of Organized Religions

Diane presently regards religion as a means of trying to control people and finds it "ridiculous" and financially driven. To her, many people may be into religion for the shared spiritual experience, but people could achieve that just as easily by getting together over coffee or in a reading group.

Diane has been very aware of her "spirit self" and has striven to let that guide her in her life, rather than how her body reacts to things. She used to find herself reacting to something from the physical part of herself more frequently, but now she catches herself and reminds herself that "that's stored reaction from somewhere."

Life Purpose

Diane frequently feels, "I can help you. It's just not time." She has thus had an underlying awareness that she would be doing something to help others, and she is just waiting for the time to be right in the world. She's trying to clear the "shackles" from her upbringing that may be in her way or that she needs to take care of before getting on to the other.

She's known that she has things (spiritual responsibilities) to do and feels that that has made her fearless in some way. She feels like she's on a mission, although she doesn't yet know what it is, and she knows that she has been able to stop some negative things from happening.

From the time she was little she's felt like the mother of the world, needing to help and protect others.

She doesn't know what her life purpose is and doesn't know if there is a specific end or destination with regard to doing one specific thing or whether it's just the journey. She often finds herself thinking, "What am I supposed to do?" when she finds herself drawn to situations. She feels that there is a pureness of being that "God loves" when we can be true to it despite the difficult layers that can be built from negative experiences. She also knows that the answers are within us if we can be quiet enough to listen and let the dust from the world settle down. So she's chewed on what her purpose is, although she has questioned whether she's been able to listen well enough to determine what it is or if she's been a little fearful of learning what it is, especially if it's fairly significant.

Kandace's Story

"I felt that there was a realization of peace—that I was actually going to be able to grow up."

Kandace remembers feeling secure and at peace when she was still in her crib with her father rocking her and singing "Teddy Bear's Picnic" to her. Additional memories include lying in her crib and watching her caretakers sneaking into the room on their hands and knees to check on her. She feels that she was less than one and knows that they did that so as not to wake her. She knew they were in the room and she would rise up to look at them. They later told her that whenever they did that she would pop up and look at them directly, as if she knew they were in the room.

When she was about one, Kandace remembers being in her high chair and having a realization of peace that she was actually going to be able to grow up—that she was going to be able to have the time to grow up into an adult (as opposed to dying young). She knew that this was an important feeling and realization for herself, although at the time she didn't know what it stemmed from.

Past-Life Recall

It wasn't until later in her life that Kandace gained some insight into what she had felt when she had that recall. She has had spontaneous flashes of past-life recall in dreams, which typically have been of moments that reveal how she might have passed on or of significant situations that might have traumatized her during other lives. Several years ago she had a dream in which she was a little girl on the outside of a really dark wooden building, in a barracks. She then knew she was standing outside of a concentration camp in Germany. Previous to this dream, she had glimmers of having been in a concentration camp in World War II, but this past-life recall in her dream confirmed it for her and allowed her to make sense of her early feeling of peace with the realization that she would indeed be able to grow up.

In addition to her recall of her life in a concentration camp during World War II, she had flashes of other past lives, including flashes of being outside a medieval castle in England or Great Britain and seeing a gypsy cart, in a chamber in a pyramid in Egypt where she was a priestess, and being a Druid priest or priestess in a sacred grove where Romans were chopping down the central tree.

Innate Spiritual Awareness

Her father was a Baptist minister, so Kandace grew up immersed in a religious tradition. When she was about four, she saw a reflection in a church window of a spiritual being, which was a profound experience for her.

Kandace tended to question everything from a very young age because she wanted to get to the root of things, and she has always been inner-guided. She's always been spiritually aware and has had moments, which have felt profoundly in the moment to her, in which she could separate her spiritual self from the world around her and see the world and trees, for example, as a "very crisp, clear world" that she was in.

She started exploring spiritual topics and information when she was eleven. She read about Edgar Cayce and studied Erich von Däniken, and she also wrote poetry. One poem that she wrote when she was sixteen was about being a star (celestial, not celebrity) and about the universe and our own individual beings as stars and light.

She also had her own spiritual knowings. For example, she knew that God was not the God that was described in the Bible and that there were greater mysteries, and she knew that people had to live more than just one lifetime. She also knew that there was one ultimate truth, although there were many different paths to it. Her concept of God has evolved, and she feels that she has been taught about this as she has gone within and asked questions. She has gradually come to understand the Divine as a Divine Creator with no gender, but one who is full of love.

Feeling Different from Others

She's always felt different from others and odd because she was hyperaware and could perceive thoughts and energy from people. She could sense what others were feeling or what they were giving off energetically. She was thus empathic from a young age. However, at the same time she wasn't sure how to deal with that information because others didn't seem to be picking up on those things and seemed oblivious to it. She felt out of place. She wasn't told that she was weird, but, instead, that she thought too much, and she was ridiculed by her family. Feeling so different and being isolated led her to have chronic illness from the stress.

Innate Intuitive Ability

When she was little, she would see someone standing next to her bed and came to realize that it was a deceased relative. She stopped being afraid after that, even while sensing a presence in other parts of the house. Additional forms of intuitive ability didn't start for her until her teens. She had inner knowings and precognitive experiences, in addition to being able to read others. She recognizes that she's an empath.

Observing vs. Engaging

Kandace frequently feels as if she's observing things around her as an observer, as opposed to being engaged. She's also good at reading other people, being able to quickly sense where people are coming from.

Additional Gifts

She has a rich dream life and experiences various types of dreams. In her dreams, she has experienced the music of the spheres, which was beautiful and had a "piercing" kind of love in it. When that happens, she feels an indescribable ecstasy. Kandace is also naturally creative and has worked professionally in interior design.

View of Animals and Nature

Kandace has always loved animals and started associating them with the spiritual world in the past several years. She's had spiritual encounters with birds, including doves and hawks, and she's learned that some animals are giving her messages at times. She also loves nature and being outside, as well as being near water and the ocean. She feels a connection with the elementals and has compassion for them.

Additional Personal Attributes

In addition to being an empath, Kandace is sensitive and compassionate almost to a fault. She's also aware that a part of her is innocent and pure.

On Feeling Protected and Guided

She has been working on feeling protected and has been gradually gaining "a peace without understanding." At the same time, she's definitely felt guided in her life, especially since her teens, and she knows that she has a very strong guardian angel who works with her while she's traveling. She's been in four or five especially "hairy" situations in which it was a miracle that she emerged okay.

View of Organized Religions

Even though Kandace was brought up Baptist, she was also exposed to some metaphysical material from a family member who was interested in Edgar Cayce and other spiritual material. Because of this she feels that she had the best of both worlds to support her search for her own truth.

At the present time I regard religion as misinformation… I think that some religions encourage avoidance of personal responsibility

... I see it as there are some innocent people that are kind of trapped in that dogma and are afraid to question because of the ridiculous Heaven/Hell concept that was set up ...: I think that it's just very limiting for people.

Personal Experience of Different Levels

Kandace has experienced conflict between her higher soul awareness and her human one, especially because her human emotions are so strong. She has been working on strengthening her spirit awareness.

On Being Spiritually Aware Since Birth

She feels that being spiritually aware her whole life is both a blessing and a curse. When she gets into those moments when "profound truth is saturating," when she's truly in touch with her higher self, it feels amazing. She feels it's also a curse when she "knows more than other people do and they don't listen." It's difficult for her when she gets warning signs and knows when somebody is lying to her or deceiving her, because she feels very frustrated.

Kandace feels that her spiritual awareness has definitely made her different from others and she's felt isolated and lonely at times because she's found it hard to convey how she sees the world to those who are caught up primarily in their daily life routines. She's found that associating with those on a more mundane level has been draining for her, especially because she's empathic.

Life Purpose

She has always felt that there was a purpose to her being here and that she came here to get back to what her core reality was. She felt from a young age that she had a specific thing to do and specific things to find out.

Kandace has been quite attuned to her life purpose. At present, she feels that it's to grow the Divine spark within herself and work toward illumination, while also coming back into her own power, which she lost in several other lifetimes. She's also working on recognizing and developing her psychic and healing gifts without being afraid; in other words, on reclaiming her natural abilities and utilizing them without a fear of retribution or persecution. She's been aware of this from a very early age and views it as her soul's project.

Alan's Story

"I have this … this memory of coming through the birth canal and being suffocated and squeezed and feeling this pressure on my head and being afraid that I would be, you know, injured for life."

Just as you've seen with others' accounts thus far, Alan also has early memories. His first memory stems back to his birth, and he has several additional early memories that show an awareness separate from his human personality—with one difference, which I'll share later on. Alan's birth was difficult because

I was … kind of turned around and I was too big.

This necessitated the doctor using high forceps to grab him and pull him out of the birth canal. During his delivery he felt that he was being suffocated and squeezed. Note that his feeling that he might be injured for life as a result of the forceps requires a cause-and-effect type of thinking that one would typically think a baby would lack.

Alan's next memory stems from the age of four to six months. He remembers being in his crib in a dark room feeling very, very uncomfortable, needing to have his diaper changed, and crying for his mother to come and change him. He remembers crying and screaming for about an hour while hearing his parents arguing. His mother wanted to go change him and his father wouldn't let her.

And finally after screaming for about an hour, my mom came in and changed me.

This was unfortunately not an isolated incident. It happened more than once, and he identified his feelings during these incidents as being those of frustration and anger, as well as feeling abandoned.

Alan's next memory is later on, although still under the age of one.

I remember being left alone for long, long periods of time.

He was lying in his playpen and he remembers looking at the toy mobile suspended above him.

I could reach up and play with that. I was so ... bored and lonely. And I remember thinking to myself that it was like being in a prison. I remember thinking, "Is this kind of what life is like?"

When he was between ages seven and eight, he was drawn to attend a Greek Orthodox church regularly. His parents did not attend church, but Alan knew the landlord's daughter, who was Greek Orthodox. Despite this acquaintance, Alan feels that it did not influence or color his desire to attend the church. Instead, he was just drawn to the church. On Sunday mornings he would get up, put on a white shirt and tie, and walk down to the Greek Orthodox church by himself. Inside the church, he would light a candle. In addition to being drawn to the church, he liked the incense, stained glass, and candles.

Feeling Different from Others

Alan always felt different from others. He's always felt that he landed on the wrong planet and was always a lone wolf.

And I wanted in the worst way—to belong ... I didn't necessarily live in the same reality that everybody else did.

In addition, he was always a romantic and a dreamer. He loved to read and always had his face in a book. He loved romantic fiction about the "knights of yore."

Innate Intuitive Ability

Alan has a natural intuition. He gets hits about people and situations and often finds that intuitive information comes to him when he's in the flow, for example being able to find hard-to-find parking places. He said that a mental voice sometimes leads him to things.

Additional Gifts

In addition to having a strong intellect, his natural gifts, he feels, lie in the areas of writing and intuition. He developed an interest in writing as a young adult. Alan also feels that he's an observer, "watching instead of participating." He feels very "simpatico" with animals and shared that animals like him, and he loves nature as well.

View of Organized Religions

While he's spiritual and considers himself to be a Christian, Alan says that he's not into religions.

> *My feeling is that religion is someone else's interpretation of spirituality—or spirituality by somebody else's rules. I think that that's manipulative.*

Later Spiritual Awareness

All of the above would appear to be natural hallmarks of being spiritual and spiritually aware. Quite obviously, Alan shares the lifelong self-awareness that the people in the previous accounts have—an awareness from infancy that is quite clear, mature, and transcends the physical human age. One major difference, however, is that Alan feels that he was not spiritually aware when he was born or as a baby. His spiritual awakening did not occur until much later in his life, between the ages of forty-three and forty-five.

His spiritual awakening was gradual, triggered by starting to do yoga and dance. He then started to do inner work through attending the Hoffman Institute, working with a neuro-linguistics programming (NLP) practitioner, and attending some of Sonia Choquette's workshops.

After his spiritual awakening began, he started doing some automatic writing. Interestingly, he wrote a poem within the past ten years in which he described remembering being told something before being born that he wasn't supposed to remember. [This, of course, evokes the spiritual directives we receive before incarnating.]

One possible reason for Alan having the at-birth and early life memories that he has without the concomitant spiritual awareness is that his early life was full of neglect and some abuse, in addition to the traumatic nature of his birth with the pain of the forceps. (He later turned to alcohol and became an alcoholic, although he eventually quit drinking through AA meetings.) I feel that the pain of the forceps may have overridden his innate spiritual awareness or the early abuse and neglect he suffered may have helped to mask his spiritual awareness, as pain will often crowd out our higher soul awareness.

Present Spiritual Awareness

Alan is quite spiritually aware and spiritually oriented at present. He wants to teach and help others live fuller and healthier lives. So his spiritual potential, which I feel lay dormant in him, has now been realized. And yet, how interesting that he had these very aware and very adult awarenesses and realizations when he wasn't consciously spiritually aware!

Part 3

Lessons from the Born Aware Phenomenon and Accessing Our Awareness

17

Initial Lessons— Attributes and Differences of Those Born Aware

You've now read accounts of people who have been spiritually aware since birth, perhaps having made note of the salient points from each person's account. If so, you will have noticed some attributes that many of us who were born aware have in common.

In this chapter, we'll begin to look more closely at some of the characteristics of the born aware phenomenon, and we'll start with the significant attributes that those who have been spiritually aware since birth tend to share.

Please note that many people have some of these attributes. They're neither special to having been born aware nor solely in the purview of us. Those spiritually aware since birth, however, tend to share most, if not all, of these attributes.

Innate Spiritual Awareness

First and foremost, of course, would be the attribute of being spiritually aware at birth. This means that those of us with this awareness didn't have to learn how to be spiritually aware or go through a spiritual awakening. We were born knowing that this physical reality on Earth was not the only reality, that it pales in comparison with higher spiritual levels. This is because we tend to remember—with varying degrees of clarity—those higher spiritual levels (i.e., the other side) and having been there before we came here. We don't come from here, but from a spiritual realm in a non-corporeal existence instead.

We have always been acutely aware of and attuned to those higher spiritual levels. This has always been uppermost in our minds without the memory or awareness fading. Indeed, our true orientation is to higher spiritual levels and it may have been difficult to be anchored solely in our human persona here (or live here at all, no matter how temporarily).

We're living in a time when increasing numbers of people are having spiritual awakenings and developing their spiritual leanings. For some, this is a natural process that proceeds from a spiritual interest or curiosity and from being exposed to spiritual material, whether books, films, friends with spiritual interests, or discussion groups, etc. In these instances, the spiritual material may fall on fertile ground that was already receptive. There are many people who are spiritually oriented, including those from a young age—the Innately Spiritually Oriented I mentioned in chapter 1.

In my private work with clients, I have intermittently read for people with whom I have sensed a deep connection with the Divine, which has been so beautiful at times that it has moved me to tears. A strong spiritual orientation can exist in people from a young age, irrespective of whether they've been spiritually aware since birth or not. This strong spiritual orientation may then be furthered by exposure to spiritual material, thereby increasing their knowledge and awareness.

Others may undergo abnormal experiences that awaken them, such as a near-death experience or spiritual or other extraordinary consciousness practices, such as meditation. Spiritual awakening, whether stemming from a curiosity or from a sudden triggering experience, can be powerful and life-changing and will usually have lasting effects.

For those of us who were born aware, however, spiritual awareness has always been with us and is ingrained in us. We didn't have to discover it or have it triggered, as we were born with it innate in us. We can't unlearn it or forget it. It is often the deepest truth we have and it colors everything in our lives because it is the overarching, transcendent truth of our lives—one that has been with us since birth and beforehand. We *know* innately that we're here just temporarily and that we have always answered to a higher power, no matter what terminology we use to refer to it. We *know* that our soul is our true identity and that our true home is on higher spiritual levels and that we're just passing through here—and our true allegiance is to those higher spiritual levels.

I must add that this spiritual awareness is neither the awareness of a baby nor that of an immature mind or consciousness. It is as adult and clear and mature as our adult consciousness and, in some ways, even more so. Various people who were interviewed for this book commented on this. Thus, it's obviously not an awareness that is a product of the chronological age or stage of brain development or accretion of experience. It's an innate clear (and spiritual) awareness.

It is also a spiritual awareness that is not the same as remembering past lives, being innately intuitive or psychic, or seeing or communicating with ghosts or other presences. I mentioned this earlier, but it bears repeating. One can remember past lives as a child or be psychic without having the innate spiritual awareness or an orientation to higher spiritual levels that those of us born aware have at birth.

Split Awareness

Our lifelong spiritual awareness has created another profound effect that never leaves us. We have an inherent split awareness while we're here as humans. This means that our awareness is split between the human part of us and our higher soul awareness. This leads us to have a foot in both worlds throughout our lives in terms of our awareness, consciousness, and orientation. In effect, we're hybrids. We will often shift back and forth between these two types of awareness: that which stems from our human side and psyche (including our emotions) and that which is our true soul orientation, our higher soul awareness.

Once again, those who were not born aware and yet have a spiritual awakening will often find it easier to tap into their higher soul awareness and may then find their human side much less confining or obscuring. The extent to which this may override their human side will vary from one person to another, as will the percentage of time spent in each mode. It also varies based upon whether having access to their higher soul awareness becomes their true orientation as opposed to a level they can access just from time to time. Tom Sawyer was a near-death experiencer whom I heard speak three times, and I could tell that his natural "home" had become his higher soul awareness as a result of his near-death experiences. Some who undergo spiritual awakenings will find themselves learning about some spiritual truths that those of us who were born aware have always naturally known. For some, this may be a cognitive awareness, whereas for others, it will be a true inner knowing or even an experiential one. I have personally been very encouraged by learning about the numbers of people having spiritual awakenings.

Because those of us who were born aware have this built-in spirit awareness, we find that we're not immune to the human experience, and we'll have a lot of the spectrum of traits and symptoms of the human experience—e.g., common needs, wants, desires, old tapes, personal issues, and fears. Indeed, while we're here in a body, we are not immune from having to focus on physical survival, and this can significantly trigger the human side of us. We may even resent or not heed the need for income and the need to garnish it because it feels that it mires us too much and detracts from our natural orientation toward higher spiritual levels.

We also have other human needs to attend to, including our relationships with other people. Survival and social needs, especially romantic relationships, as well as any attendant negative emotions, can pull us into our human side. As a result, our split awareness leads us to shift back and forth between these two modes and orientations, our higher soul awareness and our human side. We'll cover the mechanism for some of the experiences of this phenomenon later on.

We explored what the higher soul awareness is in chapter 2. I'd like to share how I came to learn that this type of awareness is both significant and a common trait of the Born Awares.

More on the Higher Soul Awareness

As I shared before, I observed over the years that on one level I felt or thought a certain way about something in the world and yet on another level I felt something different. It took me many years to determine that what I was experiencing was my split awareness. Often these perceptions, stemming from two different sources, would differ from each other or even conflict with each other.

You'll recall that I asked some of the Born Awares in this book to describe what their higher soul awareness was like. Below are the significant attributes that they shared from their own experiences:

- A lack of finiteness and boundaries

- Our true self

- The spiritual pure self that's intact

- Peaceful and centered

- Wise

- Accepting

- A place of Divine acceptance, surrender, peace, love, and knowing that everything is okay

- Angelic

- One with all that is

- One with everyone and everything else

- Encompasses everything—mind, body, spirit, emotions (but without human "stuff")

- Extremely clear

- An observer and watcher

- Objective

- Access to higher spiritual levels

- Timeless and pure

- Anchored in the present in a timeless fashion

- Vantage point devoid of self-interest or fears

- Awareness that everything we experience is just temporary

- Awareness that everything is happening according to plan

- Awareness that we each sign on for what is planned for our lives very consciously

- A replenishment of energies

- Your soul being cleared by that connection and reestablishing your priorities

Our higher soul awareness allows us to see and perceive from a higher perspective. It's one salient characteristic that we Born Awares brought in from the other side; it's an intrinsic part of us.

Those of us who have been spiritually aware since birth tend to go back and forth between our human personality and our higher soul awareness. We flit back and forth frequently and quite easily and effortlessly. However, our higher soul awareness is our natural "home," which gives us spiritual insight and clarity. It is our natural and innate orientation, and we are quite aware that the human experience and perspective is very limited and temporary. As much as we would like to stay in our higher soul awareness, we can't while we're here, as we find ourselves pulled back into our human side. That said, being able to be in our higher soul awareness as much as happens naturally for us can be very comforting—a beautiful reminder of those higher levels.

In chapter 19 I'll share some ways to groom being in the higher soul awareness.

Our Human Side

One thread that I saw running through the accounts in this book had to do with when and how we got into our human side. We were born anchored in our higher soul awareness in a clear and unwavering manner, to the extent that some of us resisted getting into our human side. How and when did the human side emerge?

In various accounts, it turned out that it was when we first encountered some form of human pain, whether that was emotional or physical. For Rosalie, it was the abuse that started when she was not quite four months old. You'll recall that I managed to stay in my higher soul awareness for a few years through feeling that I wasn't living my life here, but had already lived it and was sitting in a room watching it being projected onto a screen. It was when the bullying started that I plummeted into my human side due to the emotional pain I was feeling.

If human pain is experienced early enough, it may override the spiritual awareness. Alan remembers his birth quite clearly (and the pain of the forceps), but he feels that he wasn't spiritually aware until he had a spiritual awakening in later life. I would wonder if the pain he underwent during the birth process pulled him into the human experience and crowded out his spiritual awareness at the time of his birth. He also underwent neglect before the age of one, which may have exacerbated this.

So it would appear that it's the pain or negative emotions we experience that first plummets us into our human side. We develop the psyche and persona of a human with our human "stuff," which gets triggered and which accrues through our early and ongoing human experiences and interactions with others. At the same time we flit back and forth between our higher soul awareness and our human side. Hence, we develop our split awareness. We live our lives on two parallel—and quite contrasting—tracks.

Some people may expect that those of us who were born aware would maintain our higher soul awareness most of the time and may consequently have high expectations of us. They may be disappointed that we still have our human sides. And we certainly know firsthand that we're weighed down by that human side. Because of our human psyche and persona, we experience frustration, anger, disappointment, emotional pain, and other unpleasant feelings. Many of us strive to heal and clear our personal stuff so we can be less weighed down by it and spend more time in our higher soul awareness. Please note, however, that this is not the same as utilizing the higher soul awareness as an escape mechanism (denial) from the difficulties of our human side. It's our true orientation and home.

The truth is that when we incarnate—into *any* form (human or otherwise)—we take on the anatomy, brains, minds, etc. of the species, whereas the soul doesn't do this—it isn't pulled into the physical form—it transcends. The result is a dichotomy.

As difficult as our human side may be at times, we can't completely decry it. It exists for a reason and serves a purpose. Aside from the fact that we need it in order to navigate through our lives here, it's a mechanism for our growth and unfolding. Without the human side, we might not be able to accomplish the soul growth that we need to gain while we're here, much less play the roles that we are to play while we're here.

That said, however, Born Awares can still not completely join with the human experience. We usually can't participate in group thinking, mass phenomena and trends, blanket cultural or religious finger-pointing, or demonizing, etc. Our allegiance always tends to be to higher levels first and the spiritual truths we are aware of, and it feels too difficult and impossible to betray those spiritual truths by participating in groupthink phenomena or superficial orientations.

Additional Traits in Common

There are several additional traits that those of us who have been spiritually aware since birth tend to share, although there can always be exceptions.

Awareness of Spiritual Agency and Protection

Many of those of us who have been spiritually aware since birth also have an innate sense of being spiritually guided and protected, as well as a knowing that we have access to higher spiritual beings. For me, this stems from my direct connection to the Divine. Some may use different terms to refer to the spiritual beings "on call," guiding and protecting us, whether it's God, Spirit, the universe, guides, angels, etc.

Some of us are aware of being guided throughout our lives. Matthew was aware when he was born of the spiritual beings, the "team," responsible for the planning of his arrival here on Earth. Several people have shared in their accounts that they have been aware of spiritual beings and guides around them throughout their lives.

Unseen, invisible spiritual beings are always with us, although our attention may not always be on them. We tend to know that they're there and that we can call upon them whenever the need arises. Their presence is always sensed and in a way they are both a reminder of and a connection for us to our true home. We may even have experiences with them intervening to protect us at times. Rosalie felt this when she had her car accident, and Jemila experienced this when she was accosted at night by someone she later realized was a protective spiritual being.

As a result of our awareness of higher spiritual and protective beings, many of us have also felt protected in our lives. I have always felt protected and guided, and the feeling has never left me. As a result, those born aware tend not to have all the fears that people who don't have these memories may have. Rosalie and I have both experienced the same thing when taking airplane flights, when we have observed people on planes who may be fearful and have found ourselves wanting to reassure them that they would be okay because we were on the same flight and would be protected because we hadn't yet done what we came into this lifetime to do. Experiences of abuse may instill some fears in us, but at the same time we're able to remember our spiritual source and know that we are ultimately protected and will be fine. We may feel fear in a transient manner but then return to our natural inner set point. As a result, we aren't permanently mired in fears.

Being aware of protective, loving, and guiding spiritual beings has tended to be a blessing for us in our lives.

Awareness that We Came in to Accomplish Something

Most Born Awares have an innate awareness that we came in with a purpose or assignment. This was part of what I thought when I was born—that I didn't want to be here again, but that I knew I had to be because there was something I was supposed to do. Matthew knew when he was born that there was a template for his life because he came in to do something.

Theresa knew that she was coming in to accomplish something and that it had to do with the health of the Earth. She knew that she would be bringing people together in a way that would benefit the Earth.

Some of us are also aware that we're guided and shepherded through-out our lives so we may stay on track and accomplish our missions, as well as to go through the experiences we need to have for our soul's growth and unfolding. Jemila shared that she has always felt that she is "lovingly su-pervised" by spiritual beings, which beautifully captures this phenomenon and the feeling we have as a result.

Because we came in for specific purposes, some of us also have the sense that there's a plan for our lives (the "template for his life" that Mat-thew mentioned). We tend to sense that there's a plan for what we need to go through that will lead us to accomplish what we came in to do. Some of us remember planning our lives with spiritual beings or have the sense that this occurred even if we don't directly remember doing it, and we desire to stay on track, even while going through challenges. Others may feel, as I do, that our lives were planned for us, in accor-dance with what we were to do.

This feeling of purpose is so strong in some of us that we may feel that we're here "on assignment." I have felt this, and others have expressed it as well. This gives us not just a sense of purpose, but also a detachment from this plane (which compounds our innate detachment due to our aware-ness that this is not our true home and that we're here just temporarily). However, paradoxically, we also sometimes chafe under the responsibility and wish the human side of us could enjoy ourselves more or have more earthly pleasures more of the time. The truth is that the universe can be strict with us, and we may be held to a higher or more stringent standard.

Some of us know what our purpose is, while others are still in the process of determining what it is. We do know, however, that we will be led to it through an inevitability, and it's vitally important that we fulfill it because it's our spiritual duty—a duty we embrace, rather than rebelling against, because it stems from a higher power to which we're consciously connected. It's our sacred duty.

Innate Knowing That Everything and Everyone Is Connected

We tend to have an innate knowing that everyone and everything is connected, no matter how separate things or people may appear on this three-dimensional level. Some refer to this as oneness. This is not a mental concept for those of us who were born aware. Nor is it something we had to learn or read about. Instead, it's an inherent awareness that we have had since birth and cannot separate ourselves from.

I shared how I described this sense of connectedness. Rozlyn has always been consciously aware of the interconnectedness of everything and everyone, which she has seen as the web of connectedness, and she has been keenly aware of how anything that anyone does affects others and the whole web.

Because of this innate awareness, we tend to see ourselves as connected to others and thus tend not to see strangers. Many of us don't identify ourselves rigidly as American or any other nationality, female or male, young or old, because we tend to see ourselves as "children of the universe." We also have a tendency to want to connect with others on a pure and close level. For some of us, this is through looking into others' eyes and attempting to connect and unite that way, which is how I have always tried to connect with others and how Cynthia has. For others, it may be through feeling the heart energy of others and connecting with it, as Cheryl did when she was a baby, looking to connect with the "sparklies" coming from others' hearts.

I have always expected, as a result of knowing that we're all connected, that everything and other people would be animated with love from God, and many of us have felt this way. We may have encountered disappointment when we discovered that the innate love for others was suppressed or denied—when some people did not always act from a pureness or good intent.

Because of this awareness, connecting with others via love, positive feelings, and good will is so positive that it's an almost intoxicating feeling and one that can lead us to merge and go to higher levels (which was what we knew before coming in). As I shared, I have always felt that a romantic relationship that was pure and deep was the closest I could come—while being here—to being back with the Divine.

Some of us may even chafe against being defined as someone who is just a female or male or American or British, for example. Many of us know from our recall of other lives that we've lived as many different genders, races, nationalities, etc. We know that we're those children of the universe and being put into a category not only limits us (while we know that we're truly unlimited), but also separates us from others.

Basically, we see unity and connection and oneness, rather than separation.

Sensitivity and Compassion Coupled with a Need to Learn Boundaries

Those who were born aware also tend to be sensitive and compassionate, sometimes to the extent that we can be drained by others. This may be due to the fact that we have always known that everything and everyone is connected and we have an innate love and warmth of heart. We are naturally sympathetic and our hearts often cannot help but go out to those who are suffering or in need, whether human or animal.

We also tend to be naturally empathetic, which means that we will frequently pick up on and feel others' energy unconsciously and without intending to. We may be so sympathetic at times that we find it hard to tune out others' pain—and, indeed, we can also find ourselves attracting people with difficult issues and pain who are drawn to us and our energy. (Some people refer to the latter as "energy vampires," who latch on and drain, although I sense this is not done deliberately or consciously.) As a result, we will often find ourselves drained.

We customarily have to learn about boundaries and how to erect them so we can protect ourselves and not be drained on a regular basis. Whereas we may naturally feel that we need to help others, it can be a revelation that we need to either cut back on doing that or find a way to protect our own energy. Once we learn how to erect boundaries, we usually feel less drained. That said, we often have to tap into our own inner reservoirs through alone time or meditation in order to fill them up.

We don't tend to lose our compassion and sensitivity. It's always there. We simply find a way to manage it by utilizing boundaries. We can't be good for others if we're drained and exhausted ourselves.

Need for Alone Time

As just mentioned, those of us who have been spiritually aware since birth frequently need to spend regular time alone. This is when and how we fill up our inner reservoirs and recharge.

Our need for time alone derives not just from being drained at times and needing to recharge our batteries. It also allows us to withdraw from the physical plane and human side of our being so that our attention may more easily and without distraction go to our higher soul awareness and be in closer touch with higher spiritual levels. Being there helps to offset some of the difficulty from being on this physical level, which allows us to recharge our spiritual batteries.

Retention of Purity and Innocence

One interesting—and perhaps unexpected—attribute among those of us who have been spiritually aware since birth is the quality of still having a part of our beings that is innocent and pure. Life on this three-dimensional level can be hard and challenging at times, especially with all the pain and deprivation in the world. This is true for everyone, of course, and not just for those spiritually aware since birth. Because Born Awares have a human side and psyche, we are definitely not immune to painful experiences, disappointments, frustrations, and even cruelty and abuse.

For so many people, growing up and getting older with ongoing exposure to this world and its discordant problems (and lack of innocence) usually brings with it a concomitant loss of innocence and purity. No one tries to lose their innocence. It just seems to be hard to hold onto after we've gone through numerous painful experiences and hurts and have heard of many difficult events.

So how is it that so many of us who were born aware can still have a part of ourselves that's innocent and pure and still so alive in us?

It feels to me that it's because of our split awareness and natural access to our higher soul awareness. On higher spiritual and non-corporeal levels, we have a natural innocence and purity. That's part and parcel of our souls and on the soul level it's not lost. So the gift we Born Awares have of being in our higher soul awareness so much and remembering those other levels would appear to give us the added benefit of retaining our innocence and purity, even though we may feel down or in despair at times in our human persona. Our higher soul awareness may inoculate us somehow so that we don't completely lose our innate innocence and purity.

Indeed, the further we get from our innate innocence, compassion, and connection to others, the farther we get from God, or Spirit, and our spiritual selves. This may serve as a check at times, keeping us from straying from those qualities. Distance from God and our spiritual selves would be soul-killing for us.

I personally feel that we are fortunate to have retained our inherent innocence and purity. This is hugely beneficial and can even feel like a saving grace.

A Love of Animals

You'll recall that most of those who were born aware have a strong love of animals. Born Awares are naturally drawn to animals, not just because we implicitly know that everyone and everything is connected or because of our innate sensitivity and compassion, but also because we love the purity of animals.

In our accounts we all shared our perspectives on our love of animals and what it is about animals that we love. The factors that make us love animals include the following:

- Animals are closer to Spirit

- Animal awareness is purer than that of humans

- Animals are pure and live "as God created them to be"

- Animals tend to be pure and innocent

- Animals naturally have unconditional love

- Animals are light itself

- Animals can be wonderful teachers

- Animals are truth and have no pretense

- Animals give you a different sense of energy

- Animals can reflect back to humans what their energy is and where they are in their lives and personal growth

- Animal awareness reminds us of higher levels

- Animals have emotions and social structures

- Animals experience things similar to what we experience

- Animals have a huge capacity to connect

- Animals function on an intuitive level

- Animals are associated with the spiritual world

- One can feel a bond with animals when one touches them or looks into their eyes

- We can feel a merging energy when we connect with animals

- Animals can be a great source of comfort and companionship

- Animals can usually understand things that humans don't

- Animals are more open and less judgmental than humans

- Animals are very wise

- Animals have the same levels of depth that humans do

- Animals will often cooperate with humans

- Animals communicate with us

- Different species of animals do various, different things with regard to their energy fields and electric/electromagnetic frequencies

- Animals live in a world that is very simple and noncomplex

- Animals can be as smart (and as dumb) as humans

Many of us sense a pureness and innocence that animals naturally have. We may all feel something special when we look into an animal's eyes, especially when the animal is calm and not stressed. Doing this connects us with the energy and awareness that is implicit in everything and everyone—and, thus, as a result, helps us connect to our higher soul awareness. And this, I feel, is hugely important.

I asked some of the Born Awares what they experienced when they looked into an animal's eyes, and they shared the following:

- Animal awareness reminds us of higher levels

- Looking into an animal's eyes allows us to experience a conscious presence

- Looking into an animal's eyes establishes a bond

- Looking into an animal's eyes allows us to connect with their spirit, soul, and heart

- There's an awareness in an animal's eyes that is timeless and present (note that these are attributes of the higher soul awareness)

- When we look into an animal's eyes, we can feel love, sensitivity, and compassion, along with a sense of merging and boundarylessness (the latter being a reminder of the higher soul awareness and higher levels)

- Looking into an animal's eyes can remind us of who we really are—our soul identity

- We can see an animal's soul and purpose when we look into their eyes

- Animals can give us messages at times

Many Born Awares are able to communicate with animals in a telepathic manner, which reminds us of how we communicate when we're on spiritual, non-corporeal levels (via telepathy). Several of us have had animals (companion animals) with whom we have a strong soul connection and may have known in other lifetimes, and several of us have had animals who were more advanced spiritually. Many of us accord animals equality and don't see them as a lesser form of being.

Most of us feel that animals have individual souls, not a group soul. (The concept of animals having only a group soul has been one held by many in spiritual circles over the years.) Many people tend to feel that animals are not ensouled, but we Born Awares tend to disagree with this idea. Several of us also feel that we live different lifetimes as many different forms of beings, including being both human and animal (as well as other life forms, such as some on other planets or in other galaxies, which some Born Awares remember).

Some of us are aware that specific animals are brought into our lives for a reason, and some of us trust that the right animals (i.e., right for us at the time) will be brought to us, as they can be part of our paths and what we are to do—and *vice versa*. We may have felt soul connections with some animals and that some animals are more spiritually advanced than others, just as some humans may be "older" souls or "newer" ones.

In addition to their love of animals, several Born Awares shared some of their own experiences with them. These experiences include not just communicating with them, but also picking up on any past trauma or illness, as well as sensing an animal's soul and purpose in the present lifetime.

The experience of looking into an animal's eyes can be very powerful, and we'll come back to this topic later on.

A Love of Nature

As with animals, those who have been spiritually aware since birth also tend to love nature, feeling a sense of peace and calmness in it. The Born Awares have felt a range of effects from being in nature, including the following:

- The wind can convey a sense of things

- Nature can connect us to ourselves, as well as to higher spiritual levels

- Nature can be very healing

- Nature can trigger a palpable connection to elementals (devas, fairies, etc.)

- Nature and gardening can be a touchstone to the universe

- Nature can make us feel alive and grounded

- Nature is full of life

- Nature can lead us to get in the flow

- Nature can allow us to breathe in the energy of the planet

- There is a perfection in nature

- Nature can allow us to see the interconnectedness of everything and the continuum

- We can merge with nature and feel a part of it, while also feeling that it's a part of us

- We can feel more connected to Source when we're in nature

- Nature can renew and balance us

- Nature can communicate with us

- Nature can allow us to feel the vibration of harmony and unity that we knew on higher spiritual levels

- Earth is a living entity and has its own frequency

- Plants have some kind of energy that may be soul-like

- Earth can provide everything (as long as it's not mismanaged)

Many of us who have been spiritually aware since birth love trees and sense not just a majesty in them, but also an awareness. Some of us can sense their spirit energy and their spiritual quality. I feel that they are like silent sentinels that monitor and feed us (energetically and spiritually), and serve as a grounding point for energy. Recent research, in fact, has shown that trees communicate with each other by means of chemical signals released through their roots. (See Fleming, 2014, and McGowan, 2013.)

Many of us are so fed by nature that we feel out of sorts or drained if we are in an urban area without greenery and trees for a period of time. It's as if unrelenting concrete feels sterile and soulless.

You'll recall that Cheryl not only sees God in nature, but can also perceive the pulsating, breathing energy of nature and its representation of the interconnectedness of everything. Some of us know that the Divine fills the world and its inhabitants and is implicit in animals and nature.

Naturally Intuitive and Inner-Guided Coupled with Healing Energy

As you noticed through reading each person's account, those of us who have been spiritually aware since birth tend to be naturally intuitive and inner-guided. For some of us, our intuition started to manifest itself at a very young age. For others, it may not have become obvious until we were older, although the inner guidance was always there.

Most of us have been inner-guided from birth or shortly thereafter. Our minds have been attuned to inner knowing and guidance, even if we didn't always sense that some of this came from outside of us (from higher spiritual beings, guides, angels, etc.). I feel that this may be true because of our split awareness and inherent access to our higher soul awareness, which naturally gives us a connection to higher levels and spiritual beings.

It's important to note that being intuitive or inner-guided does not necessarily mean that one is spiritually aware, spiritually oriented, or spiritually attuned to higher levels. I have observed over the years that many people do make this assumption. Intuitive ability does not always equate to or correlate with spiritual awareness or orientation or even with ethics.

That said, innate intuitive ability is one attribute that those spiritually aware since birth appear to have in common. Many of us are quite good at reading other people. Our guts will often tell us whom to trust or distrust and whom to steer clear of. Some of the Born Awares will get intuitive information about other people in other forms as well. Some can see the energy field, or aura, of other people, while others may feel or sense what others are like. Some can even sense or see warmth or sparkles around the heart (as Cheryl does).

While the Born Awares appear to be quite naturally intuitive, the forms in which our intuitive information will present itself can vary greatly.

At the same time, those of us who have been spiritually aware since birth also tend to have a natural healing energy. Some of us have elected to use and apply it through energy work, such as Reiki. Others may not overtly use it via energy work, but choose to use it on occasion with loved ones or pets.

It feels to me that this natural healing energy may stem from both our connection to higher spiritual levels and our inherent love of others and "warm hearts." It may be that our connection to those higher spiritual levels plugs us into the healing energy implicit there.

An Inherent Sense of Right and Wrong

As I interviewed the Born Awares in this book, I was struck by another attribute that I saw over and over again: a strong sense of right and wrong and integrity. We do not like to see people treated unfairly and we adhere to honesty and integrity. We also find behavior revealing a need to put oneself ahead to the detriment of others or cheating to be repellent. As a result, we are also naturally egalitarian. We find it extremely difficult to betray our ingrained sense of right and wrong and would rather fail or suffer than commit wrong acts.

I don't know what this inherent sense of right and wrong stems from, other than our spiritual awareness and our knowing that everyone and everything is connected and that on higher levels there is always implicit integrity and fair play. As Swedenborg wrote, "Conscience is God's presence in men." So it may be our inherent spiritual awareness and orientation and/or our inherent connection to higher levels that cause it. Regardless of the cause, this is one trait that those of us born aware share.

A Tendency to Be Observers

Another thread that ran through each account was that of being an observer instead of always feeling engaged with others. This doesn't mean that we never feel engaged with people or situations, because we do at times. We also connect with others and empathize. We fall in love and feel close to people. However, we often find ourselves observing, to the extent that this is a consistent and strong attribute. We don't intend to stand back and observe. Instead, it happens quite naturally and spontaneously.

I hasten to add, however, that this trait is not the same as daydreaming or a disengagement stemming from dissociation or abuse. It's a natural attribute, rather than being a reaction to any trigger, such as abuse (from which dissociation often derives).

I feel that this trait may stem from more than one cause. The first would be our innate spiritual awareness and orientation. We have a foot in both worlds and, as a result, we are not completely here on this plane—at least not all the time. We are also frequently in our higher soul awareness, which gives us a clear vantage point and a perspective which is often that of a larger and observing view. This is our natural mode, reflective of our innate orientation to non-corporal levels.

While observing, we are also taking in information about the world and our surroundings and digesting the information. This, of necessity, requires an observational stance.

In addition, our innate spiritual orientation leads us to not always participate or engage, especially in negativity. We may want to initially get a sense of situations and people, in order to suss them out and discern where they're coming from and the tenor of a situation before participating. Knowing that our natural spiritual awareness makes us different from many others will frequently lead us to tread lightly, again to get a sense of whether the energy is positive or negative before engaging.

Some people may feel that we are detached in the sense of being aloof or unemotional. However, this is far from the truth.

Thus, there may be a multiplicity of factors that leads us to be strong observers.

Independent Thinkers and Introspective

As a rule, those of us who were born aware tend to be very independent thinkers and largely introspective. Our spiritual awareness leads us to observe and think for ourselves. The fact that we're inner-guided compounds this. We're not people to get into groupthink, fads, or trends. We have a need to think for ourselves and arrive at our own conclusions. The need to think and digest alone requires introspection.

Additionally, joining groups with a group persona is foreign to us, as it feels like ceding our independent minds and autonomy. Some of us may go through a phase in our teens of wanting to fit in and be more like other people. However, after a period of time we tend to get back into our independent modes.

Many of us have an innate maturity that prevents us from engaging in immature behavior that requires a lack of thinking or good judgment. We have a need to determine for ourselves whether something feels right before we participate in it. We tend to constantly discern whether something feels right, is okay to engage in, or is to be avoided.

We're also introspective because we can get drained unless we have enough alone time, to pause and reflect, as touched upon earlier. As mentioned, this is how we fill up our inner reservoir and we typically need to do this on a regular basis. If we don't, we tend to feel off-balance and out of sorts. Being in our center feeds us, as does our connection to higher levels—and introspection allows this.

Humility

I was struck while speaking to the people interviewed for this book by how down-to-earth, genuine, authentic, and humble they are. I've known for many years that anyone who is truly spiritually oriented is also humble and, conversely, if anyone claims to be spiritual and lacks humility, that person is usually neither truly spiritual nor spiritually aware.

We've already covered the fact that those of us who have been spiritually aware since birth know that everyone and everything is connected—and we *feel* that connection. This is not solely a cognitive awareness, but a true knowing instead. We know that on higher spiritual levels there is no grandiosity of ego or hierarchy. There may be older or younger souls or souls with varying levels of advancement or experience or growth. However, there is no ego attached to either category. There is true humility and interconnection. The souls are discrete yet connected. This may appear to be a contradiction in terms, but isn't. We are connected by our energy and hearts and consciousness, while also having a point of view which derives from being somewhat discrete (even if our diffuse energy means that there are no palpable borders).

Another aspect of humility that Born Awares tend to share appears to stem from our sensitivity and feeling different from others—namely that we often suffer from a lower self-esteem. Certainly those who were abused or even molested have had to deal with the emotional aftermath, and self-esteem often suffers as a result. We often unconsciously compare ourselves to others who may appear to fit more comfortably into society on this planet. It is true that low self-esteem will sometimes beget a compensatory mechanism of trying to feel better about oneself around others, but this typically either doesn't exist for Born Awares or does not last.

A separating lack of humility is in stark contrast to our compassionate side. The Born Awares largely have a need to connect with others (while also being observers). We seek that beautiful connection we have with other souls on higher levels. We also appear to know implicitly that ego and grandiosity separate (in addition to representing negative and isolating energy), and we tend to have a discomfort bordering on mistrust of spiritual leaders or teachers or other leaders or authority figures who lack humility. We don't consciously decide to be humble. It's just the way we came in and tend to continue to be.

Heightened Awareness and Perception

Another thread that I saw running through my interviews with the Born Awares included in this book is that of a tendency to have a heightened awareness and perception. For some reason we are quite observant, especially when it comes to details. We don't observe and "paint" with a broad stroke; instead, we notice finer details. Jimelle likened it to having a "great big thick magnifying glass that you can see all the little detail with."

At this point, I'm not sure what this attribute stems from. It could be that our easy access to our higher soul awareness and the large percentage of time we spend in it leads us to notice details. This could stem from how clear and objective our perception is when we are in this mode.

Inner Resources and Resilience

Those who have been spiritually aware since birth seem to have strong inner resources and resilience. Even when we go through challenges and difficult experiences in our lives, there's a part of us that knows we'll be okay.

This may come from multiple factors. Certainly our innate spiritual awareness leads us to know that our being here is temporary and that our experiences here, especially the difficult and painful ones, are temporal and transitory. We know on a deep level that any hardships experienced while we're on Earth won't last forever. (This too shall pass.)

Additionally, our awareness of higher spiritual levels and feeling connected to them, as well as to Spirit, God, the Divine, guides, etc., leads us to feel protected and to trust that we will always be okay.

These aspects are hugely beneficial and, I would think, lead to our having strong inner resources and resilience.

A Tendency to Be Whole-Brained and Eclectic

Many people tend to equate spirituality and inner knowing with what we term "right-brain skills." (I use "right-brain" and "left-brain" modes despite the controversy surrounding the existence of hemispheric specialization.) Indeed, many people in spiritual circles may embrace right-brain modes and look at left-brain modes (analysis, deduction, reason, logic, etc.) as being less desirable or to be avoided.

Interestingly, the Born Awares included in this book tend to be whole-brained. As you read in our accounts, we tend to have traditional left-brain intelligence (indeed, some have excelled in academic settings), as well as the right-brain skills of intuition and creativity. Many of us have had pursuits in both arenas: advanced academic degrees along with creative and artistic pursuits.

We also tend to not only have open hearts but also trust what our hearts tell us. Extensive research conducted by the Institute of HeartMath since the early 90s has shown that there is an awareness in the heart. We likewise tend to have eclectic interests over a range of topics and activities.

My sense is that some of us may have unconsciously felt that we need to utilize as much of our potential as possible and balance these seemingly distinct, yet also synergistic, modes, rather than developing and relying on one to the detriment of the others or focusing solely on one activity to the exclusion of others. There's a freedom and joy that can come from using as much of our potential as possible while we're here. This is one way in which we can make the most of our temporary sojourn here on this plane.

A Preference for Meaningful Conversations

For those of us who have been spiritually aware since birth, the most enjoyable conversations and discourse we can have with others are those in which we are discussing meaningful topics and concepts. In fact, there is a general distaste amongst us for conversations that are superficial and trivial. Several have expressed that they would prefer to be alone than have to converse superficially.

This may be due to the fact that our innate spiritual awareness and access to our higher soul awareness, as well as our easier access to spiritual wisdom, leads us to be aware of the import of events and experiences. This would appear to give us a maturity that belies our actual age. We inherently know that everything has meaning and that there is higher purpose to everything. Certainly being aware that we're here on Earth to do specific things (such as fulfill our missions and assignments) can give us substance and meaning. Focusing on trivialities just goes against our grain. We also know that true connection to others feeds us spiritually and banal conversations represent the antithesis of true connection.

Less Prone to Conflict with Others

As a general rule, Born Awares tend to be peaceful and not prone to conflict with others. There may be several factors leading us to be this way.

Certainly our innate awareness and memory of higher spiritual levels is a factor. I feel that we don't find conflict on higher spiritual levels, where there is, instead, an awareness of the interconnectedness of everyone and everything and where love and harmony seem to prevail. We may indeed have an aversion to conflict and are oriented instead toward wanting conflicts to be resolved peacefully with all parties coming to see eye to eye with mutual respect, insofar as possible. Certainly religious divisions and people fighting over religious beliefs is abhorrent to us, especially given the fact that many of us not only feel that everyone and everything is connected, but also that religions that are well-intentioned and positive tend to be delivering the same message—that unity and mutual respect are ultimately more in keeping with spirituality than infighting and divisiveness and conflict are. Our innate sense of what is right and wrong may also contribute to this.

For whatever reasons, we are simply not comfortable with any baser needs for conflict and prefer to be peaceful, and we tend to shy away from those who are prone to conflict and/or violence, as those are abhorrent to us.

Spontaneous Recall of Other Lives

Many of us, as you probably noted in people's accounts, tend to have a spontaneous recall of some of our other lives. Indeed, Cynthia has recall of a future life. Our recall is usually natural and not triggered solely through regression or any other artificial (meaning non-spontaneous) mode. Some of us have innately known some of our past or other lives. We may also have dreams of past lives—and some have had spontaneous flashes of other lives while awake.

In addition to being aware of some of our other lives, some Born Awares have what I would call an undifferentiated awareness of other lives. You'll recall that I shared a memory I always had that I thought was from my present lifetime and didn't realize until I was an adult that it was from another lifetime. This memory was undifferentiated both because I couldn't differentiate it as a past life and also because I felt that my persona was the same in both.

It could be that those of us who have been spiritually aware since birth tend to have a higher spontaneous recall of other lives because we are less anchored in or bound or constricted by the present reality or present persona and, instead, more oriented to higher spiritual levels, where we are in our soul and higher soul awareness and which is where we have access to all the personas from our various lifetimes. This recall of other lives may be strengthened by frequently being in our higher soul awareness and can also serve to keep us from being mired in our present human persona, which may be another reason why we tend to have a universal view, identity, and perspective. So it may both stem from a spiritual cause and also strengthen our spiritual orientation (by decreasing our identity with our present human persona as the only identity we have).

An Appreciation for Having Been Spiritually Aware Since Birth

I asked each person in this book whether having been spiritually aware since birth had been a blessing or a curse in their lives. Everyone stated that it had been a blessing, although some felt, not surprisingly, that it had a downside.

To have the spiritual awareness that we have, along with our memories and easy access to our higher soul awareness (which is our natural state) is a wonderful thing. It leads us to feel inspired, spiritual, intuitive, and optimistic. It has also given us strong inner resources and resilience, which allow us to weather so many of the difficulties that life presents us. We innately know that we are here only temporarily and that whatever painful experiences we go through or difficulties we face are temporary and fleeting.

Our spiritual awareness and connection also lead us to feel protected and guided and that we'll always be okay. As a result, we tend not to have many of the fears that can run rampant on this level for so many people, although some of us do acknowledge having some fears.

It is difficult to encounter ridicule or social ostracism and feel that we can't always lighten up and enjoy many of life's more physical pleasures as much as we would like to, but the positive aspects and benefits of our "condition" far outweigh the disadvantages. We wouldn't trade our spiritual awareness for anything else.

These are the attributes which are shared by the Born Awares included in this book.

It's important to note that *these attributes are not exclusive to people who were born aware*, of course, as I mentioned earlier. Many people have some of them. However, not all people who have some of these attributes will typically have all or most of them, as those who are Born Aware do.

Differences Among Born Awares

You will have probably noticed in reading the individual accounts that there are also differences in our lives and awareness. We are not carbon copies of each other. I'll share some of those differences here, as well as their implications.

Differing Ages When Aware

One of the most striking differences among us is the age at which we were aware and from which we remember. Some of the Born Awares have pre-birth memories, while some of us have memories either from the time we were born or right after birth. Others may have memories that stem from a later point after birth.

Thus there's a somewhat wide variance among the ages at which we remember being spiritually aware. Even though the age at which we remember may vary somewhat, we all share that similar clear awareness, the higher soul awareness, which is the one we had at birth, pre-birth, or shortly thereafter.

Whether We Wanted to Incarnate or Not

I've always known (and remembered) that I didn't want to be here on Earth again, as I shared in my account. However, I was quite surprised that some of those spiritually aware since birth actually did want to be here or looked forward to incarnating again. It appears that there is quite a split between those of us who did want to incarnate and those of us who didn't. Of course, there are a couple Born Awares who looked forward to incarnating, but felt after being born that it had been a mistake.

Even among those who had looked forward to coming in again or regarded it as an opportunity, it would appear that a large percentage of the Born Awares found that being here has not exactly been a bed of roses. While on the other side, we may have forgotten how difficult and painful being here in human form can be, with all the struggles and difficulties that come with being human.

As you've seen from some of the accounts of those who have pre-birth memories, we are often guided—if not gently pressured—to incarnate again, especially for those of us who feel we are here on assignment. We don't always have what we would call "choice" on the other side (or at least choice that feels free and clear), and we may view incarnating and our assignments as duties or responsibilities. Those of us here on assignment may regard incarnating again in order to accomplish what we are to do as a sacred duty and obligation, one that we may not care for but couldn't refuse. I don't feel that we're under duress or forced to incarnate. We simply know that when we're directed by spiritual beings or the Divine to come in, it's necessary for us to incarnate, and we simply do what we've been asked to do. Our innate spiritual awareness gives us this, and we know we must comply.

Varying Spiritual Orientations and Memories of Higher Levels

Another difference you may have noticed in reading people's accounts lies in what our orientation is to (or to whom) on the other side (or on higher levels). Some of us are oriented toward God (the Divine, Spirit, etc.), whereas others are oriented toward spiritual guides or angels. As I mentioned in my account, I have always felt a strong direct connection to God and haven't sought a connection to guides or any other intermediaries, which has usually felt unnecessary to me. (I never discount the aid or guidance of other spiritual beings. I have always sensed that there were those guiding me, protecting me, and arranging things. I just haven't sought specific guides out as a general rule, again, because my truest spiritual orientation and connection is to God.) On the other hand, Jimelle and Matthew have been aware of a team of spiritual beings or a council— and Heather remembers being an angel and being directed by the Creator. Carmel remembers being with Jesus and an archangel, Metatron.

Our memories of higher levels show a degree of variance as well. Cheryl is aware of the musicality of the other side. Cynthia remembers a paradise that was a community of souls. Heather stressed the beauty of higher levels. Cynthia and I remember the absolute knowledge on the other side, and Cynthia describes the "thought bubbles" with knowledge in them.

I personally feel, as I shared in my account, that this is a creative universe and that there are many levels to it, as well as a variety of possible features, some of which may be created by what we want or are to experience while we're there. (In fact, I feel that the human need for many people is to create "rules" for the universe and spirituality by seeking to codify, define, delineate, delimitate, etc., which is not congruent with the actual reality, as—again—this is a creative universe where much is possible. Creating rules may allow some to feel that they can understand or grasp or to feel more secure, but I feel that the universe is much vaster than our human need to define or limit.)

Another variance among us is that some of us remember lives on other planets or in different galaxies (with some remembering lives as other physical, non-human beings), while many of us primarily remember other lives on Earth.

Thus, there's a wide variance in what we remember and our orientations on the other side.

Varying Life Experiences While Here

You may have also been struck by the wide variation in life experiences among those of us who have been spiritually aware since birth.

Some of us have undergone abuse during our lives here on Earth, while others haven't. Rosalie and Heather experienced physical and emotional abuse. Rosalie's abuse was so severe that she was in despair for several years and has experienced symptoms of PTSD, such as hyperarousal and anxiety. Some shared that they were molested as children.

Some of us were relatively sheltered while growing up, whereas others were exposed to difficult social conditions (such as Stanislav). Some of us grew up in relatively comfortable financial circumstances, whereas others' families may have struggled financially.

Some of the Born Awares felt somewhat connected to their families, while others felt disconnected or that they had been placed in the wrong families.

Some of us despaired of being here on Earth to the extent that some contemplated suicide or tried to find a way to leave this level. Some have been told that they had a choice as to whether to stay here and live out their lives here (but that they will have to come back and do it all again, should they decide to leave). Others among us did not feel that depth of despair and did not contemplate a way to leave.

Some of us have enjoyed good health in our lives, whereas others, such as Carmel, have been dogged by health issues.

Some of us experienced the loss of siblings or parents while growing up, whereas others among us grew up with our families intact.

Some of us, although not all, went through a period of time in which we turned away from our spiritual knowing and higher soul awareness, even though we later returned to it. For those who experienced this, it usually took place during the adolescent, teen years and sometimes into early adulthood when so many try to fit in and be like others in order to be accepted socially. For Theresa, this was triggered by the death of her mother when she was young.

I tended not to share my memories with others, and others tended to be likewise taciturn. Among those who did share their memories and awareness, there was often regret as they encountered derision, disbelief, ridicule, and other negative reactions.

Some of us have known some kindred spirits throughout our lives, whereas others have felt more isolated. I was fortunate to have known some other people who were born aware in my life (although I didn't know until recently that they indeed were), whereas some of us haven't. Thus there's a large variance of experience with regard to knowing other Born Awares and the degree to which some of us have felt isolated.

Even the spiritual information that we're allowed to have access to can vary from one of us to another. Some of us may have a clearer sense of the other side, while it may be somewhat hazy for others, although the sense of it is definitely there.

So there's quite a wide variance among our experiences while we're here. We'll come back to this topic later on.

Differing Spiritual Experiences and Perceptual Modes

Another area showing great divergence among the Born Awares in this book lies in the area of our spiritual experiences.

As mentioned above, those of us who've been spiritually aware since birth tend to be naturally intuitive, whether we realize it at a young age or not. However, the forms in which we experience our intuition can vary greatly. Some of the Born Awares have always seen presences or have been somewhat of a magnet for passed-on souls wanting assistance, but not all of us have experienced this or have sensed rather than seen presences.

Some of us have had near-death experiences, while others haven't.

Some of us have been able to manipulate matter (e.g., Carmel having psychokinetic abilities and being able to levitate, even if not as high as she had wanted), whereas others of us have not experienced this. Stanislav takes anomalous photographs ("spirit photographs"), whether he is unconsciously affecting the photographs by his energy or through the agency of outside entities who are attracted to his energy.

Some of the Born Awares in this book have had direct experiences with UFOs, while others haven't.

Some of us have had experiences when angels and spiritual beings have interceded and protected us, as shared earlier, whereas others may not have been overtly aware of this spiritual intercession.

Some of us see energy, while others may sense or feel it.

Some are consciously aware of traveling and helping others while we sleep, while others may have no conscious memory of this.

Some of us have some forms of synaesthesia, in which one or more senses are connected, or a photographic memory or a spiral sense of time, while others have unusual perceptual modes, such as hearing music from nature. Others haven't experienced these.

Thus, there is a wide divergence among the types of spiritual experiences we have and our perceptual modes.

Differing Views of Organized Religion

As noted in each person's account, we often feel a direct connection to God or other higher spiritual beings. As a result, we tend to be quite independent when it comes to spirituality and often find our inherent spiritual knowing to be at odds with what many organized religions teach.

We tend to feel that we don't need an intermediary between the Divine and ourselves, especially when we can directly access Spirit and other spiritual beings—nor do we subscribe to the tenets and dogma promulgated by organized religions, since we have some of our own memories and direct spiritual knowledge. We also tend to have innate integrity and we don't need others to teach us principles or values or ethics.

It's interesting that there are differing views among us of organized religion. Some of us are okay with it, especially if we feel that it helps some people to discover spirituality or ethics who may not otherwise have been conversant with or exposed to these things. Others among us are staunchly against organized religion, for a variety of reasons—for example, that most wars have been fought in the name of religion, that it can be divisive, that it's a form of mind control or manipulation, that it can be fear-based (at least some more fundamentalist forms), that it doesn't teach or foster a direct connection to the Divine, a perceived hypocrisy, etc.

Even among these divergent views of religion among the Born Awares, there tends to be a common desire to see people find or develop their own direct, personal connection to spirituality and the Divine and for organized religions to encourage connection and unity, rather than divisiveness.

Awareness of Our Purpose

We tend to know that we're here to accomplish something specific. However, interestingly, some of us have a sense of what our specific purpose or mission is, while others have not yet been able to determine what it is. You'll recall that Diane Wulf was told that the journey itself toward her learning what her purpose was is spiritually important for her in and of itself.

So there are those of us who know that we're here on assignment, and, even though some of us would like to know what our specific purpose or mission is, we simply trust that we will be led to know what we are to do or will do it when the time arrives.

One especially striking aspect of the born aware phenomenon has to do with its spiritual implications—what we can learn from all of this, which we'll delve into next.

18

Spiritual Lessons from the Born Aware Phenomenon

THERE ARE SEVERAL INSIGHTS WE can take away from the phenomenon of being spiritually aware since birth. This means that there are many lessons implicit in this phenomenon, which derive from the born aware accounts you've read thus far.

A Clear and Mature Natal Awareness

This phenomenon certainly evidences the fact that *we can have an awareness at birth that is either separate from the body and/or not the product of an immature infant's less developed brain.*

This concept may take many people aback, and some may be incredulous about the prospect of a baby having a clear and mature awareness. I know from firsthand experience that having a spiritual awareness at birth is not only possible but is also quite real and quite natural, as do the people whose accounts appear in this book. It's our norm.

The current scientific view is that a baby's awareness has to develop over time as the brain develops and experience is accrued, which precludes any clear awareness at birth. This view stems from both conceptual models in psychology and studying human consciousness from the outside, as well as from a view that the brain, which is thought to solely produce consciousness (i.e., that consciousness does not exist separate from the brain), has to develop and that the capacity for awareness develops as the brain develops. However, those of us who were born aware know experientially, in a first-hand manner, that this type of awareness is indeed possible in infants.

We already know that variations in human consciousness exist, just as intelligence, as measured in IQ, varies. There are people who have the condition synaesthesia, in which one or more senses are connected. People who are synaesthetes may see music or colors in music, for example, or taste shapes in food.

Synaesthesia is not the only unusual type of consciousness identified by science. Some people, although very much in the minority, have what is called superior autobiographical memory (or Hyperthymesia). They remember everything in minute detail from their past. (The TV detective show *Unforgettable* dealt with a woman, who was the main character, with this condition who worked with police.)

Those of us who were born aware may likewise be very much in the minority, and perhaps our consciousness at birth is different from the norm—or, as I mentioned earlier, many babies may have an awareness at birth, but amnesia then sets in—but our memories are real. These are not memories that needed to be retrieved or triggered by regression, meditation, or any other after-the-fact mode. They are, instead, memories we have always had that have always consciously stayed with us. We have never forgotten what we thought at birth (or, in some cases, prior to birth or shortly thereafter) and our clear awareness—our higher soul awareness—has stayed with us and never diminished since that time.

These atypical types of consciousness show us that more is possible than a supposed typical human consciousness.

What Is Possible

A Higher Spiritual Awareness While Human

Those of us who have been spiritually aware since birth are very fortunate. We have retained and brought into this world glimpses and memories of the other side and of higher spiritual levels. I personally regard this as a huge gift. What we have retained from our spiritual lives on non-corporeal levels is our higher soul awareness. This shows us that it is indeed possible to have access to our Higher Soul Awareness, as well as to glimpses of higher spiritual levels and some higher spiritual truths, while we are here as humans.

And those of us featured in this book are not the only ones who were born aware. I know that there are others scattered on this planet who are, a few of whom I know. The renowned spiritual teacher Yogananda is said to have had memories stretching back to his birth and even time in the womb. There are indeed more of us out there.

It may be true that some people who are born aware and remember what they thought when they were born are not also spiritually aware, as mentioned earlier. Alan feels that his spiritual awakening did not occur until later in his adult life. I have read a few other accounts of at-birth memories that appeared to exist without a concomitant spiritual awareness. Some people may be born aware (with or without a corresponding spiritual awareness), but amnesia sets in, so the memories of awareness are lost.

Being aware at birth and remembering what one thought and perceived may derive from a source other than a spiritual awareness. It's also possible that some people may be born spiritually aware, yet not have an orientation towards higher spiritual levels or an access to spiritual wisdom or knowledge. However, the Born Awares included in this book by and large were both aware and spiritually aware at birth (or shortly thereafter) and retained these memories without lapses or a need to retrieve or recover them through artificial means such as regression, meditation, etc.

One salient hallmark of having been spiritually aware since birth is our split awareness and our prevailing access to our higher soul awareness. It is being in our higher soul awareness that maintains our strong connection to those higher spiritual levels and keeps us oriented there and spiritually sustained, even as we dip back and forth into our human persona. Our higher soul awareness keeps us on our spiritual paths, even if we can't consciously see where our paths are leading us, and it steers and guides us, in addition to the guidance we continually receive from God/Source, spiritual guides, angels, and other spiritual beings, almost by osmosis at times. It's also a source of great comfort for us. Our ever-constant higher soul awareness may make those of us born aware hybrids and never permanently anchored in our human side, but it brings great rewards.

This shows us that it's indeed possible to live a life on this planet as a human and not be completely embroiled in or blinded by or encased in our human side. It's possible to be here as a human and also have a spiritual clarity of vision, spiritual awareness, and access to some higher knowledge, truths, and wisdom.

Direct Access Spiritually

The phenomenon of the born awares also shows us that it's possible to have a direct connection not just to higher spiritual levels or to guides, but also to God (Spirit, the Divine, Source, etc.). Admittedly, this may be easier for some of us who were born aware, because we never lost our direct connection. As I shared, my direct connection to God has not only stayed with me, but is also the strongest and overarching truth of my life. I have never felt a sustained need to go through guides, except out of curiosity, and certainly not a human intermediary. Several of the other born awares have also retained this direct connection.

This certainly teaches us that we can indeed have a direct connection to Spirit and need not rely on someone else to be an intermediary. In other words, we can go directly to God for answers, support, and comfort, rather than needing to go through any other purportedly spiritual or religious intermediary or authority. It's true that not everyone may be ready for this, and some may indeed prefer using an intermediary. However, it is definitely possible to have direct access, which is quite powerful and spiritually rewarding.

Easing of Fears and Feeling Protected

Unfortunately, being a human can be very difficult. We may struggle to survive. We may go through abuse and other traumatic experiences. We may develop fears as a result of abuse or via contagion from other people's fears or mindsets, or through cultural or familial conditioning, or even through material we're exposed to (books, films, the news, etc).

One thread that runs through most of these accounts is that of feeling divinely protected and not having many strong fears. Indeed it is through feeling divinely protected that we feel less fearful, despite having experienced abuse or trauma. I personally feel that this stems from our innate spiritual awareness, access to our Higher Soul Awareness, and connection to the Divine (and/or other spiritual beings or emissaries).

Having easy access to our higher soul awareness leads those of us who have been spiritually aware since birth to innately know that everything happens for a reason. We know—and trust—that there is Divine purpose to situations here on this plane, including those things which are unpleasant or negative. As I shared, many of us naturally find ourselves asking when we see negative events unfold, whether locally or on the world stage, what the higher purpose of the event may be. In other words, what lessons, shifts, and positive changes can come out of the negative events. We innately trust in the benevolence of the universe. This also helps to stem and forestall strong fears.

This leads me to feel that, if one could foster this type of spiritual awareness and connection and, especially, the access to the higher soul awareness, one could help to ease some of the fears, whether conscious or unconscious, that so many people have. It would also lead people to feel more spiritually protected and guided.

Awareness That We're Here to Accomplish Something

Many of us Born Awares know that we're here because there is something we are to do or that we're here on assignment. We tend to regard having been spiritually aware since birth as a gift, but we are also mindful that this comes with a duty, responsibility, and obligation. We tend to know that the universe can be strict with us. As I shared above, we can't always focus on pleasure or enjoyment or be allowed to stay on a lighter level because we must always be mindful of purpose and path and what feels right. This may be especially true of us in our adult years.

For people who are aware of a higher purpose in their lives—that they're here to accomplish something—this awareness tends to color their lives and serve as a major theme. This can sometimes bring about a thread of seriousness in their lives. This certainly doesn't imply that one can't go to a lighter level on occasion; there just tends to be an undercurrent of seriousness.

This illustrates that having a sense of purpose doesn't come with "bells and whistles" or a free ride or glamour, nor does it guarantee a life of enjoyment or security. Everything has its advantages and disadvantages, even a higher purpose and spiritual awareness.

The Greater Drama and What Is Allowed

As you saw earlier in the previous chapter, those of us spiritually aware since birth have many attributes in common, while, at the same time, there are also differences in what we have experienced in our lives and in our human personas. Even the spiritual wisdom and truths we have access to may vary from one person who was born aware to another. One might expect that there wouldn't be many differences in our experiences or spiritual knowledge, leading one to wonder why we would be seeing so many of those differences.

What I have sensed is that the external characteristics of our lives and experiences, as well as our memories of the other side and spiritual knowings, are the way they need to be for what we are to experience (for our soul's growth) and for what we are to do or accomplish here, as well as for the roles we play with others—and *this is likely true for most people, whether born aware or not.*

There's a greater drama unfolding on the Earth, and we all play parts in it, whether we're born aware or not—and whether we're aware of a greater drama or not. This is because there are two levels to life here on this planet: what we are to experience as individuals (for our soul's growth) and the greater drama (for the world's unfolding and progress).

When we incarnate and come to Earth, we are in essence putting on a costume for the role we are to play. I feel that Princess Diana, for example, was an advanced soul who came to teach others about compassion and humility. While here, she may have appeared to others to be a beautiful woman with insecurities and self-doubts, who was also compassionate. On another level, however, she was playing a role to teach lessons on a larger scale, the importance of compassion being one of those. At the same time, in her human persona, her insecurities and self-doubts, as well as the painful experiences she went through in her life, happened for her own unfolding and growth, *as well as being part of her role and costume.*

It's also true that some of our greatest woundings can give us material for what we are to share with or teach to others. Some people who were abused as children and who later heal those wounds may go on to teach and inspire other victims. Our weaknesses and woundings, once worked on and healed, can then become our strengths and material for what we can assist others with. (The difficulties and any abuse that those of us born aware experience also attest to the fact that being spiritually aware is no guarantee of a life of enjoyment or one that is problem-free.) Both the painful experiences and the joyful ones exist for higher reasons—for what we are to do and how we are to affect and be affected by others.

While we all, born aware or not, wish we did not have to struggle or go through painful experiences in our lives here, the truth is that those difficulties are the raw material for our soul's growth. An easy life may be more enjoyable in some ways, but difficult lives can benefit us more with regard to the enrichment of our soul by growth. (And we may indeed have some lives that are easier mixed in with those that are more difficult—all so that our souls may experience the fullness of embodied experience.)

Thus, some of the differences in life experiences that you've seen among the Born Awares in this book exist in large part because of what we are here to do and experience.

The most important attribute that we Born Awares share—our split awareness, with its easy access to our higher soul awareness—I also feel is part of what we are here to do. I strongly feel that those of us who have been spiritually aware since birth have been *allowed* to be this way, because it is part of what we are here to do. Our higher soul awareness can show that it's possible to have this orientation and how beneficial it is (which we discussed in chapter 2).

Another factor to bear in mind is that there's also a strong sense of impermanency to our human personas. Our soul's identity transcends the human one and is our true and ultimate identity. The human persona is what we need for our role here and what we are to accomplish and how we may interact with, affect, and be affected by others. We wouldn't be unfolding much were it not for our human side (or for duality on this level). However, it is our soul and higher soul awareness that transcends and endures.

What this means is that, because of the greater drama here, there was a plan for our lives (the "template" that Matthew referred to), which encompasses the totality of our experiences here, including the people we were to interact with, as well as the attributes we were to have (what the character, our human persona, we are playing in the drama is like) and our purpose or assignment. The greater drama is complex, with all of the characters in the drama on earth and all of the "scenes" and interactions globally, and we are indeed all playing those roles.

We were all encoded with our life's plan via an energetic encoding before coming in and all our experiences with others are part of that plan and its encoding, all in order to achieve that higher purpose.

Any "gifts" we give to others via our interactions with them that are kindnesses, warm feelings, lessons learned (even if they don't seem positive at the time), etc., may endure, especially if they serve to move humanity forward. In the end, though, and as you've heard before, things on this human level are transitory. It is the soul—and love—that remain and transcend, as well as any lessons learned. The greater drama helps to create and teach humanity, all of us, those lessons—and move us all forward.

An Embrace of Being Whole-Brained

You've no doubt noticed that those of us who were born aware are whole-brained, in that we are not only spiritual, creative, and naturally intuitive, but also tend to have good left-brain intelligence (logic, reasoning ability, academic proficiency, etc.). I feel that this is because we innately value all the potentials we have and feel that we should use them.

There have been many widely-held views in the past several years that we should be either right-brain or left-brain—in other words, that we should be sensitive, spiritual, and creative and *not* analytical or logical *or* that the converse is true, that if we're logical, we should eschew spirituality or creativity or intuition. It's certainly true that in the academic arena, particularly in the sciences, there has been an attitude at times of condescension toward feelings and even warm hearts. It is the hard-core intellectual mechanisms and gymnastics, with no other workings, that may be valued. (I come from a rigid academic background and am familiar with these attitudes in some academic circles.)

Interesting, then, that those of us who were born aware tend to embrace our warm, compassionate hearts, our right-brain modes of spirituality, creativity, and intuition, *and* our left-brain intelligence and logic. In truth, these modes are not mutually exclusive and, to the contrary, can actually work with and complement each other. We may consciously or unconsciously feel that we need or want to use all of our inherent potentials, just as we often enjoy learning new things and having new experiences that can round out our life here.

Dealing with the Human Side and Our Personal Stuff

Those of us who are born aware are quite familiar with our split awareness. We greatly value our higher soul awareness, which is our true orientation, and tend to prefer being in that awareness which comes from and reminds us of a higher level. This may lead us to be less enamored of our human side at times.

As shared earlier, our human side contains our personality in this lifetime. It comes with some of the joy of human life, along with all the psychological and emotional "baggage" that being a human implies. We are intimately acquainted with the split awareness and feeling of being pulled back into our human side and stuff—quite abruptly at times. If we're fearful about being able to pay the bills, going through the angst and pain of a difficult relationship, worrying about how we'll perform on a job, finding ourselves having personal dislikes that may come from family or cultural conditioning—all of these are examples of how we can be affected by and pulled into the less desirable human side. We *know* the beauty and spiritual nature of our higher soul awareness and the clarity, insight, and spiritual information it can give us, and we find ourselves unhappy with and/or resenting that difficult human stuff.

Even though there's not much we can do about some aspects of our human side, especially those challenges connected with our need to survive on this physical level, we do know that working on healing and clearing any of our old, unresolved issues or self-hindering mindsets and beliefs can free us up more and allow us to spend more time in our higher soul awareness. And, interestingly, increasing numbers of people appear to be doing that, including those of us who were born aware. Clearing some of the personal stuff can not only allow us to perceive more clearly and be less reactive, while also finding more fulfillment, but can also serve to provide less obstructed access to our higher soul awareness.

You may have noticed that Born Awares tend to be keenly aware of spiritual agency in our lives, whether we have had direct experiences with divine intervention, aiding and even rescuing us, or not. We know that we are being shepherded to keep us on track, so that we may fulfill our assignments and do what we came in to do. We have an awareness of being guided and led. (From this point of view, we truly need not worry about knowing what our purpose is, as we know we will be led to it.) We also tend to know and accept that everything happens for a reason, as mentioned above.

Thus, we don't feel that we're all alone here on Earth or are on our own in doing things. Nor do we feel that we're here just to play and can do anything we want to do (as tempting as that thought might be at times)."

Cocreation and Awareness of Higher Spiritual Agency

You may have noticed that Born Awares tend to be keenly aware of spiritual agency in our lives. We know that we are being shepherded to keep us on track so we may fulfill our assignments and do what we came in to do. We have an awareness of being guided and led. (From this point of view, we truly need not worry about knowing what our purpose is, as we know we will be led to it.) We also tend to know and accept that everything happens for a reason, as mentioned above. Thus, we don't feel that we're all alone here on Earth or are on our own in doing things. Nor do we feel that we're here just to play and can do anything we want to do (as tempting as that thought might be at times).

Manifesting has been a very popular concept in the past several years. There are those who espouse and teach "manifesting" what you want in life. I personally have never been comfortable with this concept, for several reasons. It is certainly true that a body of research has shown that we can influence and affect things, including living beings, simply through the agency of our thoughts (or prayer). (Dr. Gary Schwartz, Professor of Medicine, Neurology, Psychiatry, and Surgery at the University of Arizona and the Director of its Laboratory for Advances in Consciousness and Health, has conducted research on the healing effect of thoughts and prayer on plants, which is summarized in his excellent book *The Healing Energy Experiments*.)

So, yes, our thoughts and consciousness can indeed affect physical reality. We can use healing energy to help others and, conversely, our negative feelings can affect others. However, the reality on this planet is a *consensual one*, meaning that it is affected by a multitude of factors, including the thoughts and consciousness of everyone. In order to manifest what we want in life, we would need to enlist the aid of many others acting on our behalf and aiding us in manifesting and affecting matter and reality. Some things that we may want will also affect other people and their lives, so manifesting would also involve our affecting others via our consciousness. (Consider the "butterfly effect," which posits that small actions can have effects universally and affect the whole.) That said, affecting beings and matter on this level may be optimally operative when we are acting in concert with others via prayer and healing energy, to help heal and aid in beneficial outcomes.

The concept of manifesting what we want furthermore omits any agency of a higher power. This means that reality on this level would be a function solely of consciousness on this level, without any outside agency of guides, angels, or even God. Many people want to be the sole creators of their lives. While this may indeed be appealing to the human side of us, the spiritually aware among us, whether born aware or not, typically have a sense of spiritual beings nudging us and helping to create experiences and events in our lives, with a view to purpose. The opposite end of this spectrum is the view that God alone creates our lives and that we humans have no choice or free will and are, instead, passive beings to be acted upon. This view rankles most people, who want to feel they have free will.

As you read in the accounts in this book, those of us born aware are quite cognizant of those unseen (and sometimes seen or sensed) spiritual beings guiding us and affecting things in our lives. This is connected to our awareness that we are here to do something specific—i.e., that we're here on assignment. This overshadows what we may always want for ourselves. We walk with this awareness daily in our lives. Thus, we know that higher agency exists and affects events on this level on Earth. I have never had a problem with it and instead treasure my direct connection with Spirit. I am very grateful for being led and guided and being protected. As mentioned earlier, the universe tends to be strict with those of us who were born aware. "We may want things in our lives, but if they're not in accordance with the plan for our lives and what we are to do (in the greater drama) we don't get them.

We also tend to be aware of the interwoven web of connection on this level, with its mutual affecting, co-affecting, and interdependence. Add to this all the events and occurrences that are supposed to happen and outside spiritual agency, and we have a hugely complex web that surpasses the ability of our human minds to comprehend. Is manifesting another factor operative in this complex web, or is it a somewhat simplistic human wish?

Another downside of the concept of manifesting involves its effect upon people when problems are occurring in their lives. I've had clients express being very down on themselves for "manifesting" such problems. This aspect of the concept can lead to fear-based thinking and represent another reason to berate oneself.

When it comes to creating our own lives or relying upon spiritual agency, I personally feel that cocreation is the optimal view and closer to the actual reality. I have always had my treasured direct connection with God and I used to feel that things would unfold in the way that they should. If anything, I used to be overly passive and felt that God would bring about what was supposed to occur in my life. I amended that attitude many years ago and now walk my life with an attitude that is in between those two extremes. I have a sense of what I want and where I should be headed, while I also listen to the guidance I receive and allow myself to be led. This approach is more in line with cocreation.

So can we just manifest whatever we want in life? I know this is an unpopular statement, but I doubt that it's actually possible, as I pointed out above. Perhaps some people have more leeway in their lives, especially if they are here primarily to gain human experience, rather than learn, grow, and unfold, as well as for the roles they play for others—*or* are here to experience manifesting. However, one would still need to find a way to enlist the aid of others, given that this is a consensual reality, as well as enlist the aid of outside spiritual agency. (And one would also be affecting others and their lives by so doing.) As a result, they might live a life without much soul growth. Being able to manifest what we want tends not to be the case, however, for those of us born aware and here on assignment.

Spectrum of Consciousness

We touched briefly on the topic of our spectrum of consciousness earlier. We discussed the spirit awareness that those of us spiritually aware since birth tend to have. However, our typical human awareness, irrespective of whether we were born aware or not, has more than one side, as most of us know. We have our conscious awareness, plus that which lies beneath our conscious mind—our subconscious and our unconscious. Research has shown that, irrespective of our tendency to identify ourselves with who we know ourselves consciously to be, most of who we are is actually that which lies below our conscious awareness. (See Timothy D. Wilson's book, *Strangers to Ourselves: Discovering the Adaptive Unconscious*.) On the higher end of the consciousness spectrum lies our higher soul awareness. I refer to these different "minds" or awarenesses as the "spectrum of consciousness."

Interestingly, while our unconscious lies "deeper" within us, in some ways it is connected to and allows easier access to our higher soul awareness, especially when we're in deeper levels of consciousness, such as sleeping or meditating. Our unconscious is thus a mixed bag, containing both our personal "stuff" and access to those higher levels that our higher soul awareness also gives us access to. Indeed, our personal stuff and old, unresolved issues tend to keep us mired in our human side, as I shared earlier. When we work on clearing and healing that personal stuff that no longer serves us, we gradually feel lighter and may find that our higher soul awareness is more and more within reach.

Thus, we humans are quite mixed while we are here, with the potential for great complexity. If we live primarily in our human side, we may be more one-dimensional, but the potential for that complexity becomes greater when we gain more conscious access to those higher levels. Working on clearing our personal stuff can definitely aid us in accessing those higher levels more easily.

Divine Spark Evidenced by a Love of Animals and Nature

People who are interested in spirituality often want to experience higher spiritual levels. We may tend to feel that those higher spiritual levels are "out there" or far away. I feel, however, that there are things on this level that can be mirrors of higher levels and that may represent entry points. In fact, we are surrounded by one of them.

A love of animals and nature is one of the attributes that those born aware tend to have in common. Being in nature not only has a calming effect on people; it can also bring us back to center and get us in touch with spiritual elements. Recent research studies have actually documented this healthful effect, to the extent that doctors in some countries are recommending and indeed prescribing that patients spend time in nature for healing purposes. (See Richard Louv, 2012, Helen Briggs, 2015, and Laura Smith, 2014.) Ralph Waldo Emerson wrote, "Nature is too thin a screen; the glory of the omnipresent bursts through everywhere." I personally feel that divine energy runs through everything and everyone, and one can sense an eternal element in nature that reminds us of the eternal and timeless quality of higher spiritual levels. It may appear to be a mute energy, but it communicates to us nonetheless, as we sense and are affected by its energy.

There can be a similar effect with animals. You'll remember that in the last chapter I shared descriptions that some of the Born Awares expressed of what they experienced when they looked in an animal's eyes. Once again, it's important that an animal not be stressed or emotional when doing this (and you wouldn't want to look in a wild animal's eyes up close or endanger yourself).

When we look into an animal's eyes, we can experience a timelessness, a presence, and a present quality that is clear and eternal—and which is reminiscent and evocative of higher levels and being in our higher soul awareness. It's an awareness that transcends this level and takes us to a clear now that has no boundaries and in which we feel a union and connection with all that is. Martin Buber must have been aware of this as he wrote in *I and Thou*, "An animal's eyes have the power to speak a great language."

I feel that the part of you that feels compassion for all animals is the manifestation of God's spark in you and in all of this physical world. The part of you that loves nature in all of its expressions is the Divine spark in you that is perennially ignited and has not been extinguished by being on this level or by the human experience. We awaken and connect to that Divine spark when we feel compassion for animals and love for nature. This is one way of connecting with those higher spiritual levels.

Implications for Parents

Unfortunately some of us who were born aware (although not all) had very difficult experiences with problematic long-lasting effects when we were very young and started to talk. Some were pooh-poohed by others when they shared their early memories, and, even worse, some were derided and ridiculed. Even being told that we have active or vivid imaginations can feel self-denying and crushing, because it feels like being told that we're foreign, different, or invalidated—an outsider, rather than one who is embraced as part of the family.

Because those born aware tend to be sensitive and tend to feel different from others due to our innate spiritual awareness and orientation, experiencing derisive and otherwise self-negating reactions from others can foster or worsen self-esteem issues and exacerbate a longing to be back home on higher spiritual and non-corporeal levels, the latter of which can lead to thoughts of suicide.

The same is true for bullying. When those of us born aware are bullied—and because of our sensitivity—we tend to lose our sense of sanctity and feel deeply violated. We no longer feel safe and begin to feel fearful and unprotected. This becomes greatly worsened if we have no parent to turn to for protection and solace or if we go to a parent and are told to ignore the bullying or that it's minor. Indeed the same is true for all children, because each child needs to have a sense of sanctity and protection. Bullying robs children of this crucial and hugely important feeling of security.

It's critically important, therefore, for parents to know how detrimental such ridicule, bullying, and other negative reactions can be. It's important for parents to be cognizant of the phenomenon of having been born aware and how it differs from other atypical attributes of young children, such as children having past-life memories and children being naturally intuitive or psychic. These are two phenomena that are quite different from having been spiritually aware since birth.

While most of the born awares have spontaneous recall of some past (or other) lives and are naturally intuitive, the converse is definitely not true: in other words, children who have past-life memories and/or who are naturally intuitive or psychic are not necessarily spiritually aware—or in possession of at-birth or pre-birth memories of the other side and of higher spiritual levels—or naturally inclined to have access to spiritual truths and wisdom—or anchored more in the Higher Soul Awareness (as opposed to the human persona). Indeed, some children who remember a past life may still associate so strongly with that lifetime and persona that they may reject their present persona, family, or other elements of their present lifetime. In other words, they have trouble accepting that they're now in a different lifetime."

That said, it's extremely important for the welfare of children not to have anyone discount any past-life memories or intuitive or psychic abilities that they have. Parents can make a positive difference for their children in this regard.

It would be helpful if parents were aware of this phenomenon—that of having been spiritually aware since birth (including at times having access to higher spiritual truths), as well as that of children having past-life recall and being naturally intuitive, and, furthermore, if parents came to view these phenomena as legitimate—not the norm, certainly, but legitimate—and credible phenomena.

Parents could lovingly tell their born aware children that their awareness is unusual and that they may not encounter many other children or adults with this awareness, but that they believe their children. Encouraging born aware children to share with them their awareness and experiences would also be validating. The same is true of children with past-life memories and notable intuitive or psychic abilities. Some parents might feel intimidated by a child's spiritual awareness and wisdom, but it's important to put that aside, respecting the child's spiritual maturity while also parenting the child in a loving and accepting manner.

Parents need to play a similar—and protective—role if their child is bullied: comforting their child, standing up for him or her, and taking concrete and strong measures to stop the bullying. Recent research indicates the bullies may derive pleasure from bullying and aggressive acts. (See Gleeson, 2016.) Thus, bullying is a serious problem that is often entrenched, with deep roots, and not easy to stop—and that has strongly problematic effects. It is not to be made light of or ignored.

Parents can play a huge role in helping their born aware children feel less isolated and more comfortable, both in themselves and around others—thus helping to forestall any potential problems later on.

We've examined the various attributes that Born Awares tend to have in common, as well as the differences, and have looked at their spiritual implications. To me, the most salient and beneficial characteristics of those spiritually aware since birth have to do with our split awareness and higher soul awareness, in addition to our easy access to spiritual wisdom and truths. I feel that being in our higher soul awareness is critical to spirituality and brings us many spiritual benefits, as shared earlier.

We'll next look at some ways to groom the higher soul awareness without having been born aware or needing to go through a near-death experience or other transformative experience that triggers it.

19

Grooming the Higher Soul Awareness and Other Recommendations

BEFORE WE EXPLORE POTENTIAL WAYS of grooming the higher soul aware-ness, it's important to note that some people may have born spiritually aware, but amnesia set in. In fact, I wouldn't be surprised if a large per-centage of babies have this awareness at birth, before amnesia erases any memory of it. If reading any of the accounts included in this book has triggered any of your own at-birth or pre-birth memories that you may have previously forgotten, allow yourself to let those memories come up to full awareness and review them, while also allowing yourself to begin embracing them. Try to identify your higher soul awareness and what it feels like and then learn and feel its ins and outs. (You'll find more recom-mendations in appendix C for those born aware.)

We know that we can't easily go back in time and redo our birth and awareness at the time, unless we do some time travel or experience an alternate dimension. Even if you weren't born aware or have forgotten any at-birth thoughts, there are steps you can take to help groom your higher soul awareness. I've shared its various benefits. It's a very desirable and beneficial attribute, especially for those spiritually oriented—so much so that it may be tempting to want to be in your higher soul awareness as much as possible and ignore or neglect your human side. I personally feel that doing this is neither productive nor advisable. We'll explore the whys of this in more depth further down in the suggestions. For now, just be aware that you want to balance your spiritual side with your life here on this Earth and its demands, rather than using your spirituality or higher soul awareness as a means of escape.

Remember, too, that the higher soul awareness is not a product of the human personality or persona, but instead transcends the human side. That said, our higher soul awareness is connected to or linked with our human side while we're here, just as our soul is, but is not a product of it. We really have to leave our human side behind, ignore it, or otherwise not allow it to get in the way or color our awareness—at least temporarily—while we're trying to access our higher soul awareness.

This does not mean that we're permanently ignoring our human side, but instead that we don't allow it to get in the way of or influence our higher soul awareness, so that they are two different types or modes of awareness. This is why the Born Awares in this book, with our spirit awareness, shift back and forth between these two modes or types of awareness. (Our human personality usually changes from one lifetime to another, whereas our higher soul awareness is pure and eternal as it's connected to our soul.) Please keep this in mind.

The following are some suggestions for grooming the higher soul awareness with the above considerations in mind.

Suggestions for Grooming
the Higher Soul Awareness

Accessing and grooming our higher soul awareness, I feel, may be a multi-pronged process, short of a transformative triggering experience. The following are some recommendations for this process. Please note that I would recommend taking all of the following steps, rather than regarding them as a menu from which to choose, as they tend to work synergistically together. I realize that following all of these recommendations would take time. However, doing at least several of them should begin to put you on the road toward an easier access to your higher soul awareness, and you can continue with the rest of them as time permits.

- **Chew on the differences between the human side and the higher soul awareness:** If you feel that you haven't yet accessed your higher soul awareness or aren't familiar with it, review the description and attributes of it shared in chapter 2. There's a qualitative difference in how each side and type of consciousness feels. Familiarize yourself with the attributes of the higher soul awareness and what it might feel like. Then take steps to feel the differences between when you're in your human persona and when you're in your higher soul awareness. Familiarizing yourself with it in this manner is a good first step.

- **Chew on what a pure state of mind is:** This may be a difficult concept to wrap your arms around, but allow yourself to imagine what it might be like. What would it feel like to perceive things without any preconceived notions or likes and dislikes or judgments—or without any fears? What would it feel like to perceive others as beings connected to you with whom you share some (perhaps indefinable) qualities? What would it feel like to both know and truly feel that you are connected to everyone and everything else in the world—and feel the same spirit running through everyone and everything else and you as a beautiful thread? How would it feel if you could drop, suspend, or forget your concerns and just be in a pure state?

Considering what a pure state of mind is and what it would feel like will help you to "prime the pump" in preparing yourself to be in your higher soul awareness. It will be less of a foreign concept to you as a result.

- **Meditate:** Allow yourself to learn to meditate and practice meditating on a regular basis. At least twice a week for a minimum of twenty minutes per session would be helpful.

  Note that this would need to be *true meditation*. I've had several clients tell me over the years that they meditate, when in actuality they are reflective and introspective at times. So it's important to note the distinction between introspection or reflection and true meditation. When we're reflective or thinking, we're in a lighter state of consciousness than the one we're in when we're truly meditating.

  With true meditation, our eyes are closed, our breathing is deeper, our mind is calmed, and we get into a deeper state of consciousness than our typical waking ones. We get into a lower alpha or lighter theta brain wave state. This is critical for true meditation and for deriving the physiological, psychological, and other types of benefits that we can gain from meditation.

  We have many different potential states of consciousness available to us as humans, and each one brings different benefits and helps with different types of activities. Dr. James

V. Hardt said, "People who can turn on the ideal brain waves to deal with each and every situation are considered gifted." Unfortunately, in our contemporary Western culture, which tends to be so stress-ridden, we may customarily get into only two of them: awake (and often stressed), and soundly asleep. Meditation allows us to get into a deeper state of consciousness (while awake), while also allowing us to begin going within. It is through going within that we can start to connect spiritually—with higher levels, with guides, and with Source—in addition to getting into our center. While we're meditating, our personal stuff is usually turned off (and I'm sure you can see why this can benefit getting into our higher soul awareness). In addition, research has shown a long list of physiological, health, and brain benefits afforded by regular meditation.

Meditation may seem that it would be difficult to do or get into to. However, most people can indeed learn to meditate. There are many classes and lessons available that can help you learn to meditate. In addition, there are several different methods of meditation, and you can try various ones to get a sense of which works best for you. (There are some good books available that detail various methods.) I personally prefer to use guided meditation, both for myself and in one-on-one work with my clients. (With guided meditation, we are guided throughout the meditation, often to go on some type of journey. We don't have to blank our minds out, as we're guided to focus on various details.)

Try not to get discouraged if you initially find meditating difficult to do or truly get into. It may take you more than one attempt to successfully get into those deeper states of consciousness. (It took me two attempts and with the second attempt, which was an individualized guided meditation led by someone else, I got deeply into it with no problem.)

As hugely beneficial as meditation is, bear in mind that you don't want to overdo it. Aside from the obvious reason for this (that of needing to focus on things in our daily lives), there are some people who have experienced a downside from perhaps too much meditation for longer periods of time than may be optimum. (See Miguel Farias, 2015.) This is why meditating for an hour or less per session or even just twenty minutes two to three times a week would be good. We need to balance meditation with our day-to-day lives, just as we need to do with our spirituality and other-world orientation.

If you're new to meditation, find a method that works for you and seek out a teacher or class or book. Keep at it and you should find success. Meditation can really pave the way for accessing your higher soul awareness. (In the appendix you'll find a meditation designed to help you access it.)

- **A suggested exercise:** Once you find yourself meditating fairly easily, you could incorporate a feature that should enable you to access your higher soul awareness and accentuate your spiritual orientation. While you are meditating, allow yourself to imagine and then *feel* Divine energy, love, and support surrounding and enveloping you and then moving into your body, filling up every part of your body with that Divine energy. Once you feel it in you, allow yourself just to be still with it and continue to feel it.

  This can help to establish your sense of a direct connection with Source and to feel the wonderful energy, love, and protection from it.

- **Pay attention to and work with your dreams:** Paying attention to, learning to interpret, and then working with your dreams can be hugely beneficial for you in your life. Your dreams can help you solve problems, work on self healing, and much, much more. Dreams can also have spiritual content and even be spiritual experiences, leading you to explore deeper levels of yourself, explore other places in the universe, connect with passed-on loved ones, and gain spiritual experience.

  Even when you're not dreaming, you can have spiritual experiences in the deeper levels of sleep. We don't always bring back a conscious memory of these experiences, but we can be affected by them and grow spiritually as a result. By placing more conscious attention on and having an interest in this aspect of your sleeping world, you can gain spiritual benefits—which can then assist in accessing your higher soul awareness. Allow yourself to embrace your sleep and dreams and the spiritual benefits they can bring you.

  I cover these aspects of sleep and dreams in detail in my book, *Dream Interpretation for Beginners: Understand the Wisdom of Your Sleeping Mind.* Your sleep and dreams can be a major portal to your spiritual world and I would urge you to value and explore them.

- **Work on clearing personal stuff:** Admittedly, clearing our personal stuff can feel like a very difficult goal. However, progress can definitely be made. Bear in mind that this is not an on-off switch and that we typically clear our personal stuff incrementally and in stages over time (aside from the gift of epiphanies). Remember that it's our personal stuff that can keep us mired in our human side and can serve to block our access to our higher soul awareness. In addition, personal spirituality that ignores the need to clear personal stuff, to me, is not a true spirituality.

Over the years I've encountered many, many people who are into spirituality. We come from many different backgrounds and may have many varied orientations. Some people seek spirituality as a respite or even an escape from their human side with its concomitant personal stuff and may seek to ignore the personal stuff, feeling that spirituality will make the human stuff go away. Unfortunately, that typically doesn't work and may bring about a bigger dichotomy between their spiritual beliefs and their human side. Still others may learn about spiritual precepts and customs and views and keep their spiritual path primarily on the cognitive level, while still retaining their personal stuff or possibly not opening their hearts. This may be more of a top-down approach, but this approach and mode feel hollow to me. I'm not convinced that a top-down approach will work, short of a transformative experience (such as a near-death experience). I personally embrace developing our spirituality in a more holistic fashion that affects all levels and layers of our lives and being.

I recommend a two-pronged approach—working on clearing our personal stuff, while also seeking greater access to our higher soul awareness. As personal issues are healed, we really do gain clearer access to our higher soul awareness and our spirituality becomes purer and more authentic as a result. This is somewhat of a bottom-up approach, if we're focusing solely on clearing our personal issues.

I feel that both working on clearing our personal issues, while also attending to our spirituality via experiential approaches, may work best. Again, working on clearing our personal issues frees us up to more easily be in our higher soul awareness (since our personal issues can represent a block), and doing what we can to access our higher soul awareness helps to strengthen our spirituality and true spiritual awareness.

There are many ways to work on clearing and healing personal issues these days. Most people may be familiar only with talk therapy and I mentioned working with your dreams, but there are many, many more, including hypnotherapy, neuro-linguistic programming, EFT (emotional freedom technique), neurofeedback, regression, polarity therapy, touch for health, PEAT, tapas acupressure technique (TAT), guided imagery, psych-K, imagery rehearsal treatment, the healing code, AFT (Aroma Freedom Technique)—and many more.

- **Work on reducing stress:** Stress can be antithetical to spirituality. Stress is obviously a tight energy and, when we're stressing about problems or an overly long to-do list, our attention is focused on our problems and issues. Stress will also pull our focus back into our human side, thereby temporarily blocking our being in our higher soul awareness. Indeed, whenever we're stressed we may find it more difficult to meditate or that it takes longer to get into a meditative state, much less access a higher state of consciousness.

    In order to reduce our stress, we need at least a two-fold process. First, we need to be able to identify what our stressors are so that we can avoid them. Reducing our sensitivity to stress would be wonderful, although that's not always easy to accomplish. Interestingly, meditation can get us into our center so it takes more or stronger external triggers to pull us out of our center, because it appears to re-calibrate our set point for stress.

Once you identify what your stressors are (and short of becoming immune to stress), the next step would be to avoid them as much as possible.

Obviously we can't always avoid all our stressors. So the final step would be to utilize stress reduction techniques. One of the best techniques for reducing your stress is— yes—meditation. Additional stress reduction techniques include the following: learn deep breathing techniques, avoid stressful or negative people, engage in enjoyable pursuits (reading, hobbies, exercise, etc.), physical affection (hugging, touching, etc.) with friends and family, reduce conflict with others, address and reduce fears, be true to yourself, practice an attitude of gratitude, spend time with pets and in nature, visualize positive outcomes, listen to relaxing music, etc.

- **Be still and calm anxiety:** Being able to be still and fully present is key to being in your higher soul awareness. Indeed, that is one of the hallmarks of it. Whenever you're in your higher soul awareness, you'll find that you're calm, still, and anchored in the present. Anxiety is similar to stress in its effects and can often stem from stress and worry. It can also be a symptom and aftereffect of difficult experiences or abuse.

  Calming anxiety may appear to be easier said than done. It's important to know what the source of the anxiety may be and then work on that cause via healing modalities. Doing some deep breathing and using relaxation techniques could help, as could meditation and reminding yourself that all is well and that any worry or anxiety is counterproductive and does not solve problems.

It may take some time and effort to still the anxiety and be calm and still, but it's very rewarding to do so and can help you access your higher soul awareness.

- **Trust that this is a benevolent universe:** I feel that this may be hugely important as an attitude to groom—and not only important, but also largely unrecognized or undervalued for its significance. One of the things that have helped me immensely in my life has been my direct connection to God.

  Trusting that this is a benevolent universe is more than a mind game or mental exercise. It helps us to calm fear and worry. It helps us to know on an intrinsic and deep level that we can trust that every move we make is happening for a purpose and that on the highest levels all is positive, while also knowing and trusting that we are indeed loved, guided, and protected by Source. This can make it easier for us to access our higher soul awareness, which rests on and depends upon that awareness and attitude. Feeling fearful keeps us bound to the human side and our personal stuff and blocks our higher spiritual access, at least to our higher soul awareness, which is one devoid of fear.

- **Recapture or retain a child's wonder:** I feel that wonder is another largely underrated attribute. It's certainly the opposite of being jaded. Wonder opens us up and leads us to observe from as much of a blank slate as possible, bypassing our preconceived notions and previous experiences. And openness is a quality of the higher soul awareness. Wonder is also built upon a hopeful or positive foundation.

There are always new things to explore and learn about in our world. Feeling that we know all about the world or that there is nothing new under the sun can close us off and lead to that jaded state, which is antithetical to being in our higher soul awareness. Our child's wonder may be lost just through the accumulation of years as we get older, along with any negative experiences we go through. It can also be contaminated by negative attitudes of others that can be contagious.

It may be important to remind ourselves of these things, while also allowing ourselves to remember how we felt as a child, when things seemed new and bright and hopeful. Looking at the world through new eyes can help, as can taking the time to look at things in full sensory detail in our world. Picking up a leaf, for example, and looking closely at it so that we see and notice new details can help to reestablish our wonder. Looking closely at a "lowly" insect and noticing details about it, as another example, could also help.

Try not to leave the child in you completely behind. There were treasures in your childlike mind and the innocence you had, and one of them, wonder, could help to open the doorway to your higher soul awareness.

- **Cultivate inspiration on a regular basis:** What is it that inspires you? I often find myself inspired by beautiful music, which can take me to higher levels. Some art, film, and lyrical writing can also inspire me, so that I find myself transported to higher spiritual levels and transcending the here and now. Inspiration can fill us with powerful, positive feelings and lift us up, while taking us to higher levels and allowing us to transcend our earth-bound existence. We can soar on our inspiration and find it leading us to those higher levels to which we aspire. When inspiration infuses us, we are just a step away from our higher soul awareness.

So allow yourself to identify what it is that inspires you. Build inspiration into your life as a regular practice—and know that it's grooming you to enter into your higher soul awareness.

- **Associate with people you resonate with:** There are many people who feel isolated these days. Some of the people in this book who've been spiritually aware since birth have felt alone. People who are sensitive or deviate from the norm substantially in a variety of ways may also feel isolated. It is through being around people with whom we feel we resonate and whom we feel "get" us and accept us that can lead us to feel less isolated, while also allowing us to feel more validated.

  The converse is also true. If we spend a lot of time around people we don't resonate with, we may feel more alone and possibly also down on ourselves, especially if we're comparing ourselves with them and find ourselves lacking. This effect can be heightened if we spend a lot of time around people who find fault with us and/or overtly criticize us. If we're sensitive or empathic, this effect can be even more potent. Even spending time around others who are negative or otherwise draining can lead to a negative effect. This problematic effect can definitely exacerbate our personal stuff, especially any issues of low self-esteem. This is why it is helpful to be around people who do indeed resonate with us and/or accept us as we are.

Feeling comfortable socially, as well as feeling validated, can lead us to feel fuller in ourselves. It can be harder to access our higher soul awareness when we're feeling drained, criticized, or invalidated. And feeling heard and validated can open up new possibilities in our lives that we may not have conceived, as well as give us the underpinning of greater confidence that we need to more freely get into our higher soul awareness.

- **Befriend your inner voice, inner knowing, and intuition:** Finding your inner voice, embracing and befriending it, and listening to it are hugely important precursors to getting into your higher soul awareness. Indeed, they help to lay the foundation for it.

  We all have an inner voice and inner knowing, whether we have found it or identified it or befriended it. It is a remnant of our awareness from higher spiritual levels and can form a connection or bridge to those higher levels. You'll recall that two things that irked me with having to be here in this lifetime were not being with God and not having absolute knowledge. On higher levels, when we're not here on Earth, we have access to absolute knowledge and complete knowing that is a true knowing and one that is pure and objective. Our inner knowing is a vestige of that.

  Intuition and our inner knowing can often help to anchor us in ourselves so we're less penetrated and impinged upon by the external three-dimensional world while we're here. When we're in our higher soul awareness, we are observing, while also feeling a connection to others. Our observing, while in that mode, can feel at times as if we're watching things on a screen. We have that complete clarity which is separate from typical perceptions and from all the stimuli coming in to us from what is around us. It's a clear, almost somewhat suspended state of observation and awareness.

So finding your inner voice and learning how to befriend, develop, and use your intuition help to prime the pump for being in your higher soul awareness. Developing your intuition is not for playing parlor games or just predicting the future. It's a doorway to get into your higher soul awareness. The advanced exercises in my book, *Intuition for Beginners: Easy Ways to Awaken Your Natural Abilities,* are exercises that will not only stretch you, as well as your abilities; they're also designed to get you to that pure level of awareness that bypasses your personal stuff and leads to clarity, objectivity, and true knowing—as well as to your higher soul awareness.

- **Try to observe clearly and objectively:** As you'll recall from chapter 2, one of the strong hallmarks of the higher soul awareness is a clarity and objectivity. When we're in our higher soul awareness, we do not perceive things through the distorting and muddy lenses of our mindsets, beliefs, past experiences, or other personal stuff. We're completely clear and objective. Thus, it's imperative to find a way to observe in as clear and objective a manner as possible.

  Working on clearing our personal stuff can lead to this. Meditation is also a strong path to greater clarity and objectivity, as well as to being less reactive. (It is our personal stuff, after all, that can lead us to react to things and people around us, as our buttons get pushed by others' actions or other external events.) As you might guess, finding your inner voice and developing your intuition can also lead to this.

We tend to trust others who are wise and give us sage advice. We deem others to be wise who are able to be objective and keep their personal ideas, wants, and agendas out of advice or counsel offered. This requires clarity and objectivity. So these are qualities you would want to develop to help pave the way for getting into your higher soul awareness.

- **Assume that good can come out of events:** Finding a way to develop an attitude and knowing that good can come out of the worst of events is critical. Some may say that this is connected to faith or trust—and, indeed, it may be connected to or an offshoot of trusting that this is a benevolent universe. If you find that focusing on faith or trust helps with developing that attitude, that's fine.

  Allow yourself to revise any assumptions about the world that may be negatively based or pessimistic, so that you become more optimistic about outcomes. The truth is that whenever we derive good from a negative experience, we're transmuting the dross into gold.

  In actuality, good can usually come out of situations and events, no matter how dire. We will usually feel dismayed about negative happenings. There are horrific events that unfold at times on the world stage, and it is perfectly natural to be upset by them and feel compassion for anyone affected. It is an awareness of our shared humanity and humaneness that leads us to feel compassion, and compassion is both healthy and spiritual. However, it is also true that positive things can come about, at times even in a natural manner, from terrible things that happen. So find a way to reprogram any negative thinking, so that you can truly know that good things can and will emerge from any problems. This is known on higher spiritual levels and is a necessary component of your higher soul awareness. Embracing it can lead you to more easily get into that state.

• **Ask yourself what the higher purpose is:** This step is built upon the previous one and may require some practice, as well as perhaps revising and reworking some of our assumptions about the world and cultural mindset. The higher soul awareness looks at events from a higher perspective. Think of this as observing from a long view or long shot, camera-wise, or as if you were way up in the air looking down on the entire world from a higher vantage point that enables you to see everything at once. It also rests upon the awareness that everything happens for a reason, with good coming out of even the worst of events.

You'll remember that those of us in this book who were born aware typically find ourselves asking what the higher purpose is when we learn about events unfolding in our world. The awareness that everything has purpose is engrained in us. We were born with this awareness and knowledge.

Allow yourself to embrace this concept and then create the habit of asking, each time you hear of things unfolding in the world, what the higher purpose is and what good may come out of it. Finding a way to remind yourself that this is true (that everything does happen for a reason and that there is higher purpose) will help to lay the groundwork for you. Then establish the habit of asking, as you observe things or hear about them, "What is the higher purpose of this?" Try to get a sense of what good may come about as a result. (Please note, however, that this awareness should never replace compassion for those negatively affected or actions to support or assist.)

Finding a way to look at purpose should greatly aid your accessing your higher soul awareness.

- **Perceive and embrace the interconnectedness of everything and everyone:** This is another prerequisite of being in the higher soul awareness. As humans and also through our cultural conditioning, we have been taught to see the differences between others (whether other humans, animals, things, etc.) and ourselves. Our human history in which tribal thinking and identification were related to survival (i.e., being able to discern which tribe others were from), which was predicated upon the assumption that people in our own tribe posed no threat, has also complicated and exacerbated this.

  In addition to a tribal mentality, our methods of classification and even science have led us to see differences, discerning, for example, which tree is an oak and which is a pine. This orientation toward differentiation is fine for science, but when applied to society has led to division. (This may seem like an oversimplification; however, from a spiritual perspective—and considering the task at hand—it's necessary to perceive and assume commonalities.)

  We humans have tended to identify ourselves with those who are like us—the same gender, race, nationality, religion, etc. We have unfortunately tended to regard people as "other" who are different in some way. Obviously this has led to discrimination, racism, religious wars—and the list goes on and on.

Similarly, our proclivity to perceive ourselves as different from—and, sadly, superior to—other beings, such as animals, has often led to abuse and misery.

In our present contemporary world, our human tendency to see ourselves as separate from and superior to our world has led to environmental degradation, pollution and poisoning of air, water, food, etc., loss of habitat, reduction of wildlife numbers, and wildlife extinction (in addition to a myriad of negative health impacts upon ourselves). Unfortunately, so many people are ignorant of the fact that ecosystems are complex, interwoven systems, as well as that destroying habitats and wildlife and poisoning air, water, etc. will ultimately and unavoidably come back to bite and hurt us as humans. As an example of how interwoven our environment is, consider that the dust from the Sahara in Africa helps the Amazonian rainforest to grow (see Philip Sherwell) or that the radiation from the Fukushima nuclear plant meltdown created elevated levels of radiation in milk in Europe within weeks.

Our human need to feel apart from and superior to our world and even from and to other humans in it has gotten increasingly damaging for us as humans (not to mention wildlife and the environment). Interesting that such a supposedly intelligent species can be so ignorant and short-sighted!

You'll recall that those of us born aware have always been intrinsically aware of the interconnectedness of life—and not just that all humans are connected to each other, but also to animals, the environment, etc.—and that Divine energy runs through everything and everyone. This is part of a higher spiritual view, an awareness that we have on those higher spiritual levels and brought in with us. It does contrast with the traditional spiritual view that if we're spiritual, we're not of this world and therefore should disregard earthly matters, to which I used to subscribe many years ago. I feel this view has been shifting and changing, especially given the factor of our interconnectedness, not just on higher spiritual levels, but also here on this level.

You'll also recall that Theresa was aware before she was born that she was coming in to assist the Earth and its health and that many other souls were coming in at that time for that same purpose. The Earth is important for our survival and Divine energy is implicit in it, so protecting it is a spiritual obligation. What we do affects the health of the Earth and all of its inhabitants. We're all threads irrevocably connected to and interwoven with each other, and this awareness is one that we born aware have always had and were born with.

Thus, it's vitally important to find a way to perceive this inescapable and inexorable interconnectedness in order to access your higher soul awareness. If it helps to visualize the web of life, as Rozlyn so eloquently described it, then you could begin to do that. If you want to build an affirmation around it, then you could do that and start to affirm it on a regular basis.

Try to identify and then root out any ways in which you perceive others as different and less than, whether this expresses itself as prejudice or a superior attitude (cultural, religious infighting, etc.). As I shared, I have always felt that all religions were talking about the same thing. From this perspective, people quibbling and even warring over religious beliefs is something that is hard to either justify or comprehend (from its irony to its futility to its non-productiveness to its ego-based negativity and need for separation).

Try to perceive the thread of both life and awareness that runs through everything and everyone. Look for what we have in common and share. The web of life is a precious one and one to be preserved, respected, and revered.

Begin to look into other people's eyes when you speak with them, as a way of trying to connect and feel a connection. Look for the good in others. Allow yourself to respect others and accord them respect.

This awareness is critical to getting into your higher soul awareness, because it's an intrinsic component of it.

- **Open your heart:** It's also important to begin to open our hearts to what lies outside of us or what we perceive to be outside of us. When we're in our higher soul awareness, our hearts are open and our compassion is activated. We perceive clearly and objectively, but this doesn't mean that compassion is absent. It isn't.

There are several factors that can lead us to have our hearts somewhat closed. Fear can lead to this, as can abuse at times. Cultural conditioning, as we discussed in the last recommendation, can also have this effect. Even our academic training can bring about a less-than-open heart if we're taught to value our intellect more than our hearts. Irrespective of which factors may have led to our hearts not being open, we can certainly move toward opening them more.

This includes opening our hearts not just to other people, but also to animals and the environment. Animals are sentient and aware, as well as being intelligent (as so much research conducted in the past several years has shown for different species), as well as sometimes having perceptual modes that we humans don't. I feel that it's important for us to accord them both respect and compassion.

You should find that an open heart leads to more easily accessing your higher soul awareness, because on those higher levels we are keenly aware of how interconnected we are and our hearts are quite open.

- **Look into an animal's eyes and connect:** As you read in several of the accounts in this book, looking into an animal's eyes and connecting can be an extremely powerful thing to do. This can actually help to take you into your higher soul awareness.

  Gazing into another's eyes in a fashion that enables you to connect with him or her can be very powerful. It allows us to see into the depths of the other, whether human or animal (who's not really "other"). As I mentioned, I have always sought to connect with others on a deep level by looking into their eyes. (This may be misinterpreted at times as romantic or sexual interest, so one has to be discerning and careful.)

  Interestingly, there's a well-known healer who has become increasingly known internationally by healing others with his eyes and gaze. His name is Braco and he has traveled extensively from his home in Croatia in the past few years offering healing gazing sessions. People who have attended his sessions in person or by live streaming have attested that it's a very powerful healing experience. (See http:// braco.me.) While Braco's gazing is focused on healing effects, gazing into an animal's eyes is focused on taking our consciousness to higher levels. Anatole France wrote, "Until one has loved an animal, a part of one's soul remains unawakened," and this is so very true. Our souls become enriched when we take the time to connect with animals and be present, especially by looking into their eyes.

When you do this, it's very important that you be calm and clear—and that the animal be calm and unstressed as well. The animal's gaze should be clear, without focusing on anything intently. You'll want to intend to connect with the animal, so that you're not looking *at* the animal, but are connecting *with* him or her, so that there's no boundary between you. You'll want to feel a true connection and merging. Allow yourself to notice the clear, calm, present, and timeless quality in the animal's eyes.

You may need to repeat this several times before you find yourself experiencing the calm and clear quality in the animal's eyes and actually connecting. If so, that's fine. When you find yourself going to that higher level, it can be powerful and have long-lasting effects. My experience looking into the depths of the manatee's eyes at Sea World has never left me.

Doing this can serve as somewhat of a portal to experiencing the still, present, and eternal quality of higher levels, a hallmark of the higher soul awareness.

- **An additional exercise:** Once you have succeeded in truly connecting by looking into an animal's eyes and have experienced that quality of the higher soul awareness, you can try another exercise, if you wish to take it further.

In meditation, allow yourself to recall the experience of looking into an animal's eyes and going to the level of the higher soul awareness. Once you feel yourself in that state, allow yourself to feel that you are looking through that animal's eyes as he or she experiences or looks at things. If you've connected with a land animal, imagine that the animal is walking, climbing, watching other beings (including humans), and doing other customary activities—and allow yourself to see what that animal is seeing and experiencing. If the animal you've connected with is a bird, imagine that they are flying and allow yourself to see through their eyes, soaring and looking at things and situations down on the ground, including humans. Likewise, if the animal you've connected with is native to water (like the manatee I connected with), imagine that the animal is swimming. This exercise can help to expand your awareness, allowing you to connect with animals in a different way.

These are the steps I would recommend taking in order to access your higher soul awareness. There's another modality, however, that can help to remove any blocks to accessing your higher soul awareness. As I shared, it is our human side that can keep us anchored and mired in our human identification. This is true because of our personal stuff, and it is even truer because of our identification with and being tunneled into our human persona. It's very hard to transcend and bypass who we are on the human level—it can indeed serve to block our being able to get into our higher soul awareness.

One modality that can help in chipping away at that blockage is past-life regression. Remember that we tend to drop the persona of a lifetime after we transition and then get into our higher soul awareness. I've regressed many clients over the years, in addition to having been regressed and having regressed myself, and can attest to how powerful it can be. By experiencing other lifetimes via past-life regression, you should also be experiencing some of your other personas.

Once you are actually able to experience other personas of yours from other lifetimes, any rigid identification with your present persona should start to soften and be less rigid. It truly is difficult to get into the higher soul awareness if we are rigidly clinging to who we are in the present lifetime and can't see past that. It's quite myopic. We have by and large lived different lives as many different personas—and also as different races, nationalities, genders, religions, etc. Allowing yourself to be regressed—more than once—can begin to free up any unyielding or ironclad identification with the present persona, as you begin to experience some of your other selves and your higher soul awareness, which contains and unifies them.

As with all other recommendations, it's important to come back to your present persona and lifetime after having been regressed. As I mentioned, it's critical to balance your spiritual experiences with the everyday demands of your present lifetime on this planet.

Closing Thoughts

IN THIS BOOK YOU'VE BEEN introduced to several people who have been spiritually aware since birth (or shortly thereafter). You've read what their lives have been like and how they have been affected by this phenomenon. Those born spiritually aware truly have a foot in both worlds, and neither are completely earthbound to this plane nor entirely free to be on those higher levels all the time. We may feel like hybrids at times.

We know directly, from personal experience, that it is possible for infants to have a clear and mature awareness—from birth or beforehand—because we all had that awareness. As difficult as it may have been for us to be here as humans, our saving grace has been our spiritual awareness and our natural orientation to our higher soul awareness. Interestingly, you've also seen that some people can be born aware yet not always have that concomitant spiritual awareness, although it may emerge at a later point.

You've read how beneficial being in our higher soul awareness can be. It enriches the Born Awares' lives spiritually, and we truly could not comprehend living without it. It's a linchpin for our lives.

And, even though we have that natural, innate access to our higher soul awareness, we don't hang out there all the time. We shift back and forth between our human side and that higher level. I personally know that the more we work on clearing our personal stuff, the easier the access is to that level—and we often find ourselves spending more time there, making the time we spend in our human persona less angst-ridden and unpleasant.

It is indeed possible to access the higher soul awareness without having been born aware. As we know, triggering events can help to bring this about, especially transformative ones such as a near-death experience. However, it should be possible even in lieu of such an event.

For anyone who is spiritually oriented or interested in spiritual matters and development, access to the higher soul awareness can open up and expand one's spirituality and spiritual understanding. It's an immediate link to those higher spiritual levels, so individuals can gain tremendously positive benefits from accessing it.

Its benefits, however, are not just restricted to individuals. I personally feel that the world could benefit greatly from more individuals gaining access to their higher soul awareness and spending more time in that awareness. It's no secret that we're living in a time of huge problems and changes. Certainly the degradation of the environment and our persistently, if ignorantly, pulling at the threads of the Earth's overall tapestry may have irreversible and catastrophic effects for life on this planet. Some scientists feel we've already reached the tipping point. And it's not just environmental concerns, with their effects on livability.

We've also been seeing a resurgence in religious-based hatred, racism, and xenophobia that go beyond intolerance or animosity; they have brought on military conflicts, wars, violence, and genocide (as if the Holocaust hadn't been enough to hammer this lesson home).

Many have written and spoken about our major paradigm shift, although it seems to be quite a prolonged process. (See Edward J. Bourne, *Global Shift: How a New Worldview Is Transforming Humanity*) I tend to be an eternal optimist. I feel that a paradigm shift is definitely underway, just as I feel that there is an inevitability about our progressing and succeeding in improving our thinking, changing our harmful practices, and reclaiming the viability of the Earth as a habitat (for starters). However, at the same time, I cannot deny the extremes to which we have been pushing negative practices that are injurious to the Earth, wildlife, and other people. To me, it's patently clear that we need to be able to make some positive changes—and quickly enough so that we're not past the tipping point.

Having more people accessing and getting into their higher soul awareness would greatly aid this process. Even if most of humanity doesn't access their higher soul awareness (which is, admittedly, a lofty goal), greater numbers of people pursuing and practicing some of the above recommendations would help. If more people worked on clearing their personal stuff, it would have a huge beneficial effect. So, too, would more people realizing and remembering that everything and everyone is interconnected. Respect for others' religious beliefs would also go a long way in this regard.

I realize that I'm painting with a broad stroke—and, as with so many suggestions, the important thing to do is to start with ourselves. We must indeed be the change we want to see in the world (a quote often attributed to Gandhi, although the phrase doesn't exist in his writings). Sage advice that we can apply. Even though I've extrapolated to the universal, world-wide benefits that could be so redeeming for our Earth, wildlife, and culture, we would always find it advisable to start on the personal level.

So, if any of this resonates with you personally, please take advantage of the information and recommendations. You don't need to save the world. It may just be a matter of starting with yourself—and you should find yourself reaping some wonderful spiritual rewards.

Appendix A:
Questions That Were
Posed to Interviewees

I GENERALLY POSED THE SAME questions to each of the people you've met in this book. A few questions I didn't start asking until about midway through interviewing people were 31–33. In addition, I spontaneously asked some questions that are not listed here.

1. *Do you remember anything from before you were born (not as a later past-life memory)?*

2. *What is your earliest memory or awareness (even if not a specific memory)?*

3. *When do you first remember thinking of God (or Source, Spirit, the Divine, the Universe) or that this was not the only reality?*

4. *Do you remember anything from your first few years of life—up until age three or four?*

5. *Were you inner-guided as a young child?*

6. *Did you feel different from others? If so, at what age did that start?*

7. *Did you feel as if you didn't belong here or this wasn't your true home?*

8. *Did you remember living anywhere else?*

9. *Did you feel that you didn't belong to your family or did you remember having any other family?*

10. *Did you have any intuitive or psychic experiences?*

11. *If so, at what age did they begin?*

12. *If so, what types of experiences?*

13. *Do you consider yourself to be spiritual?*

14. *Do you feel that you have information about the Universe—in other words, spiritual wisdom?*

15. *If so, could you put any of it into words?*

16. *Did you ever feel as if you were observing people and things around you, as opposed to being engaged with them?*

17. *Did you ever feel as if you were just passing through here?*

18. *Do you feel that you're good at reading other people?*

19. *Do you feel that your experience of life is different from other people?*

20. *Do you feel that your spiritual awareness has made you different from other people?*

21. *If so, in what ways?*

22. *Do you feel that you have gifts or abilities that others don't (who haven't always been spiritually aware)?*

23. *Do you have any special gifts, whether creativity, intellect, making things, etc.?*

24. *How do you feel about animals?*

25. *How do you feel about nature?*

26. *Would you say that you're compassionate—sensitive?*

27. *Do you feel that a part of you is really innocent and pure?*

28. *Do you have many fears or do you tend to feel or trust that everything will be okay and that you are protected?*

29. *Were you brought up in a religious tradition?*

30. *How do you regard religion at present?*

31. *Do you ever find yourself feeling one thing emotionally and a different thing on another level? (I always found myself doing that, which I later figured out was the difference between my higher soul awareness and my human stuff.)*

32. *Have you been able to detect a difference between your human psyche or persona and your higher soul awareness? If so, how would you describe your higher soul awareness/spirit awareness?*

33. *What do you feel when you look in an animal's eyes?*

34. *Have you ever had a near-death experience?*

35. *Do you have synaesthesia?*

36. *Have you felt protected or guided in your life?*

37. *If so, from what age?*

38. *Do you feel that being spiritually aware your whole life is a blessing or a curse?*

39. *Have you chewed on what your life purpose is?*

Appendix B:
A Meditation for the
Higher Soul Awareness

THE FOLLOWING MEDITATION IS DESIGNED to help you access your higher soul awareness. It's best to do this meditation after having learned to meditate, rather than as a first-time-ever meditation. Don't be alarmed if it takes doing this meditation more than once to feel that you've been able to get into your higher soul awareness. Just keep doing it until you find a shift in your awareness.

In this meditation, you can use any of your senses. You don't need to see things visually, for example; instead, you can sense whatever is transpiring.

You'll find in the meditation below that there are places with an ellipsis (...). Whenever you see this, take it to mean that you want to take more time to experience as much as you need to experience. If you're using a recording and need to take more time, just pause the recording and resume it when you're ready to continue.

Remember that you want to come back to your human side after you finish this meditation, rather than trying to hang out permanently in your higher soul awareness. It's vitally important to remember to come back and attend to those perpetual earthly matters, finding a balance between the two.

I've also made a recording of this meditation available for purchase on my website (www.dianebrandon.com) in either hard copy CD form or digital audio file.

As with all meditations, you'll want to insure that you're not interrupted by noise or other distractions.

Meditation to Access the Higher Soul Awareness

Allow yourself to get into a comfortable position, whether sitting down or lying down. Close your eyes and start taking some deep breaths, relaxing as you breathe. With each deep breath that you take, allow yourself to feel that you're relaxing more and more. If any part of your body feels tense or tight or sore, as you inhale feel that breath going to those places and softening and loosening and healing them. Then, as you exhale, breathe out any of the tightness or soreness …

Continue breathing deeply, while also continuing to relax. Allow yourself to go with this relaxation and allow it to continue and grow, knowing that you're taking this time for yourself, which you deserve and can benefit from …

When you feel that you've been able to relax deeply, allow yourself to find a comfortable breathing pattern that's a little deeper than normal, but not so deep that it's labored. Allow yourself to comfortably settle into that relaxed breathing …

As you do, find yourself in a beautiful, serene place. This should be a place where you feel completely comfortable, at ease, and peaceful. This can be a real place or one that simply comes to you, whether "real" or not. It can be a place you've been to before or one you've never visited. As this place comes to mind, allow yourself to feel that you are actually there …

Continue to feel relaxed and at ease. In this lovely place, allow yourself to notice details of this place, whether sounds, the temperature, fragrances, etc. Allow yourself to feel that you are truly in this place. You may want to walk or move around and explore this place—or you may be comfortable sitting or standing or even lying down. Fully feel yourself being in this place and note how wonderfully comfortable and secure you feel here…

You now notice that you feel completely at ease and nurtured, somewhat magically here. You suddenly find that any cares or concerns you may have had have now disappeared—just magically evaporating… You are in a place of pure being and lightness and ease here. As you realize this, now allow yourself to enjoy this wonderful feeling…

All of a sudden you feel yourself magically lifted up, rising to a place up high, out in space. You feel lighter and lighter and notice yourself feeling more and more buoyed up and positive…. You're now way up high out in space above the Earth. You may be lying down in this place or seated or in any comfortable position—or you may find that it's just your consciousness that's in this place way, way above the Earth….

As you settle into this place, you see and feel iridescent, shimmering energy and light all around you—indescribable shimmering and vibrantly alive colors and beauty. It's so beautiful—even breathtaking—and inspiring. You feel this iridescent, shimmering energy moving closer and closer to you—and you're suddenly enveloped by it. It feels so positive, energizing, illuminating, and inspiring, powerful and gentle at the same time. You feel the Divine, Spirit, God, Source with you as part of this iridescent, shimmering energy. You feel even more inspired and feel the great power, wisdom, and love within you. Allow yourself to continue to feel this wonderful Divine energy with you and through you, taking some time to fully feel this and immerse yourself in it…

You now see an animal—of any type—whether familiar or unrecognizable. As you see this animal, you feel a calm and positive energy, and you feel very comfortable with his or her presence. You now find yourself looking into the eyes of this animal. You see the awareness and wisdom, the strong, almost palpable awareness and wisdom and knowing. As you continue to look in this animal's eyes, you feel the awareness and presence. And you sense this animal being strongly anchored in the present in an unwavering manner. As you feel a timelessness in the animal's eyes, you feel yourself merging with this ever-present awareness....

You now sense other beings all around you—other humans (whether in a body or not), benevolent guides, angels, other animals, other types of beings perhaps unrecognizable, etc. All joining with you.... As you sense or see them, you find that they're no longer in bodies. You can now see or sense their souls... They're all around you, becoming beautiful—shining and shimmering—points of light. You can feel their beautiful and positive energies, so that you now feel a connection with all of them—a connection that morphs into a sense of union and unity. You allow yourself to feel this positive, yet powerful, connection and union. You know that in this place of oneness there are no concerns or worries. Instead, there is just connection and a sense of unity and support and communion—and love. You suddenly know and feel this wonderful connection...

You now find yourself far removed from events in your life—past experiences, difficulties, painfulness. All just drops away, just dissolves and melts away from your awareness...

You now understand why things have happened the way they have. You realize that you can now see your life experiences from a higher vantage point, that run along a line or a spiral, with each experience leading to another experience—and leading to a new awareness .... You now allow yourself to fully sense and know the knowledge and insights and growth you have gained from each of these difficulties and struggles...

Suddenly you can see the purpose for everything you have experienced in your life. You can see Divine purpose and how everything has added to your unfolding and enrichment... You see other people you have known—and now see and realize the complex, interwoven, and mutually affecting web connecting all of you...

You now find your focus shifting to the Earth below or in the distance. From this place up high, you can see all events on the Earth and all over the Earth, past and present, as they unfolded and unfold, including any turmoil, achievements, changes. You observe all of this in a very detached and objective manner. You notice how objective and calm you are and how any concern about things unfolding on Earth is absent. You are able to observe everything clearly and objectively without any pain or reaction or upset or judgment. You continue to observe events on the Earth with this newfound clarity...

As you continue to observe, you find yourself suddenly knowing why some things are happening and unfolding as they are—and why events in the past took place. You are suddenly flooded with insights and realizations about the higher purpose of events. You know in the core of your being why events are happening and their purpose, as well as the good that can come out of difficult events....

You allow yourself to embrace this beautiful clarity and this higher perspective, along with the insights and wisdom you are gaining. You know that you can retain this awareness and perspective and that it can benefit you in your life....

Allow yourself to stay in this place and awareness for as long as you would like. When you feel that you have gained all the richness and awareness that you need, you can come back to the room that you're in and the present time and your body, knowing that you will feel refreshed and relaxed...

Remember, once again, to come back to the present time after doing this meditation—and to attend to your life here on Earth, balancing your higher soul awareness with your human persona.

Allow yourself to do this meditation once or twice a week. You may even want to make notes from time to time about your perceptions and feelings about your life and the world, in order to notice shifts in perceptions that may occur.

Appendix C:
If You've Retained
At-Birth Memories

IF YOU'VE RECOGNIZED YOURSELF AS born aware because you also remember what you thought when you were born and/or have always had natural memories of the other side, you may wonder what to do with all of this. Here are some thoughts and recommendations.

Focus and Chew on Your Memories

Allow yourself to consciously focus on the awareness, thoughts, and memories you had at birth. Many of us may have repressed, ignored, or hidden our at-birth thoughts over the years, as a consequence of cultural conditioning or having no one else with whom to share them. Some may have felt that those memories were not to be talked about.

I feel that this is a new day. This is a time when we can embrace what we knew and remembered when we were born. So allow yourself to begin to "legitimize" those memories for yourself. Focus on them and then allow yourself to chew on them. How did they contribute to your feeling different? Embrace those memories and cherish them, as an indelible imprint from higher spiritual levels.

What do you cherish about your memories? What do they allow you to know of the other side and higher spiritual levels? Embrace what you know and remember.

Know That You're Not Alone

One of the major downsides of having been spiritually aware since birth lies in feeling different and alone. Through reading this book, you should now realize that you're not alone. There are indeed many of us with this awareness on this planet, no matter how much in the minority or geographically distant. We're sprinkled throughout this planet.

Know that there's a potential community of other Born Awares out there. You no longer need to feel alone or weird.

Connect with Other Born Awares

One of the most affirming things you can do if you've been spiritually aware since birth is to connect with other Born Awares. Even if you have never known anyone else with memories like these, you can take steps to connect with others, even if they're not in physical proximity.

Consider connecting with other Born Awares in meditation. You may not know the names of those you connect with or where they're located geographically, but you should be able to sense their energy and spirits.

If you'd like to associate with other Born Awares in person, there may be ways for you to try to ferret out and connect with other Born Awares in the area you live in. Most areas have spiritual groups founded on spiritual interests, and you may be able to find other Born Awares in such spiritual groups. Always go with your comfort level. Be resourceful!

Seek Spiritual Companions

Even if you can't find others in your area who have been spiritually aware since birth, you should be able to find others who are spiritually oriented. There are many spiritual organizations these days throughout the world and they can represent a great way to connect with others and find spiritual companions. As always, pay attention to your comfort level and seek those with whom you resonate.

Chew On Your Split Awareness

If you haven't yet thought about the difference between your human persona and your higher soul awareness, allow yourself to chew on that. Have you ever found yourself thinking one thing on one level and feeling another thing on a different level? Can you tell when your personal stuff is triggered and you're mired in your human persona, feeling pain, anger, or another difficult emotion? Can you tell when you're observing clearly and objectively and from a higher perspective?

Once you've identified your own spirit awareness, allow yourself daily to perceive the differences between these two distinctly different types of awareness. Try to remember the type of awareness you were in on the other side.

Embrace Your Memories of the Other Side

As you give more and more permission to your innate spiritual awareness, also allow yourself to remember what you can of the other side and higher spiritual levels. What did those levels feel like? What did you do there? Did you live lives in physical form in places other than the Earth? Allow yourself to remember and reclaim what you know of the other side—your actual memories, rather than what is assumed or imagined. Embrace and anchor yourself in these memories.

Get into Your Own Spiritual Knowing

You likely have access to higher spiritual wisdom and knowledge if you've been spiritually aware since birth. Allow yourself to chew on that and what you know. Try to empower yourself and trust your spiritual knowledge. You are fully capable of knowing your own spiritual truth. Trust your knowing!

Chew On Your Present Path and Purpose

As you know, those who are born aware naturally have an awareness of having come to Earth to do or accomplish something (not necessarily a grandiose purpose, but simply what we have been told to do). If you haven't consciously gleaned what you are here to do, allow yourself to chew on it, while also keeping in mind that some Born Awares don't know what their specific assignment is and just know that they will be led to it.

Those of us spiritually aware since birth tend to naturally be attuned to inner guidance. Look at the ways in which you've been nudged and guided in your life. Can you start to see purpose in your path? Whether you consciously know what your assignment or purpose is, remember that there is indeed purpose to your being here and that you're always being guided and gently nudged forward. Being consciously aware of this can be a spiritual blessing.

If You're Sensitive or Empathic

Many people who are spiritual, whether born aware or not, tend to be both emotionally sensitive and empathic (having thin boundaries and feeling others' energy, pain, negativity, etc.). (This, of course, is not true of all Born Awares or all those who are spiritual.) This sensitivity can make life difficult. How can you live your life and navigate through it without being unduly drained and without picking up on and being affected by others' energy? There are several steps you can take to mitigate and lessen the negative side of being empathic.

The first step would be to understand what being an empath means. Unfortunately, the term empath would appear to be overused these days, leading some not to completely understand it.

The term empath derives from the word empathy, which derives from the Greek for "feeling within" ("em" meaning in and "pathos" meaning feeling). We have *empathy* for others when we can understand what another person or being is feeling from the other's perspective. The term empath was coined to refer to someone who has a very high degree of empathy. In spiritual/intuitive circles, it is used to refer to those who unconsciously feel others' emotions and energy, both the positive and the negative, without trying to feel these things.

Being an empath or highly empathic becomes a problem when we unconsciously pick up on negative feelings, energy, and thoughts of others without intending to do so. This can be even more of a problem when we find ourselves feeling bad and don't understand why. Even if we can identify the source of feeling bad or down or drained out of the blue—*e.g.,* when we realize that a conversation left us drained—being affected by anything negative seemingly outside of us still leaves us feeling out of sorts.

Finding a way to reduce our empathic sensitivity can therefore be helpful. This is often not an on/off switch or easy fix and may require both a multi-pronged approach and a process that takes time.

One of the first steps to take would be to think about the situation and then decide whether you really want to lessen the effect of others on you. Think about what it might feel like were you not so affected by others. What would the benefits be? Would there be any potential downside?

If you decide that you do indeed want to be less negatively impacted by others' energy, thoughts, etc., then you'll want to affirm this. If you're less affected by negativity outside of you, you should then have more of a sense of sanctity and safety. It's important to then affirm and aver that you *deserve* to have this sense of sanctity and safety. Allow yourself to build some affirmations around this and say them daily, first thing in the morning and at bedtime. Some who are empaths may want to have boundaries and not feel drained by others, but at the same time and counter-productively may not feel worthy of having this sanctity and safety. This is why it's important to start off by affirming that you deserve to have sanctity and privacy and not be drained.

The factor of passivity comes into play as well with being an empath. We do indeed need to be receptive if we're working with our intuition or creativity, but we don't want to be open and receptive 24/7 or be a passive piece of meat to be acted upon by others. Allow yourself to reflect upon the differences between being passive and active. Then build some affirmations around not needing to be passive all the time or giving permission to others to act upon you without your consent. There may be spiritual mindsets or beliefs that can compound an orientation toward being passive. As I shared in my account, I had to work on this, as I used to feel that, because I was spiritual and divinely protected, as well as being here on assignment, that all would unfold as it was supposed to. Many years ago, I decided that I needed to amend that spiritual mindset and not wait for things in my life and needed to be less passive. I now listen to guidance and my stance is more that of cocreation.

This shift also entails taking responsibility for what we're feeling and doing. As long as we feel passive and feel acted upon, we cede our responsibility. We may allow others to do things to us, feeling that we have no say or control. We may also develop a victim mentality. When we cede responsibility for what happens to us in our lives, our focus tends to be primarily on ourselves and all the difficulties we go through. We may not take responsibility, as a result, for how we affect others through our actions. So allow yourself to know that you can improve upon this and can indeed take responsibility.

In dealing with undue sensitivity to others and a high degree of empathy, it's vitally important to erect boundaries. The term boundary is a psychological one, usually referring to a boundary between others and ourselves. It's not a physical, tangible one, but an energetic one instead. So you'll want to find a way to erect boundaries to reduce what you're picking up on from others.

In order to do this, you'll want to get into your center. Finding our center and being centered can represent a major step to erecting boundaries. And one of the best ways to get into your center is via meditation. So allow yourself to learn to meditate and meditate on a regular basis. Notice how calm and *centered* you are after you get into deeper levels of consciousness through meditation the first time.

Once you feel centered, you'll want to affirm that you don't want to be pulled out of your center. When we're centered, we can actually feel ourselves being pulled out of it, and, when that happens, we can simply energetically back up. So learn to pay attention to when you're being pulled out of your center. This observation draws upon the concept of "living consciously," meaning that we pay attention to ourselves, our actions, and our feelings in an objective manner. We can learn to observe ourselves, including our feelings and actions. If you feel yourself being pulled out of your center, observe that it's happening, back up energetically, and then get back into your center. If you find yourself suddenly drained or tired for no reason, allow yourself to consciously know that you may have picked up on someone else's feelings or energy. Affirm that it's not yours, release it, and get back into your center.

Another component of dealing with being an empath has to do with empowerment. Those who are sensitive, highly empathetic, and spiritual may also tend to have lower self-esteem and not believe in themselves. We may compare ourselves to others and find ourselves lacking or have been brought up to give others credit for being authorities, while viewing ourselves as subservient. In order to deal with this often engrained problem, it's important to perceive and know who we truly are on the inside, our true self—what I call the *essence*, who we are on the deepest level in this lifetime on the inside and underneath any of our personal stuff. Determine and know who you are on that deep level. Then embrace who you are and know that it's valid and who you're supposed to be in this lifetime. Take it further and engage in activities that allow you to express your essence.

If you find yourself customarily drained after being around one person or group, allow yourself to consciously realize that this is stemming from outside of yourself. It's vitally important if we're sensitive or empathic to develop discernment and allow ourselves to discern where others are coming from. We typically feel best if we're careful to spend time around others with whom we resonate and with whom there's an equal give and take.

Erecting boundaries and dealing with being an empath cannot be attained overnight. It takes time and persistence, but it can be richly rewarding and improve our experience of life.

A Blessing or a Curse

Having the spiritual awareness that those of us who have been spiritually aware since birth have can be very rewarding. Yes, it can have its downsides, but most of us wouldn't trade it for the world.

Allow yourself to chew on how being born aware has enriched your life. Doing this can not only enrich your experience, but also anchor yourself even more in it and bring more gratitude around it. Allow yourself to chew on what the downside has been as well and then compare that to the benefits. If you're like the Born Awares in this book, you'll likely find that the benefits outweigh the downside.

Allow yourself to embrace having been spiritually aware since birth and grow in vitality and strength with it!

Bibliography

Alexander, Eben, MD. *Proof of Heaven: A Neurosurgeon's Journey into the Afterlife*. New York: Simon & Schuster Paperbacks, 2012.

Alexander, Harriet. "Have Scientists Discovered Why We Have No Infant Memories?" *The Telegraph,* 28 Jun 2014, http://www .telegraph.co.uk/science/science-news/10932644/Have-scientists -discovered-why-we-have-no-infant-memories.html.

Atwater, P. M. H. *Beyond the Light*. New York: Carol Publishing Group, 1994.

———. *The Big Book of Near-Death Experiences*. Charlottesville, VA: Hampton Roads Publishing Company, 2007.

———. *Coming Back to Life: The After-Effects of the Near-Death Experience*. New York: Citadel, 2001.

"Babies Can Form Abstract Relations Before They Learn Words," *Sci -News.com,* May 26, 2015, http://www.sci-news.com/othersciences /anthropology/science-babies-abstract-relations-02842.html.

Bekoff, Marc. *The Emotional Lives of Animals: A Leading Scientist Explores Animal Joy, Sorrow, and Empathy—And Why They Matter.* Novato, CA: New World Library, 2007.

———. *Wild Justice: The Moral Lives of Animals.* Chicago: The University of Chicago Press, 2009.

Bourne, Edward J. *Global Shift: How a New Worldview Is Transforming Humanity.* Oakland, CA: Noetic Books, 2009.

Bowman, Carol. *Children's Past Lives.* New York: Bantam Books, 1998

Briggs, Helen. "Can You Prescribe Nature?" *BBC.* 8 July 2015, http://www.bbc.com/news/science-environment-33368691.

Brinkley, Dannion and Paul Perry. *Saved by the Light: The True Story of a Man Who Died Twice and the Profound Revelations He Received.* New York: Harper Torch, 1994.

Bucke, Richard Maurice, MD. *Cosmic Consciousness: A Classic Investigation of the Development of Man's Mystic Relation to the Infinite.* New York: E. P. Dutton and Company, 1969.

Childre, Doc Lew. *Freeze Frame Fast Action Stress Relief: A Scientifically Proven Technique.* Boulder Creek, California: Planetary Publications, 1994.

———, and Rollin McCraty. "Love: The Hidden Power of the Heart: A Scientific Perspective," *Caduceus Journal.* http://www.heartmath .com/Library/Articles/Caduceus.html.

Conger, Cristen. "Can a Person Remember Being Born?" *HowStuffWorks.* http://science.howstuffworks.com/life/remember-birth.htm.

Dombeck, Mark. "The Long Term Effects of Bullying," *American Academy of Experts in Traumatic Stress.* www.aaets.org/article204 .htm.

Eadie, Betty. *Embraced by the Light*. Placerville, CA: Leaf Press, 1992.

Farias, Miguel, "Meditation Is Often Thought of as a Pillar of Wellness, but for Some, It Has a Much Darker Side." *National Post,* June 5, 2015, http://news.nationalpost.com/life/meditation-is-often -thought-of-as-a-pillar-of-wellness-but-for-some-it-has-a-much -darker-side.

Farr, Sidney Saylor. *What Tom Sawyer Learned from Dying*. Norfolk, VA: Hampton Roads Publishing Company, Inc., 1993.

Ferguson, Marilyn. *The Aquarian Conspiracy–Personal and Social Transformation in Our Time*. Los Angeles: J. P. Tarcher, Inc., 1987.

Fleming, Nic. "Plants Talk to Each Other Using an Internet of Fungus." *BBC,* 11 November 2014, http://www.bbc.com/earth/story /20141111-plants-have-a-hidden-internet.

"France Detects Radioactive Iodine in Rainwater, Milk," *Agriculturedefensecoalition.org,* 04 April 2011, http://www .agriculturedefensecoalition.org/sites/default/files/file/nuclear _japan/114R_26_2011_France_Detects_Radioactive_Iodine_131 _in_Rainwater_Milk_April_5_2011_EurActiv_News.pdf.

Gabrielsen, Paul, "When Do Babies Become Conscious?" *ScienceNOW,* http://www.wired.com/2013/04/baby-consciousness/.

Gleeson, Katie, "Bullies' Brains Wired to Seek Pleasure from Aggression, Study Suggests," *The Independent*. www.independent.co.uk/news /science/bullies-brains-wired-to-seek-pleasure-from-aggression-study -suggests-a7114371.html.

Goldberg, Dr. Bruce, *Past Lives, Future Lives,* New York: Ballantine Books, 1982.

IHM Research Update. Institute of HeartMath, Newsletter, Vol. 2, No. 1, 1995.

Institute of HeartMath. *Freeze-Frame Training Guidebook*. Boulder Creek, California: Institute of HeartMath, 1996.

Koch, Christof. "When Does Consciousness Arise in Human Babies?" *Scientific American*. Aug 1, 2009, http://www.scientificamerican.com /artoc;e/when-does-consciousness-arise/.

Louv, Richard. *The Nature Principle: Reconnecting with Life in a Virtual Age,* Chapel Hill: Algonquin Books, 2012.

MacIsaac, Tara. "5 Stories of People with Pre-Birth Memories," *Epoch Times,* December 25, 2014, http://www.theepochtimes.com /n3/1161496-5-stories-of-people-with-pre-birth-memories.

Martin, Howard. Institute of HeartMath LLC, in "Activating the Heart's Intelligence."

McGowan, Kat. "How Plants Secretly Talk to Each Other," *Wired,* 12/20/13, http://www.wired.com/2013/12/secret-language-of-plants.

Moody, Raymond. *Life After Life: The Investigation of a Phenomenon– Survival of Bodily Death,* Harrisburg, PA: Stackpole Books, 1976.

Nakamura, Akemi, "'Forest Therapy' Taking Root," *Japan Times,* May 2, 2008, http://www.japantimes.co.jp/news/2008/05/02/national /forest-therapy-taking-root/.

Newton, Michael. *Destiny of Souls: New Case Studies of Life Between Lives.* St. Paul, MN: Llewellyn Publications, 2000.

———. *Journey of Souls: Case Studies of Life Between Lives,* St. Paul, MN: Llewellyn Publications, 1994.

The Norwegian University of Science and Technology (NTNU). "Brain Waves and Meditation." *ScienceDaily.* March 31, 2010, http://www .sciencedaily.com/releases/2010/03/100319210631.htm.

Pappas, Stephanie. "Babies Are Born with Some Self-Awareness," *LiveScience,* November 21, 2013, http://www.livescience .com/41398-baby-awareness.html.

———. "The Pain of Bullying Lasts into Adulthood." *LiveScience,* February 20, 2013, http://www.livescience.com/27279 -bullying-effects-last-adulthood.html.

"Radiation Risks from Fukushima 'No Longer Negligible.'" *EurActiv,* Apr 11, 2011, http://www.euractiv.com/section/health-consumers /news/radiation-risks-from-fukushima-no-longer-negligible/

Ring, Kenneth. *Heading Toward Omega: In Search of the Meaning of the Near-Death Experience,* New York: William Morrow, 1984

Schwartz, Gary E., PhD. *The Healing Energy Experiments: Science Reveals Our Natural Ability to Heal.* New York: Atria Books, 2007.

Sherwell, Philip. "Vast Saharan Dust Plumes Shown Heading Across Atlantic to the Amazon in Images." *The Telegraph,* n. d., http://www .telegraph.co.uk/news/worldnjews/africaandindianocean/11449918 /Vast-Saharan-dust-plumes-shown-heading-across-Atlantic-to-the -Amazon-in-images.html.

Smith, Laura. "Rx: 50 mg [sic] Nature, Ad Lib–Doctors Are Prescribing a Walk in the Park," *Slate,* July 25, 2014, http://www.slate.com /articles/health_and_science/medical_examiner/2014/07/doctors _prescribing_outdoors_time_nature_is_good_for_you.html.

Stanford, Kaitlin,. "How Fast Does a Baby's Brain Grow? Way Faster than We Thought, Says New Study." *www.bustle.com/* June 10, 2015, http://www.bustle.com/articles/89394-how-fast-does-a-baby-grow -way-faster-than-we-thought-says-new-study.

Wambach, Helen. *Life Before Life,* New York: Bantam Books, 1979.

Weiss, Brian L., MD. *Many Lives, Many Masters*. New York: A Fireside Book, 1988.

———. *Through Time into Healing*. New York: A Fireside Book, 1992.

Whitton, Joel L., MD, PhD. and Joe Fisher, *Life Between Life,* New York: Warner Books, Inc., 1986.

Williams, Kevin. "Roy Mills and His Memories of Pre-Existence." *near-death.com,* 2014, http://www.near-death.com/mills.html.

Wilson, Timothy D. *Strangers to Ourselves: Discovering the Adaptive Unconscious*. Cambridge, Massachusetts: The Belknap Press of Harvard University Press, 2002.

Wood, Janice. "What's Your Earliest Memory?" *Psych Central,* January 26, 2014, http://psychcentral.com/news/2014/01/26/whats-your -earliest-memory/64982.html.

To Write to the Author

If you wish to contact the author or would like more information about this book, please write to the author in care of Llewellyn Worldwide, and we will forward your request. Both the author and the publisher appreciate hearing from you and learning of your enjoyment of this book and how it has helped you. Llewellyn Worldwide cannot guarantee that every letter written to the author can be answered, but all will be forwarded. Please write to:

Diane Brandon
℅ Llewellyn Worldwide
2143 Wooddale Drive
Woodbury, MN 55125-2989

Please enclose a self-addressed stamped envelope for reply,
or $1.00 to cover costs. If outside the USA, enclose
an international postal reply coupon.

Many of Llewellyn's authors have websites with additional information and resources. For more information, please visit www.llewellyn.com.

Intuition

For Beginners

Easy Ways to Awaken Your Natural Abilities

DIANE BRANDON

Intuition for Beginners
Easy Ways to Awaken Your Natural Abilities
DIANE BRANDON

Have you ever known who was calling when the phone rang? Or have you ever made a decision on an absolute whim—and later felt that you made the right choice? Perhaps you've had an immediate good or bad feeling about a person—and then had that instinct confirmed? Most people, whether they acknowledge it or not, have some degree of intuitive ability.

Diane Brandon has spent the past two decades studying intuitive development. Whether your intuition is naturally accessible or hidden, this comprehensive and approachable text offers strategies to elevate your level of conscious awareness. Dispelling the myths of intuitive and psychic knowledge, Brandon focuses on how intuition can be applied as a tool of empowerment and self-improvement. Get in touch with your inner voice to improve relationships, solve problems, make well-timed decisions, and more.

978-0-7387-3335-7, 312 pp., 5¼ x 8 inches   **$14.99**

Dream
Interpretation

For Beginners

Understand the Wisdom of Your Sleeping Mind

DIANE BRANDON

Dream Interpretation for Beginners
Understand the Wisdom of Your Sleeping Mind
DIANE BRANDON

Decode the messages that your dreams may be trying to give you. Exploring your world of dreams, as well as your world of sleep, can enrich your life, improve your relationships, and help you achieve a sense of personal unfolding. *Dream Interpretation for Beginners* shows you how to use dreams for personal and spiritual growth, as well as improved problem-solving and deeper insight into your life.

978-0-7387-4191-8, 312 pp., 5¼ x 8 inches   **$15.99**
